CARE, CRISIS AND ACTIVISM
The Politics of Everyday Life

Eleanor Jupp

P

First published in Great Britain in 2023 by

Policy Press, an imprint of
Bristol University Press
University of Bristol
1–9 Old Park Hill
Bristol
BS2 8BB
UK
t: +44 (0)117 374 6645
e: bup-info@bristol.ac.uk

Details of international sales and distribution partners are available at
policy.bristoluniversitypress.co.uk

© Bristol University Press 2023

British Library Cataloguing in Publication Data
A catalogue record for this book is available from the British Library

ISBN 978-1-4473-5300-3 hardcover
ISBN 978-1-4473-5301-0 paperback
ISBN 978-1-4473-5303-4 ePub
ISBN 978-1-4473-5304-1 ePdf

The right of Eleanor Jupp to be identified as author of this work has been asserted by her in accordance with the Copyright, Designs and Patents Act 1988.

All rights reserved: no part of this publication may be reproduced, stored in a retrieval system, or transmitted in any form or by any means, electronic, mechanical, photocopying, recording, or otherwise without the prior permission of Bristol University Press.

Every reasonable effort has been made to obtain permission to reproduce copyrighted material. If, however, anyone knows of an oversight, please contact the publisher.

The statements and opinions contained within this publication are solely those of the author and not of the University of Bristol or Bristol University Press. The University of Bristol and Bristol University Press disclaim responsibility for any injury to persons or property resulting from any material published in this publication.

Bristol University Press and Policy Press work to counter discrimination on grounds of gender, race, disability, age and sexuality.

Cover design: Liam Roberts
Front cover image: istock

Contents

List of figures	iv
Acknowledgements	v
Introduction: sticking plasters and cotton wool	1
1 Care, austerity and the politics of everyday lives	11
2 Citizenship and community in times of crisis	23
3 Journeys into and through local activism under austerity	38
4 Austerity politics and infrastructures of care: Children's Centre closures and activism	60
5 Small stories and political change: local activism across time and space	74
6 Provisioning in times of crisis	99
Conclusions: a politics of everyday life?	119
Appendix: overview of research projects	136
References	138
Index	158

List of figures

3.1	Image from the Coastal Arts project's 'period poverty' campaign video	56
5.1	Protestors campaigning to save Children's Centres in Buckinghamshire	80
5.2	Photo of a placard made at a campaign event in Area B and then circulated on social media	83
5.3	Post from National Children's Centres campaign Facebook site	89
5.4	Images from Save Our Sure Starts animation	92
6.1	Leaf-printing, April 2020, made during home-schooling with my daughter, Caitlin	100
6.2	The organisation of the town mutual aid scheme	109

Acknowledgements

My first thanks go to the many research participants across all the projects discussed in this book, for their time, energy and generosity in engaging with me and my research. Thanks also to those who gave permission for images to be used. Aspects of the research were supported both by the Open University and the University of Kent. In particular, the research on Children's Centres was supported by a grant from the Faculty of Social Sciences at the University of Kent. I would also like to thank colleagues and students in Engineering and Digital Arts at the University of Kent for their work on the Children's Centre animation.

Julie MacLeavy, Janet Newman and Julia Twigg all read an entire draft and gave me hugely helpful feedback which has improved the book – I am very grateful to all three of them for their support and engagement. I have collaborated on other publications and research on these themes with Sophie Bowlby, Sarah Marie Hall, Jennie Middleton and Jane Franklin, whose own rich ideas and research in this terrain have helped shape my understanding of the politics of care. I am also very grateful to a wider group of scholars whose diverse research has been so valuable in shaping both my own and broader academic engagement with matters of austerity, including (but not limited to) Esther Hitchen, John Horton, Helena Pimlott-Wilson, Andy Power, Ruth Raynor, Alison Stenning and Eleanor Wilkinson. Both their written contributions and discussions at conferences, seminars and in between have been much appreciated. Most recently I have benefited from fantastic discussions on the politics of care with Amy Clark and Carolyn Pedwell while supervising Amy's doctoral research project.

I would like to thank Laura Vickers-Rendall in particular and all at Policy Press/Bristol University Press for their support and patience in working with me on this book over some years. In terms of the practicalities of writing, the bulk of the book has been written very much 'in the middle of things', to borrow a phrase from Joan Tronto which I use elsewhere. The COVID-19 pandemic and associated disruptions of care, work and education have made this a challenging process. I am very grateful to Kate Bradley, Dawn Lyon and other colleagues at the University of Kent who supported my research leave in autumn 2020 – without this the book would not have existed. In the middle of things with me have been my children Jake, Anna and Caitlin, and my partner Rowan, as well as my parents Tom and Cressida. I can't imagine a better crew to be at sea with and I would like to thank them all for their support, care, love and fun, especially Rowan in the final stages of the book.

Introduction: sticking plasters and cotton wool

Approaching a politics of everyday life

This book is concerned with matters of community, local action and practices of care, and their relationship to matters of austerity, crisis and transformations of the welfare state. I begin with two quotes from Sandra, a community activist running a residents' group in a deprived neighbourhood in Stoke-on-Trent, a case study discussed further in Chapter 3. I had known Sandra since 2005, when I had first undertaken research in her neighbourhood. She spoke to me during a second round of research in 2013, about the impacts of austerity cuts on the projects they ran in her community. Much of their energy was now spent on a food redistribution project, collecting surplus food from supermarkets and making it available at very low cost to residents. Yet she told me:

> 'It's a *sticking plaster* [my emphasis] and it's never going to achieve the outcomes of making somebody self-sufficient. You're not going to get to the stage where they don't need that service. Until they get a job, until the benefits are paid properly, until they're not ill anymore, until the families are grown up, there are so many things that impact on why people can't feed their families that we're never going to solve that.' (Sandra, Community activist, Stoke-on-Trent)

In the same interview, Sandra also mentioned that they were no longer able to run a youth club because of loss of spaces at the local school. However, she said that they had now found different ways to run sessions with young people:

> 'So we lost all those facilities. We didn't let that stop, we delivered projects in open space, whether it be overgrown doesn't matter, you know if the grass is four foot high you can go bug hunting. If it's cut down nicely you can play cricket and ball games, it doesn't matter, there's going to be some sort of green space somewhere that can be used, which is what we did.'

Sandra's words here demonstrate some of the issues at the centre of this book, of the immense pressures on communities and community action under austerity, but also the creativity and persistence demonstrated by local activists. Her points about the food redistribution project show her frustration with, and critique of, a new discourse of 'self-sufficiency' and 'social enterprise' that her group was now subject to, as part of a reconfiguration of their roles under austerity governance (see Jupp, 2021a). They had been told to work towards 'outcomes of making somebody self-sufficient', yet their activities were increasingly about crisis provisioning. Sandra identified that the problems of food insecurity that they were trying to tackle involve far wider structural problems of work, ill-health and inequality, and this limits what they could ever achieve. At the same time, the second quote shows how the group did manage to continue to work with young people, in the material and relational spaces that emerged as other spaces were being shut or no longer maintained. Overall, her group demonstrated enormous capacity to change and refocus how it operated, in continuing to provide different forms of support and care to local residents.

The two quotes reveal different senses of agency and the politics of community action under austerity. They also reveal the intimate links between shifting forms of community action and shifting provision by different aspects of the welfare state, including welfare benefits, health and family services, and local authority governance. Such forms of local activism thus operate within the 'shadows' of the welfare state (Wolch, 1989; DeVerteuil et al, 2020; Power et al, 2021), and are clearly intertwined with matters of social and public policy. When I had first met Sandra, eight years previously, her concerns were quite different, and more to do with power, voice and democracy within the context of 'neighbourhood renewal' programmes of the New Labour government of the time (Imrie and Raco, 2003), as will be further explored in Chapter 3. Other forms of activism discussed in this book involve more conventional protests and interventions against austerity cuts, yet they all therefore involve engaging with the shape and reach of the state.

At the centre of such changing forms of activism and changing relationships with the state are matters and practicalities of *care*. What kinds of care are being offered or withdrawn by the welfare state, and what does this mean for the caring practices and interventions of community activists? More broadly, what visions and understandings of collective care arise when listening to community activists? Puig de la Bellacasa proposes using metaphors of touch to explore such matters, 'thinking with touch' (2017: 95–8), and indeed there is a wider interest in 'haptic' methods and knowledges within geography (Paterson, 2009). Applying this idea to Sandra's first quote at the start of this chapter, the care she feels they are now offering involves 'sticking plasters'. Indeed, this was a phrase that I heard repeated by both resident volunteers and professionals working in the shifting context of austerity. No longer were they able to engage with the problems they faced in an holistic manner that might resolve suffering in the long term. A sticking plaster is a temporary and short-term fix that responds to immediate embodied pain.

However, Sandra's second quote suggests a more persistent and longer-term caring orientation (see Jupp, 2020). Indeed, a contrasting and related metaphor that was used by staff I met working in a Sure Start Children's Centre (to be further discussed in Chapter 4) was the notion of providing 'cotton wool' for their service users. A head of a Children's Centre told me that, at least in their pre-austerity services, 'we are like the invisible cotton wool that wraps around our communities'. This was within the context of a discussion about how difficult it could be to prove the worth of the support work that they did with families, given that such work could be low key and 'invisible' within formal evaluations. Unlike a sticking plaster, cotton wool does not necessarily have an immediately apparent function, it could be useful 'for a range of health and beauty purposes' (as stated on packaging). It has soft, comforting and cushioning qualities. These are the qualities of care which seemed to be under threat at a moment of austerity cuts to the welfare state.

The sticking plaster and cotton wool metaphors therefore suggest two contrasting visions of collective care that might be provided by community organisations and by structures of the welfare state, and suggests the shifting of roles and responsibilities under austerity. However, there is perhaps more to consider in relation to the politics of the 'sticking plaster'. Cloke et al, analysing foodbanks, propose that the 'sticking plaster' analogy (that they had also heard in analysis and everyday discussions) is not sufficient:

> the tendency has been to dismiss the caring work concerned as short-term pragmatism, an incorporation into neoliberal policies and postures to perform 'sticking plaster' work. … However, our analysis of food banks indicates that these 'in the meantime' activities are capable of opening out rather more progressive and hopeful spaces of political conscientization, invention and reorientation. (2017: 721)

Foodbanks are clearly part of a system of crisis welfare provisioning, indeed could be seen as supporting an austere and neoliberal state (Garthwaite 2016). However, Cloke et al (2017) point to emergent forms of subjectivity and relationality in the foodbanks that suggest a more hopeful and transformative everyday politics (see also Cloke et al, 2020). While not necessarily involving explicit 'resistance' to political systems either, they argue that this politics can be captured by 're-reading seemingly mundane spaces of care and welfare that are ill-served by analytical binaries of incorporation and resistance' (Cloke et al, 2017: 721).

In this book, I follow this kind of analytical approach to community-led spaces of care and welfare, although I would categorise them as 'everyday' rather than 'mundane'. I also consider more conventionally 'political' spaces of local organising, protest and resistance to austerity cuts. In bringing together spaces and practices of everyday provisioning with spaces and practices of activism, I seek to work across boundaries of 'incorporation and resistance', as well as tracing different (and perhaps co-existing) visions of care such as 'sticking plasters' and 'cotton wool'. The 'politics of everyday life' that is the terrain of this book is therefore 'entangled' (Sharp et al, 2000; see also Hughes, 2020) and messy.

This entanglement involves both the shifting practices of the welfare state and collective organisation of care in society, as well as the personal lives and subjectivities of citizens. In among these domains, and across a series of case studies of community organising and action, I draw out emergent visions and knowledges of an everyday politics. Such a politics concerns how care can and should be organised in society, including the reach and role of the state and other institutions and infrastructures, and the potentials and problematics of local activism and action as expressions of citizenship. Matters of the gendered aspects of these questions are also considered throughout, with a particular focus on diverse women's lives, as impacted by austerity cuts and as activists resisting austerity in different ways. While the 'crisis' at the centre of the book concerns austerity, Chapter 6 considers the 2020 COVID-19 crisis, and how it has shifted, and will continue to shift, these matters. My overall argument, therefore, is that within the practices and spaces considered, a messy but ultimately hopeful 'politics of everyday life' can be traced, and that such a politics should be taken seriously.

The rest of this Introduction discusses the case studies and research projects via which this analysis takes place. Chapter 1 then considers theoretical questions of care, the welfare state and austerity cuts, drawing on wider research and writing. Chapter 2 explores matters of community action and activism, citizenship and political subjectivity. The four empirical chapters at the centre of the book present case studies focused on different forms of community action and activism via which to trace such a 'politics of everyday life': the case studies on which they are based are introduced in the rest of this chapter.

Methodological background: researching crises

In the rest of this book, I draw on research projects undertaken over the past seven years of researching within contexts of austerity, and then very recently within the context of the COVID-19 pandemic (see Appendix for further details). These different research engagements were not undertaken as one project and are being brought together in new ways here. This means that there is a level of unevenness in how I draw on research material, which reflects both the shape of the analysis and the shape of the research material available. Matters of methods and my positionality as a researcher are integrated throughout the empirical chapters, and returned to in the Conclusion. Some brief comments are included here about the particular political and relational contexts that shaped the research.

In the first instance, it should be noted that all the projects took place within the UK, and indeed more specifically within England (given policy and political differences across the UK nations). The crises of austerity and the COVID-19 pandemic are global, but clearly inflected in significant ways by particular political and welfare settlements (Clarke, 2005). In terms of the geographies and contexts within that, all my research projects spring from engagements with communities and individuals who might be understood as 'marginalised' in some way. Locations include Stoke-on-Trent, a post-industrial city in the Midlands, migrant communities in North London and coastal towns and urban areas in South East England. The notion of 'marginality' in this framing is complex and intersectional: the projects include some individuals who were middle class and resourceful in a number of ways, as detailed analysis shows. Others were working class, including those in post-industrial Stoke-on-Trent where the neighbourhoods were predominantly White and might currently be framed as 'left behind' within contemporary UK policy discourses (Raynor, 2021). Indeed in terms of ethnicity, the main participants in the research in Stoke-on-Trent and in the voluntary sector in South East England were all White British, although their wider community engagements involved more diverse groups to some extent, as subsequent discussions show. The research on migrant women involved individuals from a wide range of backgrounds including Latin America, Turkey and Somalia, as discussed. The interviewees for my research on Children's Centres were predominantly White British but included two participants from Asian backgrounds, and the wider ethnographies and community engagement involved were also more diverse to some extent. The lack of ethnic diversity in my sample relates partly to the locations of my research largely outside of diverse metropolitan areas. However, it is also important to note that there is further research needed to engage with the experiences of the welfare state, austerity and community activism from the perspectives of racialised minorities, building on the crucial work of Bassel and Emejulu (2017, 2018; Emejulu and Bassel, 2020) in this terrain.

In terms of wider political and economic contexts, a broader common context across all projects was 'austerity', a shorthand term for the contraction and reshaping of the welfare state following the global financial crisis of 2008–9 (Farnsworth and Irving, 2015; Gray and Barford, 2018). Austerity as a phenomenon will be explored further in the proceeding chapters. At this point I wish to note that researching within and on austerity poses some particular methodological and ethical challenges (Hall, 2014, 2017, 2019a; Jupp et al, 2019). Austerity involves a diffuse set of changes and shifts in political, economic and governance regimes and is therefore not necessarily an identifiable phenomena, rather its impacts are 'knotted within' (Hall, 2019a) the textures of intimate lives, relationships and experiences, for example shaping horizons and constraining choices (Horton, 2016). A number of other researchers have experimented with methods including participatory theatre (Raynor, 2017), and creative forms of 'life mapping' and biography (Hall, 2019a; Taylor, 2020) in order to render visible the impacts of austerity. Indeed as discussed later in this chapter, I myself used animation to explore the everyday yet powerful impacts that the closure of a Children's Centre had on a community, having provided friendship, and forms of care and support that might be invisible beyond the centre itself.

In some ways, however, austerity seemed more 'present' within my projects than other research looking at the impact of austerity on everyday lives, given my focus on forms of local activism and action which were all an explicit response to austerity. Nonetheless, across the different projects, for my research participants, from supporting others struggling with mental health problems in a low-income neighbourhood, even to fighting cuts to family services, the issues at stake were not necessarily experienced as an encounter with austerity (Hitchen and Raynor, 2020). After ten years, austerity may be experienced as the normal workings of the state, and this can make it hard to make austerity 'visible' within research. I noticed that with community organisations in particular, new governance arrangements, ways of working and accessing funding demanded by the austere state (see Milbourne and Cushman, 2015), for example through forms of 'commissioning' and monitoring of outcomes, had become accepted as the normal way of working.

One way to make such changes over time more visible then, is through a longitudinal approach to research, as drawn on in discussing community action in Stoke-on-Trent in Chapter 3 (see also Jupp, 2020). Revisiting fieldwork sites over years and following government, policy and economic change can highlight the impact of these changes on everyday lives and everyday experiences of places (MacLeavy and Manley, 2018). The processes of longitudinal research and fieldwork interactions can in themselves make visible such changes, both for researchers and research participants. For example, my embodied presence in the neighbourhoods in Stoke eight years after my original project prompted reflection among my participants about what had changed, in ways that were not always comfortable for them to reflect on, as the loss of resources and economic hardship being suffered was brought into focus (Jupp, 2020).

For the COVID-19 pandemic discussed in Chapter 6, almost the opposite could be considered to be true – the pandemic (while paradoxically an invisible airborne disease) has been a hugely 'visible' crisis and event which has impacted on people's lives in a very dramatic fashion. At the time of writing, and while interviewing during the pandemic, it became very hard to discuss anything other than the pandemic itself, and all discussions of community action and citizenship circled around this topic. Yet of course many of the issues that have come to the surface during the pandemic, for example of burdens of care, of isolation, inequality, precarity and poor mental health, are in many ways intensified by the virus, but not caused by it, as I discuss in Chapter 6. The pandemic both shines a light and intensifies existing social and economic issues, as will be further explored.

These two inter-related crises, the crisis of the austerity and the crisis of the pandemic, both involve intimate and personal matters of everyday lives, including matters of care, health (both physical and mental), household and family dynamics and 'getting by' in material and emotional ways (Jupp et al, 2019). In terms of methods, this means that particular emotional and ethical considerations are brought into fieldwork, potentially involving entanglements with people's vulnerabilities and intimate lives (Hall, 2014). As well as researching with individuals and families, researching with community organisations and campaigns in extremely pressurised circumstances, lacking funding and support, brings into focus ethical – and epistemological – dilemmas about the status of academic knowledge and the value of research in the context of crisis. What is the role of the researcher in a context where crises are unfolding in real time? Is 'witnessing' (Robinson and Sheldon, 2019) a sufficient position to take? Or should researchers adopt 'scholar-activism' (Derickson and Routledge, 2015) as a position within research – and dissemination – strategies? While it is not possible to fully resolve these matters, reflexive considerations around my own positionality and ethics are woven into the chapters that follow and returned to more explicitly in the Conclusion.

Introducing case studies and methods

Across the four empirical chapters a number of activists and organisations are introduced, all referred to using pseudonyms (see Appendix for an overview). The names of a number of geographic areas are also not used in order to protect participants' identities who might otherwise be identifiable, although larger urban areas including London and Stoke-on-Trent are referred to. Chapter 3, 'Journeys into and through local activism under austerity', draws on three separate research projects, with a focus on women, the lifecourse and their movements in and out of activism.

The first project, mentioned at the start of this chapter, involved research with two small community groups in Stoke-on-Trent that I first met as part of my PhD research in 2004–5 (see Jupp, 2006, 2007, 2008). The project involved extended ethnography. I essentially became a volunteer with them, helping out at a wide range of activities including kids' craft sessions, a teenagers' film-making project, Christmas parties and gardening clubs, as well as assisting with office-based tasks such as newsletters and funding applications. This volunteering was punctuated by interviews and discussion groups of various kinds, especially with the groups' 'chairs' or leaders, Sandra and Jill. In 2013 I returned to visit the women and projects after a gap of eight years, specifically because I wanted to research the impacts of austerity on their work. This was a much smaller piece of research, involving interviews, a small discussion group and some ethnography with each of the groups.

The second piece of research discussed in Chapter 3 was undertaken in 2014 and was a pilot project for an envisaged wider project on women and austerity activism. I worked with one social enterprise that ran a network of migrant parents (overwhelmingly mothers) supporting others in North London primary schools. I led one half-day workshop and then did four in-depth follow-up interviews. The workshop focused on mapping communities and activism, asking the women to reflect on how they understood these terms and their positions and practices in relation to them. The interviews were in-depth interviews focused on the lifecourse (Worth, 2011). I asked the women to tell me their 'stories' however they wished to, and I then interjected to follow up aspects of interest to me. The experience of migration was generally the central narrative in these interviews, as the data shows. In terms of my own positionality, I was invited by the organisation to come and do the research, and there was a high level of willingness among the participants to be involved, I believe because of their desire to understand and extend their own activism.

The third project discussed in Chapter 3 formed part of a small-scale project on researching the impacts of austerity on community and voluntary sector projects in south-east England, during 2019–20, with a particular emphasis on projects focusing on women. I interviewed two women from an organisation I call the 'Coastal Arts project', initially about a 'period poverty' project that they had run. This had involved using creative and social media to raise awareness of how poverty impacted on women's access to sanitary products locally, and setting up a new network for individuals to donate and access products. During the pandemic I returned to do a further interview about their activities under COVID-19 (this is also discussed in Chapter 6). Plans for a more extended ethnography of the period poverty project with the organisation had to be abandoned because of the pandemic.

Chapter 4, 'Austerity politics and infrastructures of care: Children's Centre closures and activism', and Chapter 5, 'Small stories and political change: local activism across time and space', draw on the research project mentioned concerned with Children's Centre closures (see Jupp, 2020,2021b). The research was undertaken during 2017–18, on the processes of Children's Centre closures centrally in two localities in South East England, which I call Areas A and B, with a small amount of research on a third Area C. There is therefore a much closer focus on one empirical context and set of issues in these chapters. In Chapter 4 I focus on the politics and discourses of care at stake in closures, and in Chapter 5 I focus on activism and organising tactics that might take activism beyond the local.

Overall, I undertook 12 in-depth interviews, did social and conventional media analysis, and became a participant/observer/activist in relation to the campaign against closures in Area B. I also observed a court case and did one in-depth interview in a third area, Area C. Over the course of a year of research, I therefore started off undertaking more conventional research interviews, and then moved to participant-observation as an activist and campaigner, in a 'scholar-activist' position (Routledge and Derickson, 2015). This was partly due to beginning the research in an area where the campaign has essentially finished and centres were closing (Area A), to then researching in a local authority area where closures were being threatened (Area B). This involved giving evidence to the local authority as an 'expert witness', giving media interviews, and disseminating my research findings. As part of this I developed a co-produced animation using interview material, as further discussed, as an aspect of my commitment to seeking to use the research process to 'give voice' to my research participants as far as possible (see Cahill, 2007). In order to shape the 'stories' at the centre of this animation I used in-depth interviews to enable participants to discuss the importance of the Children's Centres in their lives. These narratives generally had the experience of becoming a mother at the centre of them.

The final empirical chapter is Chapter 6: 'Provisioning in times of crisis'. This chapter draws on my own experiences of volunteering under COVID-19, three in-depth interviews within a mutual aid scheme, as well as drawing more material from my research with the Coastal Arts project. Chapter 6 includes a reflexive discussion of this positionality, and I also draw on my own (shifting) feelings about mutual aid as part of the research material. This autoethnographic approach enabled me to include my own embodied and emotional responses as research data (Longhurst et al, 2008). However, as I note in Chapter 6, there is clearly a risk of researchers' own emotional experiences of a collective crisis such as the COVID-19 pandemic colouring all analysis. Such methodological and epistemological issues therefore form part of the challenges of researching a politics of everyday life.

As this summary has shown, the book's focus ranges across different forms of local action, activism and intervention – only some of which would normally be recognised as 'political'. As already noted, there are different ways to 'read' or analyse these activities, ranging from notions of 'resilience' or 'innovation' to 'survival' and 'resistance' (Vaiou and Kalandides, 2017; MacLeary et al, 2021). In order to trace the politics of everyday life that I wish to draw out, in the proceeding chapters I explore conceptual and theoretical questions of care, the welfare state, austerity, citizenship and activism.

1

Care, austerity and the politics of everyday lives

Introduction

This chapter considers a politics of care, firstly via a discussion of care ethics and conceptualisations of care in broad terms, before moving on to consider care and transformations of the welfare state and economy, including in relation to gender roles and processes of austerity. Care is an everyday and ongoing set of practices and relationship. In this book, the forms of care at stake include caring for children (especially as a mother), care for neighbours, care for older people and those with disabilities, 'young carers' supporting their parents, forms of community care, especially among migrant families newly arrived in the UK, and notions of 'self-care' and nurturing. All these forms of care involve vulnerabilities, needs and dependencies. However these forms and practices of care are not individual relational matters but in themselves caught up in wider structures and institutions that may be caring or uncaring. Forms of care may be sustained in the most hostile and uncaring environments. As such, a politics of care, as Joan Tronto (2015: 4) writes, must 'start in the middle of things. Care practices don't suddenly begin, they are already ongoing'. Within this book, the research projects discussed did not initially have a focus on care, rather I came to see that care practices and politics were crucial both for the actions of local activists, and the wider economic and political structures that framed these actions.

How, then, to approach this diffuse and everyday terrain? Theorising care has been a key concern for feminist scholars over decades. A starting point for recent discussions of care has often been Fisher and Tronto's definition of care as 'everything that we do to maintain, continue and repair our "world" so that we can live in it as well as possible' (1990: 40). As can be seen from this definition, feminist analysis since the 1980s has been concerned to define care in expansive and wide ranging ways, that place it at the centre of how society, politics and ethics are conceptualised (for example Noddings, 1984; Gilligan, 1993; Held, 1995), recognising that it has often been excluded and marginalised.

These approaches therefore represent a challenge to dominant understandings of care as a banal, everyday and practical matter, undertaken within a largely 'invisible' private sphere. Maintaining this private sphere has fallen crucially mainly to women, separated from politics and ethics within a notional 'public sphere' that has sought to deny human vulnerability and frailty (Davidoff, 2003; Pateman, 2016). A public–private divide in how care (and indeed politics more widely) is understood has been challenged by feminist writers and activists, yet remains a key dynamic in a politics of care. Another way to consider these lines is via notions of the 'visible' and the 'invisible' in society (see Newman, 2012; Jupp, 2017). That which is 'visible' in society might be considered a matter for political and media debate, while that which is 'invisible' may feel marginalised from mainstream political and media discourses, hidden in the home or domestic sphere.

Seminal feminist writing during the 1980s and 1990s brought care into the realm of politics by defining an 'ethics of care' as well as related normative questions of how 'good care' should be recognised and evaluated (Tronto, 1993; Svenhuijsen, 1998). These contributions sought to challenge the invisibility of care and place it at the centre of debates about justice, democracy and equality. These debates involve issues of needs, voice, power and inequality within caring relationships and within how care is organised in society more broadly.

These contributions were radical and far-reaching in the propositions they made about reframing the value that society generally places on care, demands that feminist analysis continues to make today (Care Collective, 2020; WBG, 2020b). A key challenge for analysis since has been to connect such thinking with already existing empirical practices, structures and spaces of care 'in the middle of things'. Indeed as Tronto (1993) does point out, care always involves embodied practices and emotions and feelings, as well as matters of politics and ethics (also quoted by Puig de la Bellacasa, 2017: 4). Embodied/affective and political/ethical dimensions of care can therefore be seen as often knotted together and inter-related, within particular spaces and places.

Sophie Bowlby (2012) and colleagues (Bowlby and McKie, 2019) seek to address this via the notion of 'caringscapes', a multifaceted approach to the everyday contexts, resources and relationships via which care is achieved in people's lives. More broadly place-based approaches to the 'geographies' or 'landscapes of care' (for example Milligan and Wiles, 2010; Power and Hall, 2018) offer opportunities to consider these multifaceted dynamics of care within specific contexts. Extending these conceptualisations has been Power and colleagues' (Power and Mee, 2018 ; Power et al, 2021) work on 'caring with', and 'infrastructures of care' approaches, which draw attention to the need for different kinds of material resources and structures in order for care to take place. This takes us into an analytic which grapples with the unequal and shifting contexts of care, and a need for a critical approach to the practices, politics and ethics of care in relation to specific sites, beyond interpersonal caring dynamics.

To return to the example at the start of the Introduction, Sandra and her group may have been providing important caring support to fellow residents through the food-sharing project, but the context of austerity which shaped this initiative means that the project is perhaps problematic in terms of the politics and ethics of care. Is it right that a small community group becomes responsible for the failures of the benefits system? And how sustainable is the care that they are offering? Indeed Sandra also spoke to me about feeling burnt out and exhausted from the current pressures on the group, as explored further in Chapter 3.

Recognising both the broader political, ethical and everyday and emplaced aspects of care can also help us to recognise its *ambivalent* and multifaceted nature. As these early feminist contributions pointed out, care can be viewed as a vital and progressive lens via which to frame new politics and ethics, involving recognising our human vulnerabilities and interdependencies. The joyful and life-affirming nature of care can be seen as a challenge to an individualistic and competitive neoliberal society (Care Collective, 2020). On the other hand, there is a risk that such approaches to care are over-celebratory, and lose sight of the sense that care is burdensome, potentially exploitative and often unrewarding embodied labour which is unequally distributed in society. Emejulu and Bassel capture this ambivalence with their propositions around seeing care as a 'double-edged sword' (2018: 9).

Care and inequalities

Caring labour, especially without an accompanying notion of self-care (Lorde, 1988; see also Ahmed, 2014), can be mentally and physically damaging to care-givers, and is a key site of oppression and inequality. As Raghuram (2019) points out, while debates on the ethics of care focus on the need for good care to be recognised as such by the care-receiver, there has been less focus on a recognition of the care needs of the self by the care-giver. This process of recognition may be challenging for those whose everyday lives and identities are tied up with the labour of care-giving; Raghuram (2019) argues that this applies especially to women of colour.

Indeed, while much analysis of care begins from the starting point that care has historically been associated with women, more recent analysis has called for an intersectional approach, recognising that differences of power and resources between groups of women may be as significant as gender differences overall with regards to care (Raghuram, 2019). Raghuram (2019: 626) argues that a 'normative white body' has been centred within debates about care. Intersectional approaches have therefore focused particularly on race and class and to the differential burdens of care that are experienced by groups of women, particularly women of colour and migrant women (Lonergan, 2015; McDowell, 2015). Not only does the work of care fall onto particular groups of women, but more privileged women can be seen as complicit in such burdening. The caring labour of racialised women has been differentially valued (Raghuram, 2016, 2019). This is shown, for example in research on nannies and domestic workers from the Global South (Pratt, 1997) and the treatment of au pairs in middle-class households (Cox, 2011).

Unpicking gender identities around care also means that there is a need to consider the role of men in relation to care, as in work on 'caring masculinities' as a challenge to normative male identities (Elliot, 2016; Tarrant, 2018; Jordan, 2020). More broadly, there is a danger of essentialism in defining gender roles within discussions of care and a need to contribute to a project within which care can be more equally distributed in society, partly via a transformation of gender roles and identities (Prügl, 2020). This raises wider questions for feminist analysis, and the study of women's lives, as the categories which animate such analysis may no longer hold together (Brown, 2003; MacLeavy et al, 2021). Indeed, more recent writing on care (Care Collective, 2020) has in many ways re-animated categories of analysis through drawing specifically on queer, post-colonial and critical race approaches that do not begin from potentially normative assumptions about the role of women in society (Robinson, 2020).

Demands for a more equal distribution of care in society, independent of particular axes of identity, have been at the centre of a somewhat different strand of feminist thought, that has called for care and housework to be recognised as labour with economic value. The term 'social reproduction' has been proposed to capture the labour of care and housework that supports all other productive labour within society and the economy (Laslett and Brenner, 1989; Bezanson and Luxton, 2006; Hall, 2020c). A view of care as work continues to inform strands of feminist analysis, therefore, and of the varying and unequal ways that such work is patterned (for example Kofman, 2012; Henry, 2018). And just as work on the ethics of care has argued for a new political and ethical settlement based on care, so have economists and care analysts argued for a new approach to the economy which places care at its centre, for example via the idea of the 'foundational economy' (Foundational Economy Collective, 2018). Considering questions of how care is valued and resourced in society takes analysis into the realm of political economy and the role of the state in relation to care, further explored in the next section of this chapter. Nonetheless, at this stage it is worth noting that there are perhaps dangers in seeking to focus primarily on the economic value of care (however 'the economy' is conceived) in that it potentially instrumentalises care, losing sight of the joyous and pleasurable aspects of care practices and relationships, as well as the promise of a more hopeful politics.

Overall, therefore, in the case studies that follow, matters of care will be considered as they arise within processes of austerity cuts and within practices of community activism and resistance. Care is central to the 'politics of everyday life' that I am seeking to illuminate. Such matters of care always involve embodied practices and emotions, but also politics and ethics. These politics and ethics concern questions of work and labour, power and inequality, and gender, class and race. They also concern the potential for visions of more care-full societies to provide a challenge to contemporary political and economic structures and suggest alternative futures. An important focus of both care in the here and now and in terms of imagining caring futures concerns the welfare state, which is explored in the following section.

The state, gender and care

The 'welfare state' is not one entity, and while political, ideological and economic shifts matter, a diversity of spaces, practices and relationalities may nonetheless co-exist (Clarke, 2005; Newman, 2012). Individuals and organisations may find themselves on the edges of welfare state arrangements, partly through increasingly complex governance arrangements. For example, the migrant parents' support network in schools, discussed in Chapter 3, was funded through a European funding stream that was delivered through a social enterprise. It would be hard to make a judgement about whether the network was acting within or outside a welfare state. Newman (2012) uses the idea of 'border work' for such arrangements and practices, an idea I return to at various points in this book. Furthermore, welfare and indeed nation states also have differing 'affective' as well as institutional and material patternings (Closs Stephens, 2016). In other words, how people feel about the welfare state and their relationship to it is also important. These ideas about the differentiated qualities of the welfare state will be returned to later in this chapter as well as throughout the book. Before this I turn to recent critiques of the contemporary welfare state in relation to care.

The welfare state in contexts such as the UK has played a key role in mediating boundaries between public and private spheres, and in some ways promises to resolve some of the inequalities of care already outlined (Fink, 2004). Social welfare, and its key concerns of housing, education, poverty, work and health, clearly seeks interventions into the household and home, and into intimate and 'private' matters of family, relationships and care. Therefore critical analysis of the welfare state in relation to care has been a focus for feminist analysis (for example Lister, 1998, 2003b; Twigg, 1999, 2000).

The development of the welfare state in mid-20th century Britain clearly had profound impacts on women as care-givers, both in their everyday or home lives and in their working lives too (Thane, 2016). Yet the gendered nature of the issues at hand was little acknowledged by the early architects of welfare, and arguably often continues to be silenced. Nancy Fraser (2016) explores this territory in her essay 'Contradictions of capital and care', which examines the links between care, economy and the welfare state. While in the mid years of the 20th century questions of 'public welfare' began to enable state support for women and the terrain of 'social reproduction' previously considered, Fraser argues that these regimes in many ways bolstered normative ideals of patriarchal family life. In the early days of the welfare state, men were expected to earn a 'family wage' that would cover women's unpaid reproductive labour, within a normative ideal of the heterosexual patriarchal family. Therefore, while on one level, the development of the contemporary welfare state made aspects of women's lives matters of public and visible concern, on other levels it shored up these aspects of lives within traditional unequal and exploitative models (Fink, 2004).

Overall, Fraser (2016) argues that shifting forms of capitalism, the welfare state and caring labour (or social reproduction) have resulted in a series of settlements between these aspects of society, settlements which have not necessarily improved women's everyday lives. Fraser (2016) also critiques a veneer of women's empowerment under a neoliberal political economy that may benefit individual (already privileged) women but does nothing to contribute to collective change, indeed undermines it. She describes this as 'a perverse configuration, in which emancipation joins with marketisation to undermine social protection' (2016: 114), a dynamic that she terms 'progressive neoliberalism'. This essay sits alongside Fraser's critiques of contemporary versions of feminism (Fraser, 2013) that she sees as complicit in these shifts: promoting superficial versions of empowerment that bolster neoliberalism and failing to address collective issues of welfare and care that remain central to women's lives. Mary Evans (2015) has made a similar argument about the 'entrepreneurial' turn in feminism that serves to bolster neoliberalism and excludes many women (see also Dabrowski, 2020).

Such a 'perverse configuration' involves pushing women out of the home into paid work in the 'dual income' household model, meaning that care becomes commodified and outsourced to other women, working for low pay and at a cost to their ability to care for their own families. As Fraser writes (2013: 116), 'typically, it is racialised, women from poor regions who take on the reproductive and caring labour previously performed by more privileged women'. As noted in the previous section about how groups of women might be unequally burdened by caring labour, so the welfare state has shaped different relationships of power with different groups of women. Gunaratnam and Lewis (2001), for example, analyse the racialised subject positions at the centre of caring labour within social care and social work.

Alongside such exploitation of certain groups of women, Fraser argues that various 'technical fixes' have been proposed to overcome these 'contradictions' that arise between care, capitalism and the welfare state (see also Dowling, 2018). For example, Fraser discusses breast pumps and technologies of breastfeeding available to women working in corporate jobs in America (where there is very little entitlement to paid maternity leave). While seeming to promote 'flexible working', which enables women to both undertake caring labour (albeit at a distance) and paid work, Fraser argues that essentially such 'fixes' promote the march of neoliberal capitalism while systematically de-valuing care. Fraser's argument therefore suggests that the welfare state continues to evade real responsibility for care, despite the rhetoric of gender equality. Care continues to be undertaken by women either within their own home or commodified within the homes of others or in privatised institutions, while the state overall promotes forms of neoliberal capitalism. Implicit in Fraser's analysis, then, is the need for a rethinking of the state and of its relationship to care, to shape a more progressive and collective political and economic settlement around care.

However, as well as these calls for an entirely new politics and economics of care, there is also value in paying more attention to the diverse political and economic practices which may co-exist in the here and now. Newman (2012) argues, in relation to Fraser's analysis of the complicity between feminism and neoliberalism, that there is a danger in glossing over the differentiated nature of strands of feminist thought, which may or may not be complicit in neoliberal capitalism. There is also a danger, as already outlined, of not paying sufficient attention to the differentiated nature of the welfare state and the forms of care, as well as citizenship or empowerment that might emerge from within it, around it and despite it. This means more attention to the micro-politics of care and welfare. This argument is further developed at the end of this chapter, after a discussion on the impacts of austerity on the issues already considered.

Care, the welfare state and austerity

It is clear that the 'place' of care within society has shifted again with austerity (Power and Hall, 2018). Austerity is a shorthand term for the programme of cuts and retrenchment of the welfare state that has taken place in the UK, and across Europe and other economies of the Global North since the global financial crash of 2008 (Farnsworth and Irving, 2015; Gray and Barford, 2018). This has been an economic, political and ideological programme to shrink welfare provision (Clarke and Newman, 2012). As well as cuts and changes to welfare benefits and services, UK local government lost over half its central government income between 2010 and 2016 (Centre for Cities, 2019). As Annette Hastings and colleagues (2017) evidence, these impacts fell most heavily on cities and on disadvantaged populations, although they also show that many more progressive local authorities have sought to protect the poorest communities from aspects of these cuts. Nonetheless every aspect of the welfare state that might provide and enable care has been reduced or reshaped in the UK, from benefits and social housing, to social care of different kinds, and many of the spaces and resources that provide the overall structures of care within communities and localities (Hastings et al, 2017; Jupp, 2019). At the same time, the level of needs within disadvantaged communities has increased exponentially, as the opening example in the Introduction showed, creating a 'perfect storm' (Lowndes and McCaughie, 2013) of increased pressure on service providers and decreased resources to respond.

As analysis in this book will show, austerity involves not just cuts to spending but reshapes the rationalities and practices of different aspects of the welfare state. Some public sector workers and particular community organisations reliant on public funding may resist funding and programme cuts with new practices and ethics of care, and, like the residents' group at the opening of this book, find creative ways to keep going (Morse and Munro, 2018). As the central state withdraws and cuts resources and services, there may be the possibility of new local alliances and practices, in what Featherstone et al have called 'progressive localism' (Featherstone et al, 2012). Such potentialities for new forms of citizenship and community action under austerity are discussed in the following chapter.

Nonetheless, whatever might emerge via the actions of citizens, there remains an underlying reality that decreased capacity and funding inevitably has a detrimental impact on the ability of public sector workers and services to engage in sustained and meaningful caring relationships with service users, in whatever sector (Clayton et al, 2016). Public sector workers from youth workers (Horton, 2016) to social workers (Bywaters et al, 2018) may have less time and emotional capacity to care, potentially exhausted and drained by the cuts and pressures wrought on services by austerity (Hitchen, 2016).

Furthermore, with austerity comes not just less capacity and resources to care, but also new ideologies and politics of care that shift the emphasis and orientations of many services. For example, retreating from widespread concern to support families in need of care, new rationalities of services move to a focus only on what Emejulu and Bassel (2018) call 'failed care': households that require 'interventions' in order to avoid risks to children and vulnerable groups, and indeed risks to the reputations of welfare services. These debates have perhaps been particularly acute within social work (Featherstone et al, 2018) which navigates this emotionally complex terrain of potential abuse and neglect of children and others (Warner, 2013) and has arguably become increasingly focused on avoiding risk rather than providing care and support for families. Outside social work too though there is an increased emphasis on 'targeted interventions' aimed at those 'most in need', although such interventions may be experienced as more controlling than caring for needs (Gillies et al, 2017). These shifting ideologies of care (explored in more detail in Chapter 4 in relation to Children's Centres) therefore seek to rework the links between families and their domestic spaces and the welfare state (see Jupp, 2019).

In this situation, everyday care (as opposed to those falling under judgements of 'failed care') moves back into the household, what England (2010) calls the 're-privatisation of social reproduction'. This therefore involves a shrinking of the structures of care via which households might experience collective support (Jupp, 2019). This means that austerity is encountered, felt, experienced and perhaps resisted (or at least endured) within the gendered and domestic spheres of everyday lives (Hall, 2020a; Stenning, 2020). As noted in the Introduction, this can mean that austerity is not necessarily readily 'visible' within media and policy debates, or even within research. The 'crises' of austerity may be everyday and seemingly mundane (Jupp et al, 2019) although they may also be dramatic at times, when certain moments (such as the closure of a centre or service) bring impacts into new focus (Needham, 2014). Closures of services are discussed in Chapter 4.

Women are therefore impacted unequally by austerity in a range of ways (Boyer et al, 2017). Firstly, as much research has shown, on a very material level they have been unequally impacted by benefit changes, loss of employment in the public sector and the withdrawing of resources from public services (MacLeavy, 2011; Greer Murphy, 2017). As Women's Budget Group (2016) analysis also shows, different groups of women have been differentially impacted, with minority ethnic women particularly hit. Bassel and Emejulu (2017) have also shows how the voluntary and community sector around Black and minority ethnic women has also been particularly impacted by austerity cuts, undermining these organisations as sources of support and resources for women of colour (see also Lonergan, 2015; Vacchelli et al, 2015).

On the level of labour, therefore, there is the sense of women needing to do more care as state resources and structures are withdrawn via austerity from an already neoliberal state. And this care involves not just everyday practices and resources, but the more affective labour of keeping households going when times are difficult, of 'managing' the impacts of austerity overall. This may range from the decisions involved in shopping and feeding a household (Cappellini et al, 2014), often involving sacrificing personal nourishment, to various forms of 'thrift' and 'make do and mend' (Tosh, 2013; Holmes, 2019) As subsequent chapters in this book show, women may also be at the centre of efforts within communities to resist austerity politically (Watt, 2016; Jupp, 2017) and this may offer up possibilities for women's citizenship to be expressed in new ways, as further explored in Chapter 2. As I go on to discuss, structures of anti-austerity activism beyond the local may nonetheless exclude women (Craddock, 2020).

The crisis of austerity has now been overlaid with the crisis of the COVID-19 pandemic, which, as emergent analysis has shown, has also impacted on women in unequal ways (WBG, 2020a). Indeed, many of the issues already discussed around inequalities, care and the unequal values of different forms of work have been brought into sharp focus as everyday lives have come under extreme pressure during the pandemic (Care Collective, 2020). As many of the normal systems for organising social reproduction, including education and care, were shut down or massively reduced because of the health crisis, research has shown that it has been women's caring labour that has disproportionately filled the gaps (Bowlby and Jupp, 2021; Brickell, 2020a). For example many more mothers than fathers have undertaken homeschooling with children while schools have been shut (Petts et al, 2020). At the same time, women, and especially women of colour, undertaking waged frontline care work in the social care and health sectors have been extremely vulnerable to the virus (Ahmed, 2020; Dobusch and Kreissl, 2020). To return to Fraser's argument, the pandemic has exposed some of the failures of the 'fixes' proposed by the contemporary welfare state to truly address inequalities around care, labour and bodily vulnerability. Furthermore, the impact of austerity in stripping away much of the infrastructure that had been provided by the UK welfare state, around, for example public health and social care, has been seen as a factor in the UK's very high death and infection rates (Bambra et al, 2020).

Conclusion

On the one hand, therefore, the welfare state and the caring structures it promises are in crisis. Beginning from that place, however, one of the purposes of this book is to illuminate how the crises of austerity and of COVID-19 might also be seen as politically productive moments. While not in any way to be celebrated, focusing on these crises can bring to our attention matters of care, citizenship and the welfare state in new ways. Indeed, as Fraser (2016) acknowledges alongside her critique, there is a value in paying attention to the micropolitics of debates and activism around welfare services, as containing within them contested visions of how the welfare state and care might be differently imagined. As she argues, struggles over social reproduction (housing, community services, childcare, etc) involve summoning up new visions of society and care: 'taken together, these claims are tantamount to the demand for a massive reorganisation of the relation between production and reproduction ... involving a new alliance between social protection and emancipation' (Fraser, 2016: 116). The even more immediate crisis (at the time of writing) around the COVID-19 pandemic, has prompted renewed expressions of and discussions around these matters too (for example Care Collective, 2020). The Conclusion discusses the crisis of the pandemic in more detail.

Moving on from Fraser's (2013, 2016) critiques discussed earlier in this chapter, despite the failures of the welfare state to address inequalities, it seems clear that it is desirable to have collective structures of care in society, away from the unequal and exploitative contexts of households and family. New visions of the welfare state and the economy are needed, but these might arise from paying attention to 'entangled' practices and politics of care in the here and now as well as looking to the future. Indeed much analysis has already discussed how a more radical politics of care can exist within and through the spaces of public service provision, perhaps through the kind of 'border work' already mentioned (Barnes and Prior, 2009; Newman, 2012). Through various kinds of policy experiments and programmes, both long-standing and more recent, welfare services can and do provide spaces of care – not just commodified forms of childcare or for other groups, but care among carers, those being cared for, and state professionals (Jupp, 2013b). These sites and spaces might be taken seriously in providing 'prefigurative' resources to enable us to imagine the welfare state differently (Cooper et al, 2019).

In terms of how such experiments and programmes might be thought through more systematically, Tronto (2010) has discussed the principles for 'caring institutions'. Crucially she argues that such institutions need to hold open democratic spaces, within which matters and experiences of care can be debated and contested from a range of perspectives. More recently, analysis has focused on notions of 'infrastructures' of care (Lopes et al, 2018; Alam and Houston, 2020; Hall, 2020c), that might configure households, institutions and community and voluntary sector structures, spaces and resources in a range of ways, placing care more centrally in the organisation of society. This notion of infrastructure potentially enables an holistic consideration of what is needed to support the caringscapes (Bowlby, 2012) or landscapes of care that individuals or households operate within, which are at present hugely unequal. This notion of 'infrastructure' will be further explored in the book and returned to in the Conclusion.

Taking seriously such a politics of care requires a different orientation to care that sees it not solely as 'unwaged labour' (although it is that too), but also holding within it radical forms of empathy, community and connection across difference (Lawson, 2007; Morrow and Parker, 2020). Indeed, as Emejulu and Bassel argue in relation to women of colour in particular, there is a need to think critically about how care can both subordinate and repress women, but also to think more hopefully about care as resistance and political agency: 'Care is a double-edged sword of domination and resistance. Care is a politics of becoming' (2018: 9). This may require thinking again about what is meant by 'resistance' and 'political agency' as well as attending to the ways that lines between public and private spheres may be further shifting in new modes of activism. Such a politics of care as it might enable new expressions of citizenship is discussed in more detail in the following chapter.

To summarise, this chapter has discussed the question of the place of care in society. It has focused on how care has been conceptualised, particularly within feminist analysis, in relation to the inequalities it entails and how it might be differently valued. The place of the welfare state in both overcoming and exacerbating inequalities of care has been discussed. The crises of austerity over the past decade, as well as the much more recent crisis of the COVID-19 pandemic, have both intensified and exacerbated many of the problematics of care. Nonetheless, as discussed at the opening, care contains within it the promise of new forms of connection, community and relationality, indeed new forms of citizenship. It is key to the 'politics of everyday life' at the centre of this book. Such promise of new forms of citizenship is clearly complex and it is to this terrain that the next chapter turns.

2

Citizenship and community in times of crisis

Introduction

This chapter continues the themes of the previous chapter, but with a focus on how the issues discussed, of gendered dynamics of care in society, social welfare and conditions of austerity, create a context for forms of political subjectivity and action, or citizenship. This begins with a focus on the specific context of the UK state, and its relationship to the scale of community and local action. The second section focuses on more conceptual issues around citizenship and the 'politics of everyday life', including notions of vulnerability, the lifecourse and storytelling as forming aspects of political action, that can enable us to trace this emergent politics.

'Community' is obviously a contested term (Joseph, 2002), suggesting both a local scale and also a social entity denoting belonging and inclusion or exclusion. Communities may be based on locations or on identities or both. For the purposes of this book, community represents a space for action, a space both material, but also emotional, relational and political. As will be further explored, the spaces of community potentially offer spaces for political action and citizenship to those who are unable to participate in more formal and wider scales of politics (Staeheli, 2008). There are debates around the definitions of 'activism' at such a scale (Martin et al, 2007), an issue discussed further in the next section of this chapter. For the purposes of this book, I generally use the terms 'local action' or 'activism' as opposed to 'community action', as I feel these terms enable links to wider debates around politics and citizenship that the term 'community' can render problematic, as will be explained.

As subsequent chapters will show, for those undertaking forms of activism and local action, 'community' might be defined in a wide range of ways, from a fairly large urban area to a small neighbourhood (indeed 'community' is sometimes used interchangeably with the term 'neighbourhood' in policy), from online spaces, to service users of a particular 'community centre', to a diaspora stretching across continents or an axis of identity. Community is clearly 'imagined' (Anderson, 2006), and a notion of a settled and non-conflictual community is a fiction. Therefore acting in the space of community involves grappling with these conflictual dynamics (Staeheli and Thompson, 1997). The conflictual nature of community also represents a challenge for social science research. Since an era of 'community studies' within the social sciences in the second half of the 20th century (see Lawrence, 2019), there has been some wariness of the politics of community within social science research. This is because of the dangers of romanticising or essentialising a scale of politics often seen as politically regressive, and a sense of the limitations that analysis at this scale offers.

Community, local action and the welfare state: the third way

A wariness around community from contemporary social scientists may also be linked to its close association with particular policy discourses in recent decades (Imrie and Raco, 2003). Just as the previous chapter discussed shifting and often uneasy settlements between matters of 'care' and the welfare state, so has there been a related and often uneasy set of settlements between dynamics of 'community' and the UK welfare state (Rose, 2000). Like care, and 'the home' (see Franklin, 2019), 'community' has proved useful to policy makers in promising to provide resources of care, connectivity and belonging which fill in the gaps of what the state might provide. However, such a dynamic has shifted considerably over the past 20 years in UK welfare policy, creating very different contexts for community and local action (Levitas, 2012). One of the projects discussed in Chapter 3, the residents' groups in Stoke-on-Trent, spans the years of such policy changes and provides an empirical example of the shifting impacts of policy regimes on local action. The discussion here sets out some broader context, which also provides relevant background to more recent research material.

A concern with 'community' has been apparent within UK urban and social policy at least since the 1980s, when processes of de-industrialisation were seen to be destroying traditional working-class neighbourhoods (Meegan and Mitchell, 2001). Alongside such communities as sites of economic and social concern, practices of state-funded community organising and 'community development' also worked with more radical rationalities of empowering or giving voice to excluded communities (Gilchrist, 2003). Yet in the UK at least, it was during the 'New Labour' centre-left government (1997–2010) that 'community' became more central to social and urban policy.

This government drew on the ideology of the 'third way' (Rose, 2000; Giddens, 2013) in emphasising the importance of 'community' as a site between the state and the market. As Prime Minister (1997–2007) Tony Blair said in a speech in 2005, his policy programme had sought in many ways to reduce the involvement of the welfare state in people's lives: 'Today is not the era of the big state, but a strategic one: empowering, enabling, putting decision making in the hands of people, not government' (see *Guardian*, 2005). As he also outlined in this speech, his government sought to enable mechanisms of the market, such as choice and competition into public services. Nonetheless, public spending increased considerably during the New Labour government, within a programme of 'modernisation' of public services (Newman, 2001), and investment in aspects of services such as education in particular (and early years, as in the Sure Start centres discussed in Chapters 4 and 5).

Such programmes fitted broadly within a 'social investment' model of the state (Lister, 2003b). This was therefore in many ways an individualistic vision of providing 'opportunities' rather than equality. The state would invest in citizens' and families' lives, but would not necessarily provide an overall supportive framework for lives, and nor indeed would it seek to shift the overall balance of the economy and resources available. As a buffer against this rather individualistic and atomised view of society, 'community' programmes and activities were invested in, within an often rather moralistic vision of communities (Wallace, 2010), alongside an agenda focused on shaping behaviour through mechanisms such as 'Anti-Social Behaviour Orders' (Squires, 2006).

In concrete terms, between 1997 and 2010 there were swathes of neighbourhood and community programmes, generally aimed at the 'most deprived' or 'most disadvantaged' areas (Lupton, 2003; Lawless, 2006), although some (like the Children's Centre programme) were extended to become universal programmes. Initially, these programmes, such as the New Deal for Communities, were 'area-based', bringing new resources to an area but often accompanied by very complex systems of 'partnership' working and indeed forms of bureaucracy and managerialism (Newman, 2001; Lawless, 2006). Community organisations, including residents' groups and charity and voluntary sector organisations, became more firmly emmeshed in governance strategies, creating complex partnership arrangements on the edges or 'borders' of the state, as already mentioned. Area-based programmes were then gradually replaced with other forms of 'neighbourhood management', again based on targets and central management of 'outcomes' (Sullivan, 2002; Griggs and Roberts, 2012).

As will be shown in the discussion in Chapter 3, this meant that for residents in such areas involved in local activism, these programmes were often experienced in very ambivalent ways (Jupp, 2013a). On the one hand, new resources and personnel were present in their areas, and in theory at least, there was a desire to listen to the voices and perspectives of residents in allocating such resources. On the other hand, the programmes were overly bureaucratic, creating a complex web of funding pots and target-driven programmes (Newman, 2001). This meant that the programmes could feel exclusionary for the very residents they were seeking to empower. As wider evaluation has shown (Lawless, 2006), the programmes were often grappling with far wider structural issues, such as problems of employment and health inequalities, that could not effectively be tackled on a local basis. In this sense, 'community' could be seen as a 'fix' for far wider problems, like the 'fixes' for care discussed in the previous chapter, or the even more short-term 'sticking plasters' mentioned in the Introduction.

However, as my previous research (see Jupp, 2013b) showed, if nothing else, the programmes could enable the formation of new relationships and connections between residents and community workers employed on the programmes. Individual workers could create caring and solidaristic relationships with residents, even if these did not reflect the overall rationalities of the programmes they were working under (Barnes and Prior, 2009). Such connections could therefore enable small community groups to access funding and resources in new ways, often working in complex arrangements on the 'borders' of such programmes (see Newman, 2012; Jupp, 2020).

Local action and austerity governance

So while community programmes under New Labour were partly framed by a narrative of reducing reliance on 'the state', they nonetheless took place within a context of relatively generous state spending. Under the Conservative coalition and then Conservative governments from 2010 onwards, this narrative persisted, but framed by the programme of austerity cuts and reductions discussed in the previous chapter (Levitas, 2012; Hastings et al, 2017). At a neighbourhood level, this involved the loss of the infrastructures of community development and support that had grown up during the previous government (see Jupp, 2021a) as well as closures of spaces and massive reductions in services, alongside benefit cuts and reductions in other forms of state support.

David Cameron's coalition government in particular (2010–16) promoted notions of the 'Big Society' and 'localism' to express a vision of communities, volunteers and local agencies stepping in to fill up the gaps as the state withdrew from whole areas of public services (Lowndes and Pratchett, 2012; Williams et al, 2014), as mentioned in the previous chapter. The discourses around these programmes also functioned as a critique of New Labour's policies (Newman, 2014) with programmes promising 'freeing from red tape' and a more meaningful transfer of decision-making powers to localities and communities. Volunteering, voluntary action and the 'transfer of assets' that had belonged to local government to community groups or charities have been key actions under the discourses of localism (Wills, 2016).

Therefore, as discussed in the previous chapter, austerity involves not just reductions in spending but new governance arrangements and modes of operation for the welfare state. As the discussion of Children's Centre cuts in Chapters 4 and 5 shows, the politics of austerity has certainly involved a distancing of central government from local decision and actions, with local authorities 'free' to make their own decisions about the future of such services (Clayton et al, 2016). However, this is within a context of the severing of resources from central to local government and to grants and funding available to communities, as well as increased need due to benefit cuts. Local authorities experienced overall falls in income of nearly 50 per cent between 2010 and 2017, depending on how it is calculated (Hastings et al, 2017; Centre for Cities, 2019). Therefore groups and local government have been working within extremely constrained contexts, and the de-centralisation of power involved can be experienced more as an abnegation of responsibility (Penny, 2017). As Clayton et al (2016) show, local government ends up feeling more 'distant' from localities as it works with increasingly stretched resources.

As will be seen in Chapter 3, as well as in the example at the start of the Introduction, under austerity, community groups have therefore been expected to become self-sustaining and independent, perhaps 'social enterprises', while they are also more depended upon than ever to meet material needs in communities (Milbourne and Cushman, 2015). Such material needs include food and sanitary products (Briggs, 2021). Indeed foodbanks, and the exponential increase in their number and their use since 2010 (Trussell Trust, 2020), have come to be seen as a central and almost symbolic example of the dynamics of austerity and community action in particular, as discussed in the Introduction (Garthwaite, 2016; Cloke et al, 2017; Strong, 2019, 2021). Mostly run by a Christian network, the Trussell Trust, foodbank usage has a clear link to failures of the welfare state, often used by individuals and households experiencing delays and problems with accessing the state benefits system (Butler, 2016).

So, to return to one of the central questions of this book, what is the meaning of local action and activism within this constrained context? Are there possibilities for empowerment and agency for local activists and community organisations at such a moment, or are organisations such as foodbanks essentially complicit in regimes of austerity (see Strong, 2020)? Analysis (for example Cohen et al, 2017), has both critiqued the rise of community action under austerity from this perspective, but also traced the contours of emergent forms of local activism, solidarity and empowerment. On a material level, there is no doubt that the community and voluntary sector are working in extremely constrained circumstances, losing grants and income while grappling with increased social need. This has fallen in uneven ways, across regions (Centre for Cities, 2019) as well as across different groups of the population. As previously mentioned, Vacchelli et al (2015) have traced the impacts of cuts on women's organisations, and within that, the disproportionate impact on minority ethnic women's organisations. Emejulu and Bassel (2018) have also traced the political and financial constraints of minority women's organisations through austerity.

As well as material financial constraints, the context of austerity has been seen to produce a kind of deadening of political energy and horizons. Horton (2016) talks about the affective sense of the 'current climate' permeating all senses of what the youth group he was researching might do in the future. Hitchen (2016) and Wilkinson and Ortega-Alcázar (2019) have both written about austerity as producing a wearying, exhausting set of dynamics among those encountering, coping or seeking to resist it.

On the other hand, research has shown that volunteers or those taking local action are often resistant to the policy regimes that they are working within, and may, perhaps in small and embodied ways, exert their own senses of citizenship and agency (Newman, 2012; Cohen et al, 2017). For example, as I have argued elsewhere, in some ways the context of austerity enables new creative forms of home-based and very localised activism, engaging with matters of care, housing and social isolation for example (Jupp, 2017). New organisations operating as 'social enterprises' or very localised charities may indeed be able to meet local need in ways quite different from the bureaucracy and constraints of conventional local services. As will be explored in relation to the 'Coastal Arts project' in Chapter 3, new organisations in this space may draw instead on informal relations and connections around the home, family and community. And there are no straightforward answers to questions around the politics of foodbanking, as briefly discussed in the Introduction. As a number of research projects have shown, they do have the potential to function as spaces of political and consciousness raising on some level (Cloke et al, 2017; Strong, 2019). Nonetheless, as Bock and Cohen (2017) argue, while community action under austerity may shift 'small scale realities', it does not necessarily impact on wider political discourses and spheres.

This then raises questions of different forms of action and activism under austerity, including grappling with the broader matters of what constitutes and activism and also 'resistance' to dominant political and economic regimes. During the first few years of austerity in the UK in particular, there was a rise in anti-austerity activism, partly linked on a national level to a number of networks including 'UK Uncut' and 'People's Assembly against Austerity' (see Ishkanian and Peña Saavedra, 2019; Craddock, 2020). As well as participating in a number of large demonstrations, these networks co-ordinated playful and localised interventions into public space, highlighting the social and spatial injustices of austerity cuts (see Cammaerts, 2018). In particular this has been a politics which has worked across public/private boundaries and spaces and circulated around the kinds of matters of care discussed in the previous chapter (Jupp, 2017).

Specific local issues have also at times brought to national attention, for example the eviction of a group of young mothers from a hostel in East

London, who became known as the Focus E15 mums and took part in actions including squatting empty local housing and legal action (see Watt, 2016). It is perhaps hard to assess the overall impact of the anti-austerity movement, which is ongoing (especially in areas such as housing, see Nowicki, 2021) yet has not necessarily coalesced into a longer term movement, while austerity cuts have persisted (Cammaerts, 2018). Nonetheless, via circulation on social media and digital spaces in particular, such groups have developed a repertoire of local anti-austerity activism that has been taken up by other local struggles, such as activism against Children's Centre cuts discussed in Chapter 5. Legal challenges have also been part of such a repertoire, as further explored in Chapter 6. In any case, as already set out, struggles against austerity might also be understood to take place within a wide range of contexts, not just explicit 'activism', but within and among the kinds of community and local action already discussed. Indeed, as already suggested, it is one of the contentions of this book that it is more helpful to consider citizenship and political subjectivity across a spectrum of activities, from very 'everyday' forms of coping to more explicit and conventional activism. The case studies that follow clearly span these practices. Such a spectrum then raises wider questions about definitions of politics and citizenship. The next section of this chapter places these questions within a wider conceptual vocabulary of the meanings and registers of 'political' action.

Rethinking citizenship and the politics of everyday life

On what basis can those marginalised from mainstream politics enter spaces of political agency, inhabit identities of citizenship? This is a question which has been considered historically in relation to women, again drawing on notions of the public and private as discussed in Chapter 1 (Davidoff, 2003; Pateman, 2016) and the exclusion of women from sites of formal citizenship and public representation (Lister, 2003a; Roseneil, 2013). Such analysis begins with the exclusion of women from the Greek agora and some of the foundational sites of contemporary Western democracy. As discussed in the previous chapter in relation to care, women's association with private spaces, and the supposedly non-political realm of domestic life, led to them being seen as ill-equipped to inhabit realms of properly 'political' and public decision-making.

One strand or narrative, therefore, of feminist analysis and action would be of the struggle for women to enter realms of formal citizenship and enfranchisement – claiming the right to vote, to hold public office, to participate in decision-making (see Roseneil, 2013). To return to the argument of the previous chapter, these changes have gone alongside the entry of women into the labour market, of economic 'empowerment' (Fraser, 2016). Yet equally, as Fraser's (2016) analysis shows, strands of feminist critique have questioned the extent to which marginalised groups of women (and other marginalised groups in society) have been empowered and enfranchised by such changes (Lister, 2007; Lister et al, 2007). In addressing this, such analysis also seeks wider definitions of citizenship, to extend what might be thought of as moments of political subjectivity and agency for those still excluded from conventional public spheres. These strands of analysis therefore extend and critique T.H. Marshall's (1964) propositions of citizenship that have been so very influential in policy and welfare thinking. Moving beyond rights, responsibilities and legal status, new approaches point to the importance of subjective experiences of participation, belonging and political action, with regards to both state and civil society (Abraham, 2010).

Engin Isin (2017; Isin and Nielsen, 2013), for example, has proposed the notion of 'citizenship acts', emphasising the diverse practices and processes of claiming political space that cannot be equated with formal demands and processes of state recognition and representation. Citizenship therefore becomes a series of processes, which might include formal democratic processes of recognition of identity, democratic representation and rights, but also potentially involving a multitude of both everyday and overtly subversive acts. These might range from forms of community organising and relationship building to acts of protest in public space and in media spaces (Isin, 2017). Such an approach also ties in with Nancy Fraser's (1990) conceptualisation of 'counter-publics' that sit outside mainstream public spheres. These are important not just in relation to making demands on hegemonic public spheres, but also seeking to reconfigure the rules by which they operate, the 'genres' of public-ness at stake.

One example of such an approach would be Umut Erel and colleagues' (Erel, 2011; Erel et al, 2018) work on 'migrant mothers' in a UK context. The category of 'migrant mothers' she sees as encompassing women from a range of backgrounds but drawn together by experiences of migration and care for children. She sees the mothers as 'enacting citizenship' or undertaking citizenship acts through their practices of care for their children and their everyday negotiation of aspects of life in their new home cultures, as well as negotiating relations with others in the cultures from which they migrated. These everyday acts can be seen as carving out a space of political agency and articulation from a subjugated and marginalised set of positionings, around gender, ethnicity, economic and migration status and more. Their particular kinds of citizenship acts reflect these positionings, 'enacting subjugated knowledges' (Erel et al, 2018: 69).

Erel's work can be seen as tracing examples of the kinds of feminist politics which MacLeavy et al (2021) draw attention to, as comprising (entangled) practices of 'resistance, reworking and resilience' rather than what might seem explicit politics. Their analysis sits alongside that of other feminist commentators within the social sciences who have developed a vocabulary to consider how 'everyday' (see Dyck, 2005) and intimate lives can be the site of expressions of (subjugated) citizenship. This is a vision of citizenship as tied up with matters of care, of everyday relationality and connection associated with matters of 'getting by' and 'helping out' that can sustain everyday life in communities grappling with material deprivation (Jupp, 2012).

Alongside this sense of the politics of the 'everyday', another important theme within the research presented in the rest of the book is around how the lifecourse (such as migration) might shape, disrupt or produce forms of local action and activism (Woolvin and Hardill, 2013). As will be seen, many of my research participants spoke about the impact of having children on their activism and engagement, as well as migration, starting or losing other forms of paid work, or being reliant on particular services and therefore becoming aware of different kinds of need in society. Citizenship may therefore be expressed in different ways at different points in the lifecourse, within the shifting spaces and times that everyday life makes available, and entangled with matters of care. This disrupts a notion of empowerment and citizenship as necessarily a linear process.

Related to matters of what counts as 'citizenship' are clearly questions about what counts as 'activism', already touched on in this book (Martin et al, 2007). The label of 'activist' can clearly exclude as much as it might include (Craddock, 2020). While most research on activism and social movements focuses on more conventional interventions, there has been discussion on notions of 'horizontal' activism (Fincher and Panelli, 2001) taking place in the background of other more visible forms of activism and involving practices and matters of care. These notions have a particular history in a US context, and among the struggles and histories of Black organising in particular, whereby grassroots community focused activism might stand in contrast – or background – to more confrontational activism which targets structures of power (see Morrow and Parker, 2020). Amy Howard (2014) discusses 'affective activism' among tenants of San Francisco housing blocks, involving building relationships and provisioning through activities such as communal barbeques and everyday forms of support, in a situation of feeling abandoned by those in power. In a UK context, recent researchers in geography have identified practices of 'quiet activism' (Askins, 2014; Pottinger, 2017). Hughes (2020), in a review of understandings of 'resistance' in human geography, argues that these approaches also involve thinking differently about intentionality and reflexivity within activism. In a discussion of the Women's March in Washington in 2017, ostensibly an explicit and conventional form of 'resistance', she argues that those taking part could not 'fully know what claim [they were] making now, nor the conditions of possibility for future claims' being created (Hughes, 2020: 1141).

Such analysis therefore blurs the boundaries between conventional activism and other practices of everyday lives. In relation to practices of collective care and survival, a slightly different strand of thought has figured such everyday practices as involving 'prefigurative politics' – an enactment of a better society in the here and now (Cooper, 2017; Ince, 2012). Such a formulation potentially reframes community, care-based and local activism as not secondary to 'proper activism' involving explicit ideologies and visions and programmes of political change (although see Hughes, 2020), but rather enacting both alternative visions and modes, in a 'minor' rather than major key (Katz, 2017; Secor and Linz, 2017). Certainly of the local activists interviewed in this book, very few would have called themselves 'activists', or even have described themselves as doing anything political. However their actions may still be enacting or bringing into being alternative ways of being, 'new ways of being in the world' (MacLeavy et al, 2021: 9) at whatever scale. The notion of prefigurative politics therefore enables modalities of politics that can be occupied by those completely outside conventional public or political spheres.

Vulnerability and storytelling

A further development in understanding political action among those conventionally excluded from politics has been Judith Butler and colleagues' recent work on 'vulnerability' as a starting point for political action (Butler, 2014; Butler et al, 2016). Matters of vulnerability and dependence clearly relate to the matters of care already discussed. Bodily vulnerability has often been hidden in the private or domestic sphere, managed by the caring labour of women and framed by the categorisations of the welfare state (Twigg, 1999).

Butler's work on the politics of vulnerability also draws on a far wider orientation towards 'affect' and 'emotions' within social science theory, demanding that these aspects of experiences and their political power are taken more seriously (for example Gould, 2009; Greco and Stenner, 2013; Pedwell, 2014). Rather than seeing vulnerability or weakness as an opposite to the possibility of empowerment and resistance to dominant power regimes, they suggest seeing vulnerability as 'in fact one of the conditions for the possibility of resistance' (Butler et al, 2016: 1). Politics takes place via a recognition of human needs and interdependency. Butler and colleagues discuss new forms of activism within public spaces (with a focus on protests in Gezi Park, Istanbul in 2013), which they argue show that 'vulnerability is part of resistance, made manifest by new forms of embodied political interventions and modes of alliance that are characterised by interdependency and public action' (Butler et al, 2016: 7). Butler also links a politics of vulnerability to a politics of infrastructure – that by being and exposing vulnerabilities within political spaces, citizens can highlight the losses of 'infrastructural support' in society, be it from the state or other forms of institutions and resources that provide collective care (see Ortega-Alcázar and Wilkinson, 2020). Butler also links such a loss of infrastructure to austerity and welfare state retrenchment. This notion of 'infrastructure', discussed in relation to collective care in the previous chapter (Alam and Houston, 2020), will be returned to a number of times in the rest of the book, including the Conclusion. Thinking about infrastructures potentially provides a way to consider the materialities and practices of the welfare state alongside other forms of collective resourcing and structures.

One space in which such a politics of exposure and loss of infrastructure might be enacted would appear to be digital spaces (for example Gerbaudo, 2012), the forms of online culture which are now heavily tied up with many forms of activism and local action. For example, the discussion on 'mutual aid' under COVID-19 in the Conclusion shows how its practices are heavily dependent on connections via social media and messaging services, in a sense remaking 'infrastructures' at the moment they are falling apart. As well as connecting activist practices, digital spaces and social media potentially also offer opportunities for marginalised and 'hidden' voices and experiences to enter politics and arenas of debate, reworking lines between public and private or intimate lives (Wright, 2009).

For example, online spaces offer opportunities, as will be seen in Chapter 5, for 'storytelling' – presenting accounts of experience in ways unmediated by formal spheres of politics and the media. Such storytelling (Cameron, 2012) as it might form part of activism, can be seen as stemming from longer traditions of 'experience sharing' (Sargsyan, 2019) within the women's movement and other minority struggles. Storytelling within public and counter-public spheres enables stigmatised and marginalised experiences to be rendered visible, and potentially connects individual and 'small stories' to wider matters of politics and political change. As Cameron (2012) also argues, stories have the power to move and 'affect' the listener. This then raises wider questions about emotions, affect and the public sphere, and the possibilities for progressive politics such modalities might contain.

Sabsay (2016), writing in the same collection on vulnerability as Butler, sounds a note of caution about a politics of embodied vulnerability and affect (see also Brown et al, 2017; Gibbs, 2018). She talks of the dangers of a 'new sort of naïve empiricism' linked to the affective turn in social sciences, and the 'fantasy of an unmediated material reality' (Sabsay, 2016: 293). Overall, she insists on the ongoing importance of the 'judging subject', within a framework of democratic debate, mediation and judgement. This recalls the discussion about the conditions and structures needed for 'caring institutions' (Tronto, 2010) in the previous chapter. Without spaces for the evaluation of needs and demands within public spaces, or infrastructures, there is a danger that the underlying hierarchies of representational politics, of whose voices and experiences get heard and attended to, will simply be replicated in new ways.

Sabsay therefore argues for a recognition of the 'entanglement of discourse and affect' (2016: 282), and the need for the discursive mediation of spaces of 'affective articulation' (2016: 293). This then points to a politics of listening (Bassel, 2013), which is not just about attending to the loudest voices but seeking out marginalised experiences and subjugated knowledges. Sabsay also calls for a recognition of questions about what forms of politics and democracy might emerge *after* affective articulation, the structures and infrastructures of society, which a turn to 'affect' does not necessarily resolve. This cautious approach to a politics of vulnerability is all the more important given the wider eruptions of emotions into contemporary political and media spheres, as will be explored further in the next section.

Emotions, politics and activism

There is no doubt that, linked to digital culture already discussed, the public sphere is now far more emotion-filled than previous conceptions of the public/private sphere divide might suggest (Jupp et al, 2019; Jupp, 2021b). This is evidenced across other forms of conventional media and across political discourses. Alongside the rise and mass accessibility of digital culture, such a change links to other changes in society and economics, as Davies (2018) documents, from a loss of faith in institutions and expertise of various kinds, to the centring of the lived experience of marginalised groups within forms of identity politics as discussed. Across the social sciences, too, emotions are now being taken more seriously (Greco and Stenner, 2013), not just as indicative of the interior states of interest to the 'psy' disciplines, but as aspects of social, political and economic realities.

The 'political' impacts of the eruption of emotions into public life are complex and contested, and it is clear that a more emotional public sphere is not one thing and does not equate to one particular form of politics (Gould, 2009; Askins, 2016). From one perspective, Lauren Berlant (2008, 2009) has written critically on 'the intimate public sphere', focusing in particular on genres of media representations, including books, TV shows and films aimed at women which claim to represent female experience and even empowerment. However, Berlant sees these as ultimately a weak and depoliticised sphere which may 'claim to reflect a kernel of common experience and provide frames for encountering the impact for living in the world as a woman', yet ultimately should be understood as 'female realist sentimentality ... that sees the expression of emotional response ... as achievement enough' (Berlant, 2008: x). In other words, Berlant sees such genres as sites for expression and emotion, but not of politics and citizenship, recalling the points already discussed about the 'judging subject' (Sabsay, 2016).

Yet while the specific genres of media Berlant is analysing may not provoke new progressive collective politics, emotions clearly do animate political movements and action in a range of ways (Jupp et al, 2016; Davies, 2018). 'Populism', the rise of nationalistic, anti-immigration and anti-progressive politics, often centred around charismatic individual leaders, has thrived on emotional registers, often explicitly opposed to 'science' and 'expertise' and a notion of 'elite' knowledge which excludes followers (Clarke, 2020). As Newman (2016) argues, a politics of 'rage and resentment' has been enacted via appeals to collective emotional dynamics and experiences, finding expression in the election of leaders such as Donald Trump in the US and in 'populist' decision-making in the 'Brexit' referendum in the UK, both of which have proved enormously divisive and fuelled anger and division on both the left and right. Paradoxically, perhaps, such seemingly raw and unmediated emotions can in fact be seen as highly orchestrated by technology (Davies, 2018), making use as they do of the 'big data' on emotions and identities available via digital culture and the possibilities for the micro-targeting and shaping of subjectivities and subjective responses (Pykett, 2015).

However, it is also worth noting that more progressive leaders and politics across the world have also begun to draw on more emotional registers, for example via discussions of empathy, care and love in the public sphere in new ways (Nussbaum, 2013; Pedwell, 2014). To some extent this can be seen as a reaction to the division and resentment circulating linked to the discourses discussed, and, as argued in the previous section, the fact that conventional institutions and sites of power in society have historically excluded emotions and the lived experiences of many groups. Such new registers of politics therefore potentially offer progressive possibilities for their inclusion. All this means that there is a complexity and an ambivalence to making sense of such emotional registers in terms of their wider political impacts (Jupp et al, 2016; Jupp, 2021b).

This is also the case in relation to much 'smaller-scale' experiments in political organising and activism linked to 'positive' emotions such as kindness and empathy. As well as new discourses surrounding the transformative qualities of such human emotions and instincts (for example Bregman, 2020), there has been the rise of small-scale community projects and initiatives, linked to positive human emotions. Examples would include 'kindness' and 'sharing' community initiatives (Ince and Hall, 2017) that seek to help those in need on a micro-level, as well as initiatives such as 'the Big Lunch' and 'the great get-together' (Parry, 2020) that promote community connection and cohesion. These emotional registers can be seen in the Coastal Arts project discussed in Chapter 3. They might also be linked to the wider landscape of austerity discussed earlier in this chapter, whereby communities feel more aware of needs in their communities and the inability of the state to meet them. Such initiatives also tend to rely on social media and digital culture to enable sharing and connections (Koch and Miles, 2020). These dynamics can also be seen in expressions of community solidarity and mutual aid during the pandemic, as discussed in Chapter 6. There is no doubt that such initiatives have an instinctive appeal and can be effective at meeting needs at least in a small-scale and localised way. They are also invariably fragmented, uneven and cannot claim to meet needs in society in the ways that wider infrastructures, including the welfare state, might be able to. Indeed Muehlebach (2011) sees such affective labour as firmly incorporated into modes of 'humanitarian capitalism' whereby citizens' emotions (as well as voluntary labour) are called upon to fill the spaces left behind by the austere state.

Conclusion

To sum up, overall, this chapter has provided a set of contexts for the analysis of local action, citizenship and activism in the empirical case studies that follow. Firstly, I have shown how such action has been shaped in a UK context by shifting political and economic regimes, which have variously invested in such action as part of political strategies, and also relied on it to take up the spaces left behind as the welfare state shrinks. This context therefore shapes an ambivalent politics, inevitably entangled with the shifting structures and atmospheres of welfare provision, perhaps finding spaces of action on the edges or borders of the state.

Secondly, I have sketched out some conceptual questions and approaches which draw attention to marginalised and subjugated practices of citizenship and political action. These include seeing citizenship as comprising a multitude of 'citizenship acts' that involve political subjectivity and agency in a range of everyday practices, perhaps involving dynamics of 'resilience, resistance and re-working' (MacLeavy et al, 2021). I also suggest the need to pay attention to modes of storytelling, and qualities of vulnerability and embodied and emotional experience more broadly as constitutive of forms of political action. This then suggests a politics of the self and the intimate before other spheres of politics might be entered. However I have also drawn attention to the importance of the 'judging subject' (Sabsay, 2016), or at least spaces or structures of deliberation which are still needed to evaluate needs within such a politics.

These key terms and debates will be threaded through the analysis that follows in the empirical chapters at the centre of this book, as I trace an emergent 'politics of everyday life' within the case studies of local activism. Overall, I am interested in how moments of crisis, including austerity and

COVID-19, can be seen to illuminate wider understandings of collective care, and of political action, subjectivity and citizenship. This politics includes matters of care, gender and the welfare state; and austerity and COVID-19 and their impacts on community groups and activism. Via a close analysis of empirical contexts, the book demonstrates how modes of citizenship and political action can be understood to include the experiences and practices of those often excluded from politics. Case studies explore the potentials and problematics of such modes of politics on a local level. The research material is also used to explore matters of how collective care is and should be provided in society, including the role of the welfare state, and of other structures and infrastructures.

3

Journeys into and through local activism under austerity

Introduction

In this chapter I explore experiences of local activism among diverse women, with a focus on care, the lifecourse and the self, as part of the patternings of the politics of everyday life I am concerned with. I follow individual research participants' 'journeys' or 'stories' into and through local activism and action of different kinds, presenting interview and other data across a number of research projects. In so doing, I draw out common themes about how different individuals might enter and sustain activism at a range of scales. This also involves considering how different organisations and infrastructures support and position such action, particularly with regards to aspects of the welfare state. All the primary research participants in the chapter are women. While I draw attention to gender as a key issue here, as discussed in Chapter 1, I am not arguing that all women share experiences of activism and citizenship. Nor do the women discussed here share a cohesive identity. Differences around race, class, location, age, work and migration status are all apparent in the accounts presented in this chapter.

Indeed none of the organisations involved had an overall remit to focus on women, although the 'period poverty' project which formed one strand of the Coastal Arts project discussed in this chapter, was clearly gendered. Rather the dominance of women within groups working on issues of neighbourhood, community and family support reflects the often gendered nature of local activism (Martin et al, 2007). This relates to matters of care and gendered divisions between public and private lives, and between different forms of work, as discussed in the preceding chapters. As the analysis in this chapter will show, there are also gendered aspects in how the women discussed in this chapter entered and sustained activism on a personal level, for example in relation to being a mother or carer for others.

Crossing public and private lives in this way involved forms of what Newman (2012) calls 'border work', drawing together subjectivities and resources from across different spheres, including domestic lives, institutions and forms of work (Jupp, 2017). Such transitions and movements were not straightforward or painless. A number of the women discussed in this chapter entered local activism from a place of struggle, trauma and distress

(Jupp, 2017). As will be further discussed, the movement into and through activism was often tied up with the recognition that individual experiences reflected collective realities and structures of experience. This dynamic of relating personal experience and feelings to collective emotions and processes might be seen as key to the forms of political subjectivity and citizenship of interest (Bosco, 2006). As noted in the previous chapter, these forms of activism were not necessarily conscious or reflexive political interventions (Hughes, 2020).

In the first section, I briefly introduce the women from the research projects as discussed in the Introduction. For each of the projects under discussion I then explore issues of how they moved into activism, the nature of the spaces of community within which they operated, and aspects of identity and 'boundary' work undertaken by the women.

Approaching women and community action

This chapter draws on data from three community projects in particular, which involved different methods and different positionalities for me as a researcher. Firstly, the research project involving a network of migrant women based in primary schools in London (see Jupp, 2017). The network was run by a social enterprise, and involved employing part-time 'support workers' of parents within schools whose remit was officially to support other families whose first language was not English. This was therefore essentially a peer support scheme, with the support workers helping others in a similar position. The support envisaged by the scheme was around social and educational integration for families newly arrived in London. In practice, the women employed as support workers interpreted their role as wider than this, but also with more personal dimensions, in terms of empowering other women who were struggling with experiences of migration, dislocation and care, as the further discussion will show. For this project I undertook one afternoon workshop with approximately 20 women, and then followed up with four in-depth interviews with women who had participated in the workshop too.

The second project drawn on here focused on two community groups in Stoke-on-Trent, and involved longitudinal research over eight years, tracking the changing contexts and practices of their activism. At the centre of the groups, Sandra and Jill were two women whom I interviewed extensively as part of the research. The sections that follow draw on ethnographic research and a number of interviews, including one in-depth interview undertaken jointly with both them, which took place in 2013 (see Jupp, 2020). In this interview they reflected on over a decade of community action and activism. All of their work was entirely voluntary and unpaid. I finish by discussing an arts charity in a coastal town, that I call the Coastal Arts project, run by two women, Claire and Rachel. Their community activism took place within the framework of a more formally constituted organisation and paid work; the women paid themselves on a freelance basis to run the sessions and projects involved, although this was not a stable or regular income. The Coastal Arts project will also be discussed in Chapter 6, focusing on their response to the COVID-19 pandemic.

These projects took place in different contexts, and as already mentioned, the women at the centre of them were different in a multitude of ways: age, ethnicity, migration status, class and privilege, and I therefore take an intersectional approach to analysis (Raghuram, 2019). As discussed, the category of women as activists is not a coherent one and it would be problematic to present it as such. In relation to the last axis of difference, around class and privilege, none of my projects have measured the class position of my participants in any systematic way. However, in general I have worked with women whom I would classify as 'marginalised' from a socio-economic perspective. Class position in a straightforward sense may shift with migration (Raghuram, 2004). So while it is clear that the 'migrant mothers' project involves women marginalised by UK culture and society (Lonergan, 2015; Burrell and Schweyher, 2019), this may not have been the case within the countries and cultures they moved from.

The exception to this marginality would be the women working within the Coastal Arts project, Claire and Rachel, who described themselves as privileged and middle class. As will be shown, their activism partly sprang from a place of reflection on their own privilege in terms of resources and class, and a desire to connect with others who have less. Yet there were nonetheless similarities across the projects in the dynamics of activism. Some of the same dynamics of empathy with those in need could be seen among women from much more marginalised positions. The Coastal Arts project sprang from informal and home-based practices that are common to the other projects too (see Jupp, 2017), and was led by Claire and Rachel as individuals, drawing on personal capacities and connections. They were not in secure paid work when they started the projects, and they were primary carers for children. There were therefore (gendered) aspects of marginality in how they operated. However, it would be a mistake to gloss over the different kinds of resources available to the women in entering and sustaining activism, particularly in terms of social and cultural capital. In what follows I will seek to keep the differences as well as points of similarity between groups of women at play in the analysis, and analyse the projects separately for these reasons. These differences and similarities concern not just the women themselves but also the communities they are operating in and the impacts of austerity.

"I want to start exploring my life": trauma and empowerment among migrant women activists

For all of my research participants, they became engaged with collective and community action of various kinds because of events within their own lifecourse, often of a gendered nature, that altered their orientation to their local community and to the lives of others around them. Elsewhere (Jupp, 2017) I have discussed these events in terms of the notion of trauma, of experiences which disrupt or break down a stable sense of self. This was often how it was narrated by participants – experiences which required some kind of transformation or re-orientation of self and identity in order to move on. However, given that trauma can be understood as an experience that fragments the self (see Coddington and Micieli-Voutsinas, 2017), in the case of these women it is important to recognise that they had clearly in some senses 'moved on' from their own trauma, or arrived at a position from which they were able to speak and place these experiences within a narrative. Activism and community engagement were often discussed as in themselves transformative experiences, that enabled the women to regain a sense of self.

For the group of migrant women, it was the experience of migration that was often described in these terms. Migration itself can be experienced as a trauma, a loss of self and identity for women who might be marginalised in the UK not only by race and ethnicity, but also gender, class and immigration status (Erel et al, 2018). Alongside conditions of austerity, migrant women have also had to negotiate the increasingly 'hostile environment' of UK policy (Yuval-Davis et al, 2018; Burrell and Schweyher, 2019). Umay, from Turkey had been studying at university and then working in the travel business in Turkey, before migrating to London. She spoke about losing all aspects of her identity through the process of migrating with her husband:

> 'My working life was so busy and I really enjoyed it. Then I met my husband and that's how I came to London. When I came here, my old life ended, and my new life started over again. I left everything behind, my job, my friends, my family, my life … and I started another one.'
> (Umay, Support worker, North London)

Obviously because of the location of the project in a school, all of the women involved with the school support project were mothers, and the loss of self involved in becoming a mother was talked about by interviewees as compounded by the dislocation and rupture linked to migration too. Umay also spoke to me about her experience of motherhood, and her experience of migration, as part of the same sense of trauma and loss:

'When I first had my baby, that was the hardest time. It's the time when you need someone to support you, I didn't have my family … it was a hard time. I couldn't go out, I was losing my confidence. It was a difficult time for me. I had no time for myself, only taking care of my daughter, housework, shopping.' (Umay, Support worker, North London)

Umay summarises her feelings of loss from these experiences by saying "I was lost for a couple of years". It is striking that her material losses of time, relationships and structures of care were experienced above all as a loss of self. For Umay, rebuilding a sense of herself as a person, and reconnecting with others was tied up with becoming involved with a sphere of community work and activism, in common with other research participants. Initially Umay volunteered in her daughter's nursery and school and then started working for the bilingual support programme. Ana, from Colombia, had a similar experience of isolation and loss associated both with migration and with becoming a parent: "When my daughter was young … it was difficult, a very difficult time. I didn't know anyone. Then slowly, slowly I began to meet other people."

For both of these women, it was their recovery from forms of personal trauma in their home lives that formed the catalyst for, and spur to, activism and wider engagement. The connections they began to form with other women in similar positions produced a collective consciousness around the similarities of experiences for migrant women, even from very different backgrounds. For example, both Umay and Ana reflected on the burden of care work and wider emotional labour born by migrant mothers such as themselves, with both of them commenting that "women do everything". For example, Ana mentioned, "They go to work, cleaning, take children to school … fathers just work, have dinner, bed". The 'everything' could be seen as including the work of navigating a new cultural context, and the institutional and personal barriers that needed to be overcome in order to build a life. As Erel et al (2018) have argued, and discussed in the previous chapter, migrant mothers' labour can be seen as involving acts of citizenship, their care work a form of political intervention operating at multiple levels of belonging, from family, to local community, to the national and transnational.

For the support workers involved with this project, they had therefore gone through a process of reflection on their own experiences and those of others, and found new ways to articulate and name the issues they faced. Ana spoke quite extensively about domestic violence and the patriarchal oppression that might be intensified under the strains of the migration experience for women from her background. She also pointed out that migration might shift traditional gender roles within a family for both men and women (in contrast to her point in the previous paragraph about women doing 'everything'): "In my country, men looking after children and shopping, that's a no-no, that's not a man ... here they do ... maybe mummy's working, they have to look after baby, go shopping. ... Sometimes we [women] are the first ones to find a job, and then they are depending on us."

The support workers' activism therefore involved, in the first instance, this reflexive labour on their own and others' experiences and the complexities and difficulties that other women faced. Much of the work of the project involved very everyday tasks to support others. During the workshop, the women worked collectively on descriptions of what they did to help others in their communities. The activities listed were a mix of emotional and affective labour, and practical, domestic-based tasks, for example being patient, being friendly and kind, developing trust, getting to know women 'on their level', to more practical tasks such as collecting children from school, gardening, cooking, housework, socialising, chatting to neighbours, looking after pets. Umay explained that activities involving very everyday practices and care, for example cooking for each other, could lead, over time, to profound processes of empowerment and fulfilment for the women they supported: "Our job, first thing is you are building a friendship. Then trust between parents and us, it comes afterwards. We spend time together: weeks, months, maybe years: then we can push women to do something else."

The 'something else' might involve forms of paid work, or training, or a sense of individual and collective empowerment and confidence, and agency. Nadifa from Somalia spoke about the need for 'self-care' among the women she worked with: "When you are caring and you are responsible for everyone it's really difficult ... the difficulties women have are about forgetting yourself."

It is interesting that she again uses a language of loss of identity and of self here. In order to inhabit practices of citizenship and participation, Nadifa identifies needing to nurture a sense of their own selves, a grounds or position from which to speak. This involved a recognition of their own care needs (Raghuram, 2019). Indeed Nadifa also spoke about helping women to communicate and claim their rights, especially when dealing with bureaucratic systems and institutions. She saw this as an issue not just of language (although translation was a task that all the women undertook both in formal and informal roles), but broader issues of self-expression and confidence in the face of an often unwelcoming and hostile sphere. She told me about giving women advice on how to access healthcare and how to navigate systems at the local council. The sense of confidence and agency that she wanted to instil in the women she worked with clearly related to her own developing sense of agency. She had arrived in the UK as an asylum seeker and undertaken various forms of education and training. With her children now older, she told me, "I am now living my own life". Umay, similarly, told me that looking forward, "I want to start exploring my own life ... and do things just for myself" (as opposed to care work).

This sense of the oppressive nature of care which also formed the basis of their activism ties in with the notion of care as ambivalent 'double-edged sword' (Emejulu and Bassel, 2018: 9). Another way to consider the practices of the women involved with the project would be the practising of 'border work' (Newman, 2012), connecting up the boundaries of domestic and public spheres, across cultural and international contexts, and across everyday life and institutions such as schools and the spaces of social welfare. During the workshop, the women made maps of their 'personal communities' – all of which spread outwards from immediate family to spheres of local, national and transnational networks. Online interactions, particularly via their mobile phones, were central to this labour of holding together such scales and spheres: as one workshop participant mentioned, "my phone is at the centre of everything" (see Hall, 2020b). Their work therefore involved trying to support other women to move across these boundaries too – Ana mentioned that recent migrants tend to stay "in their own little communities" and she saw her role as encouraging them to connect with others outside of these groups. She therefore occupied a number of different positions with different communities and spheres, telling me: "I have different roles, different hats I put on: chair, governor, school inclusion worker, friend, mother" (Ana, Support worker, North London).

Spanning these different roles might though mean that it was difficult to not be 'working' or to have your own sense of boundaries. Umay told me: "You can't draw the line, you just do it constantly ... especially if you were helped yourself before you want to give things back" (Umay, Support worker, North London).

As this quote shows, the emotional and material proximity of the women to those they were supporting and their own experiences of support or empowerment were tightly bound together: the women's senses of self were tied up with their work. This might also lead to a sense of exhaustion and continuous labour. In relation to austerity, the women told me that as formal services were shut down, more work had to be undertaken by them as volunteers or informal advocates, in relation to translation and accessing services in particular. Ana also mentioned that austerity in other parts of Europe, for example Spain and Portugal, had led to migration from those countries to the UK. This context of increased material pressure on migrant women increased the burden of everyday care work (Lonergan, 2015), rather than giving them the space to develop a more expansive sense of their own agency and citizenship, as Bassel and Emejulu point out (2017). This theme can also be seen in the case study discussed next.

"I always say the resident's association saved my life": neighbourhood action in Stoke-on-Trent

Sandra and Jill, as already introduced, were at the centre of residents' groups based in two marginalised, predominantly White post-industrial neighbourhoods in Stoke-on-Trent, UK. At the time of my initial fieldwork, unemployment figures were high in their neighbourhoods (see Jupp, 2006) as was the percentage of people classified as having a long-term illness or disability that prevented them from paid work. This was the case for both Sandra and Jill, as will be discussed further in what follows. The personal experience of unemployment for these women was therefore clearly connected to wider structural social and economic issues in their neighbourhoods – as indeed could be considered in relation to the personal experience of migration for the women in the previous section. Again, such connections between personal experience and wider social issues might be considered a starting point for forms of local activism, or a politics of everyday life.

Receiving benefits relating to ill-health is a particular feature of post-industrial areas such as Stoke-on-Trent (Warren and Garthwaite, 2014). The manual labour of its traditional industries (in this case the ceramics industry) had damaging impacts on workers' bodies, but the new precarious forms of manual labour (such as warehouse and construction work) that might replace it could also be very damaging (Rowland, 2019). In relation to Sandra, Jill and many other research participants, it was striking that illness or accidents abruptly cut short working lives in ways that would not have occurred in a context where non-manual forms of labour, or indeed training and education, had been available. Despite these collective and structural experiences, the category of 'long-term sick' within welfare benefits can be experienced as personally stigmatising and shameful (Garthwaite, 2015; Raynor, 2021), even more so since austerity cuts to the welfare state have focused on reducing and restructuring this category of benefits in particular. Claimants are now made to undergo more frequent 'assessments' with the aim of moving them into benefit categories under which they are compelled to find work, in order to reduce the costs of these benefits (see Garthwaite, 2014). The caring voluntary labour which my research participants were involved with was clearly positioned outside the conceptions of 'work' in relation to the benefits system and welfare state.

Jill came to the residents' association after being involved with a road accident in which she hurt her back, meaning that she could not continue with her job in a shop, an incident which led to a breakdown of her mental health: "Then I lost my job and became depressed ... I don't know what I would have done. I always say that the RA [residents' association] saved my life."

Sandra had also begun to become involved with the group following both herself and her partner (Mick) becoming ill with long-term health conditions and needing to leave their jobs. Sandra mentioned that she had wanted to find something for both her and Mick to do together, and the residents' association had provided this.

Moving into the sphere of voluntary rather than paid work in their communities drew on different kinds of capacities and orientations towards a locality. As Jill commented: "When you're working you don't take so much notice of what's going on in your local area ... when you're at home like we are now, you see it all the time."

More profoundly, the kinds of activism and local action undertaken by the groups drew on their subjectivities and practices as mothers and as caregivers to older generations of family too. Both Sandra and Jill had teenage or young adult children, so were no longer involved with caring for young children on a day-to-day basis. However, Sandra told me that when her kids were little, "there was always a crowd of kids round ours ... and I used to take them on adventures". These informal practices of collective childcare informed her practices as a community activist. Furthermore, advocating for the rights of teenagers, as well as connecting their concerns with those of older generations, was central to both groups. Teenagers and young people in both areas were seen as often demonised or stigmatised, within wider neighbourhood discussions, meetings and the local press. Both women wished to take a more sympathetic stance. Jill told me: "I originally got involved because I was just so sick of the kids on the estate having nothing, then it just grew from that."

Both Sandra and Jill could be seen as approaching their roles as advocates and activists in their areas from within extended forms of caring – supporting young people, but also other women and older people in particular, through long-term and caring forms of support. Both groups were based in 'community houses', ordinary houses within their council-owned areas of housing, that were given over to the groups for community use. This in itself linked their activities to an extended sense of the domestic sphere. Many of the sessions run by the groups focused on particular age groups, connecting with everyday lives and practices, for example through group cooking sessions, cross-generational gardening and wildlife and crafts. Howard (2014), analysing neighbourhood support projects in San Francisco, calls such modes 'affective activism', tied up with domestic spheres and practices. 'Mothering' identities and practices could also therefore be seen as central to the motivations behind and catalysts for local activism (Wright, 2007).

However, it would be a mistake to overlook the contributions of men and fathers to the groups too, although women were the most visible and vocal group members. Like Mick, a number of other husbands, partners and relatives of group members took on roles within the two groups, for example supporting activities with children and young people and elderly people. At Riverlands, a male committee member ran an allotment project aimed at young men, and he spoke about his own memories of gardening with his father as the inspiration for it. Via such individuals and spaces, the groups offered possibilities for 'caring masculinities' (Tarrant, 2013; Elliot, 2016) in relation to providing local and community support. However there remained barriers to their involvement in these activities. As Bell and Braun (2010) point out in relation to community activism in Appalachia, post-industrial regions in particular may frame or produce certain forms of masculinities which preclude involvement in community activism. The spaces of the groups' activities in Stoke could be experienced as uncomfortable for boys and men. For example, my fieldwork notes include an incident at a play session in Southfields when a father came to collect his daughter from the community hall. It was raining outside and the volunteers invited him to come in to wait for her while she gathered up her belongings – "no, you're alright, I'll stay outside", he responded, presumably not feeling comfortable enough to enter the space. I also recorded an incident when a male volunteer was involved with a craft session in Southfields, which was unusual. He obviously felt frustrated by finding the task difficult, gave up and went to play pool with two teenage boys instead. This raises questions about who might be included or excluded from activism based on caring everyday practices, in particular how far these are available to men.

Indeed the close connections between family caring identities and the work of local activism was not unproblematic. Similar to the migrant women discussed earlier in this chapter, there was a material and experiential proximity to the other families and residents that they were supporting, which could make their work overwhelming, again evidencing the 'double-edged sword' of caring politics (Emejulu and Bassel, 2018). Both Sandra and Jill often spoke about being exhausted and continuously "on call" for residents with any issues and problems. Sandra and Mick lived next door to the community house where their activities were based and "were in and out all the time". They also commented that "there's no cut-off, we're just next door". Family identities and practices were closely linked to their identities and practices as community activists (Jupp, 2017). This provided resources for their activism, but such linkages could also be problematic. Jill commented on one occasion that she wished less volunteers were parents, as "it makes everything so personal". Decisions about the group's activities could become too tied up with the particular needs and perspectives of the families involved.

Nonetheless, on the other hand, the groups offered opportunities for those involved to connect their domestic practices with other families and wider neighbourhood contexts, and in so doing to develop their own senses of confidence and empowerment. In Southfields in particular, Jill spoke about the mental health issues that she and other volunteers had had to overcome in order to act within the residents' association, as well as barriers of lack of confidence: "People have been put down all their lives ... I've banned certain words, 'thick', 'can't', banned them in the building ... now if I say I'm thick I get my wrist slapped, we can't put ourselves down, we have to be positive" (Jill, Community activist, Stoke-on-Trent).

There was a gendered quality to these women's discussions of confidence and mental health, with talk of being "put down all our lives", and the women talking about being "stuck at home" and burdened with care across generations. Pat, one of the volunteers at Southfields, said that she had been "out of circulation" before getting involved with the group, and indeed had been diagnosed with agoraphobia. Again, as seen in relation to the migrant women's group, personal lives, confidence and a recognition of the self were inevitably bound up with processes of collective action.

As well as developing their own capacities and sense of agency, the activism of the groups was also very much concerned with supporting and empowering other residents within their place-based communities and improving facilities and resources for the areas. Indeed, the women's own agency was often expressed through speaking out for resources and support for their areas, which they both felt were often overlooked within funding and service decisions. Jill told me, "I'm at my best when I've got my back against the wall, when I've got my teeth stuck into something." The women had very strong commitments to their localities and to an idea of community which consisted of extended caring networks and relationships. This was in the face of senses of stigma surrounding their neighbourhoods and abandonment by political and economic structures via de-industrialisation (Pain, 2019). One community arts worker whom I interviewed told me she felt that the neighbourhoods had been "traumatised and abandoned" via the process of de-industrialisation as the ceramics industry shut down.

This kind of advocacy work meant engaging with the shape and reach of the local state. And as discussed in the previous chapter, at the time of my initial fieldwork (under the New Labour government) there were opportunities for their groups to try to lever resources into their areas via a range of neighbourhood programmes. Under this policy regime such communities had become a (contested) site of governance. As discussed, 'third way' and 'communitarian' approaches to urban policy (Imrie and Raco, 2003) had ushered in new programmes in marginalised and disadvantaged neighbourhoods, involving partnership working and new forms of community engagement. During my initial round of fieldwork there was therefore a dense network of actors involved in community initiatives and projects in both neighbourhoods. These included various kinds of community workers, supporting the groups, as well as forums and partnership meetings of different kinds (Jupp, 2013b).

At the time of this earlier fieldwork, therefore, much of the work of the groups consisted of negotiating with and managing sometimes fraught relationships within this complex sphere of 'the local state' (see Ormerod, 2021), another form of 'border' or 'edgework' (Brown, 2009) in connecting this sphere with everyday lives. As resources became available for neighbourhoods via regeneration schemes there were often tensions with what resident-activists sometimes called 'the suits' – the officials and professional bureaucrats tasked with managing regeneration schemes. This related to some of the references to 'fighting' and 'battling' for resources from these schemes. However, there was also evidence of care, solidarity and support between residents and professionals. This was particularly in relation to community development workers who spent time and energy building relationships with activists such as Sandra and Jill in the spaces around and between policy programmes (Jupp, 2013b). For example, community workers connected the groups to new resources and initiatives that they could benefit from, and helped them form alliances with other residents' groups. As such they drew on more radical traditions of community empowerment as well as the forms of neighbourhood governance that shaped their work (Gilchrist, 2003).

Neighbourhood action under austerity

This 'thick' and complex sphere of partnerships, individuals and relationships that circulated around the neighbourhoods was massively diminished at the time of my second round of fieldwork in 2013, when austerity cuts at local government level had essentially stripped away this sphere entirely. This initial sphere was clearly problematic in many ways, as previously discussed, in its attempts to instrumentalise community relationships and capacity. Nonetheless, the loss of staff, networks and resources was experienced as a huge loss for groups, a profound 'thinning' of the infrastructures of care and support surrounding the neighbourhoods. As Sandra commented:

> 'I wouldn't say there's any real support network for any community groups at the minute. There's something called a Community Matters Group that consists of three people who cover the whole of city basically ... but obviously you can't get support. All the support's been withdrawn, so Neighbourhood Renewal, the Area Implementation Teams they've all gone, so there is nothing left.' (Sandra, Community activist, Stoke-on-Trent)

The three people replaced a network of approximately 36 community workers in post at the time of my initial fieldwork, and this was only one network (called the 'Community Facilitation Service') within the wider web of networks and partnerships previously engaged with neighbourhoods in the city. As discussed previously, such individuals created connections, contacts who could enable the groups to access resources, ideas and wider networks. As Sandra also explained, it was not that the previous community workers did the work for them, but that, "in the past, if you needed something, there was someone you could ask how to go about it, someone would help you".

Austerity has therefore led to such groups operating in a much more fragmented and isolated manner outside of such webs of connections and solidarities with others (see Raynor, 2021). During the first round of fieldwork the group took part in workshops and initiatives with other groups, for example via various initiatives around 'community cohesion' (Robinson, 2005). These initiatives connected the predominantly White neighbourhood groups with predominantly Black and minority ethnic neighbourhood groups from other parts of the city. The loss of such initiatives can be seen as an example of austerity cuts hampering the ability of small-scale community groups to become involved in wider political and especially progressive agendas and alliances, potentially producing more divisive feelings of community (Raynor, 2021). On my return visit, the only outside worker I encountered was a public health worker engaged with an anti-obesity project. This can be seen as indicative of a very much diminished approach to social policy at a community or neighbourhood level, wherein it is only via a fairly narrow health agenda that social and community spheres are considered, presumably because of a focus on 'lifestyle' and 'behaviour change' as connected to public health (Pykett, 2015).

Instead the groups were increasingly operating in a context of material poverty, and dealing with short-term needs around this. This was especially the case in Riverlands. Southfields had somewhat changed since my previous fieldwork, because of new (private) housing development there, which had both changed the demographics of the area and led to investment in some new community facilities (see Jupp, 2020). By contrast, Sandra at Riverlands spoke about her group focusing increasingly on very short-term matters of survival and basic provisioning: "The agenda used to be, say traffic calming, people were worried about kids getting knocked over, now it's just, there's not going to be food in bellies … the social and economic situation of households now is so bad, we can't really address anything else."

Indeed issues of food and hunger had become central to the work of the Riverlands group under austerity, including providing food for families during the school holidays (when families who would normally access free school meals were not able to). They also worked with a food redistribution project that enabled them to collect excess food from supermarkets and sell at a very low price, as discussed at the opening of this book. As also noted, at the same time as responding to this increased material dependence on them from residents, the group itself was supposed to be becoming more independent from outside support and funding. The Riverlands group had been encouraged to become a 'social enterprise', charging for some activities in order to run others. This had not been successful, as Sandra told me:

> 'All activities with kids we give out food, we charge 60p per head for playgroup but for that we have to pay £19 per evening to the church hall. Then some people haven't got 60p, I'm not gonna turn them away am I ... so the whole thing just doesn't add up.' (Sandra, Community activist, Stoke-on-Trent)

The food redistribution project was also supposed to be charged for, and to be a 'self-sustaining' project. However, Sandra said that they struggled to ask residents for money for the food, and were funding it through other activities including running events for other community groups.

> 'The problem with ours, the food redistribution project is a sticking plaster. ... It will alleviate an immediate need and that's all it does, and a lot of people that come in haven't got £2 to pay for a food parcel, so you're having to give it away, which continually adds pressure on our group to fund raise and subsidise that project, that *need*, so we do events all over the city. ... Now the majority of it would go directly on the food redistribution project. There's very little left for any other projects and that's the one project we cannot allow to fail, it has to continue.' (Sandra, Community activist, Stoke-on-Trent)

As Sandra points out, the food projects are not developing the capacity of residents in the ways that previous projects might have done, and nor are they addressing the root causes of hunger and deprivation, but rather acting as the 'sticking plaster' discussed at the opening of the book. The groups' own proximity to the residents they were supporting in this material way meant that to imagine their practices as 'enterprising' activity overlooks the felt obligations and concern felt by the group to keep providing food for neighbours, that 'need', as Sandra puts it. They were therefore unable to feel that they were 'moving forward', either as a neighbourhood or as a group, "there are so many things that impact on why people can't feed their families that we're never going to solve that, so we're not going to reach those outcomes".

The group had therefore become a provider of last resort, using their own 'affective labour' (Muehlebach, 2011) to pick up the pieces from far wider failures within the economic and political systems which have failed residents of the neighbourhood. This was not an empowering position for the work of the group, and did not allow them to make long-term meaningful interventions into the lives of residents and the wider community. Indeed while the group were actually supporting residents more directly, paradoxically this move into short-term provisioning coincided with a loss of support from other residents for the group. Sandra felt that this was because of anger circulating within the community because of the loss of services and wider experiences of poverty. Having stepped into a role as service provider, such anger was now being directed at the community group themselves: "As more and more things are withdrawn from people they get despondent, disheartened and apathetic. Now they will either walk away, or they will become angry, and expect us to provide all the things that were provided by the statutory services but we're not there to do."

Overall there was a sense (for both groups) of 'going backwards' rather than forwards, and of acting in a sphere of the present without a clear sense of the future. Sandra described a community in social and economic crisis, and this meant that in terms of temporality, short-term needs had become dominant and undermined the group's previous investments in the future, in what Knight and Stewart (2016) analyse as a 'slowing down of the present' under austerity (see also Jupp, 2021a). This example of youth work (a key concern for both groups), illustrates this.

Sandra: [In the past] there were large groups hanging about the streets and the people in the houses were intimidated, so we had to do a lot of inter-generational work to ease those barriers, and it got an awful lot better, as we had the Youth Clubs, we had all these projects, we had the Play Club and everything else. We now don't have a Youth Club, because we don't have the facilities to have a Youth Club. It's resurfacing, those issues are coming back, and you can see the next generation, they're going to have the same issues that the last one did.

Jill: I do feel quite sad for our area in respect as I feel we're going back … we're taking steps back instead of steps forward.

Sandra: Yeah, it is regressing.

Jill: I feel that we're starting completely from scratch again.

While the groups' work did persist, as in the example of organising 'bug hunting' in the long grass discussed in the Introduction, Sandra and Jill overall were operating within increasingly constrained and marginalised spaces, suffering huge economic and social deprivation. In very material ways, as the discussion shows, their activism was enabled or quashed by the shifting framework of state governance and resourcing around their neighbourhoods; in this they were always acting on the edges of the welfare state. The withdrawal of resources under austerity therefore had multiple impacts on their ability to continue to provide care and support to others around them. The groups also moved from being somewhat central to how neighbourhood governance was imagined under New Labour (see Chapter 1) to essentially being abandoned, as new models of 'social enterprise', completely unrealistic for such groups, became the desirable partners of governance. Soon after my fieldwork with the Riverlands group drawn on here, the group closed, officially because of lack of support from other residents, although this was clearly tied up with lack of support from local agencies and governance structures.

"You automatically think, 'how would I cope with that?'" Empathy and solidarity in a community arts project

The final community group I will focus on involves women who are less marginalised by class, race and work/migration, as set out at the opening of the chapter. As introduced in Chapter 3, the women involved with what I am calling the 'Coastal Arts project' talked about themselves as privileged and middle class, and in this sense different from the communities they were working with on their projects, in contrast to the sets of activists discussed in the previous sections. This gives them a different orientation to activism, community and care.

As discussed, the Coastal Arts project was a charity that raised funds and was formally constituted. While the migrant women's network also involved paid work to some extent, the two women who ran the Coastal Arts project (Claire and Rachel) undertook their community work largely within the framework of paid work on a freelance basis. However, the project began because of their desire to undertake a different kind of paid work, which fitted into gendered issues of the lifecourse and care for children:

> 'The catalyst was lack of opportunities for jobs when you're a mother!! And sheer boredom of always being late for my job in a school as my children were never ready on time (they were only four) … this idea of a flexible job then turned into an art project to give all children the opportunities my children had … so in March 2013 we sold a heap of our kids' old clothes on eBay, bought paint and told everyone we were a new art project … lovely lady councillor had faith in us … and gave us a grant of £2k to run a project in local schools in deprived areas to give kids the opportunity to explore where they live in a positive light using art and creativity.' (Claire, Community arts worker, Email communication)

As this quote shows, the project sprang from experiences of being a mother in a couple of ways – issues of accessing paid work, but also feelings of empathy and solidarity with other families who had access to less resources. Similar to the other forms of community work mentioned here, their community activism also consisted of practices that they were already doing in the domestic sphere (such as art and crafts) and taking these practices into new contexts, involving other families and spaces. However, unlike the previous projects discussed, there is an immediate sense here of recognition and support by authorities even within a context of austerity ("a lovely lady councillor had faith in us"), evidencing the more privileged positionality that the group began from.

As should be clear, the women's major concern was not to work in their immediate community, but in the more deprived and disadvantaged areas that bordered it. The town in which the women live, like many other coastal towns, is to a large extent characterised by poverty and disadvantage, including lack of well-paid work, opportunities for local young people and issues of housing inequality (McDowell et al, 2020). Alongside this, though, there are enclaves of more expensive housing and wealthy households, often clustered around schools that perform better within local rankings and evaluations. As Claire told me, the physical geography of her town (hills and cliffs) also played a role in keeping different communities separate, with the location of the 'village' where she and Rachel live (essentially on the outskirts of the town) reinforcing the social, economic and class divides at play.

In crossing these divides, the women very much drew on their own experience of motherhood and of empathy with others, as already discussed. Identities as mothers were therefore important to their approach to activism, as well as extended practices of 'care'. For example, Claire mentioned that they had recently begun working with women who had suffered domestic violence and had been relocated into the town due to leaving abusive relationships. While women arriving in town had been provided with housing through a domestic violence service, they often had nothing else. Claire commented:

> 'We want to do a basic care package for people fleeing domestic violence ... you know a kettle, a toaster, a duvet, real basic, basic stuff, so it's immediate ... so they can move into the house *and can immediately do what anyone would want to do*, put the children to bed and have a cup of tea.' (Claire, Community arts worker, Coastal Town; my emphasis)

This quote shows the senses and practices of care which underpinned much of the work of the Coastal Arts project, via dynamics of embodied empathy that attempt to imagine the feelings and needs of a woman in a different situation to her own. As discussed in Chapter 2, empathy as a starting point for activism is clearly not in itself unproblematic (Pedwell, 2014) and certainly does not guarantee a particular form of politics. However, within a context of increasing inequality and especially a culture of competitive and intensive middle-class parenting (Jensen, 2013), for the women involved, this reflexivity on their own privilege was at least a starting point for progressive intervention. Again, the women were involved in forms of 'border work' (Newman, 2012) between communities and across boundaries of class and privilege.

As the quote suggests, the idea of 'basic' and 'immediate' embodied and material needs were at the centre of a number of the Coastal Arts projects, and using creativity of different kinds, art and care practices to address such needs. For example, they ran a 'period poverty' project (see Briggs, 2021) that highlighted the fact that girls and women were using tissues, toilet rolls, tea towels and other inadequate materials instead of sanitary products which they couldn't afford. In order to highlight this the group made a short film for distribution on social media, holding up some of these items, saying 'this is not a sanitary product', and explaining how shocked they were to hear about these products being used locally. The film was well produced and used the group's trademark heart logos and a playful use of tampons and other sanitary products (see Figure 3.1), to make visible both the material matter of sanitary products themselves (as something that is still stigmatised within society) and the immediate need for them within their community. The film appealed to local businesses and individuals to support the project, which they did through donating products and providing spaces around the local area for those who needed free sanitary products to access them.

After their initial work in schools, the group had developed a number of long-term projects with disadvantaged and marginalised groups in the area, always with art and creativity as both part of what they offered groups but also how it was communicated or expressed. These projects included work with a group of 'young carers' (children and young people caring for an adult in their household); with older people living with dementia; and with homeless people. Claire and Rachel were based in a small gallery space, and they both ran sessions within the gallery and visited people in their communities. Such engagements enabled the women to deepen their understanding of the inequalities around them and in the lives of those they were working with. Claire spoke to me about the level of trauma and disadvantage in the lives of the families with 'young carers', for example interactions with social services and the criminal justice system. As she explains, she was shocked not just by what happened to the families, but by the lack of emotional and material recognition of this trauma, how it was weighted within what was considered 'normal' for these families: "There's been lots of tears … from me, my tears, in the car afterwards when I've visited a family. You automatically think, 'how would I cope with that'? These things, *if they happened in our family, a privileged family, it would be massive, it would be recognised as a trauma.*" This quote points to the way that it is not only the material but also the

Figure 3.1: Image from the Coastal Arts project's 'period poverty' campaign video

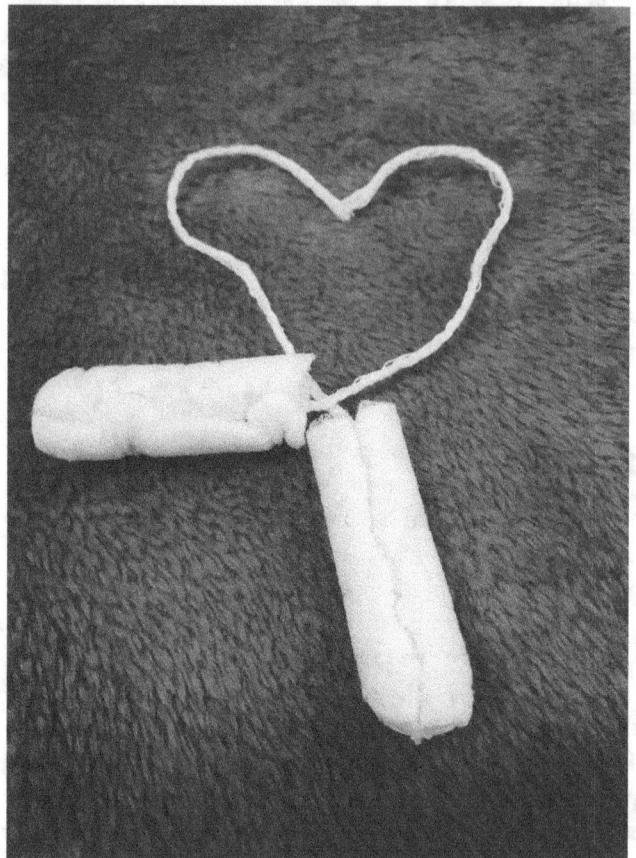

Source: Jo Godden

emotional needs of families that can be seen as unequally attended to by society, and might form a catalyst for local action.

Indeed, emotions overall were one of the key registers of the group's work, captured in their use of hearts on publicity material and project descriptions, and their emphasis on 'kindness', 'love' and 'care' in how they talked about their work, linking in to a wider contemporary discourse, as discussed in Chapter 2. During COVID-19 lockdown (discussed further in Chapter 6) the group distributed 'creative care' packages to families they were aware were in need. These included art materials but also food and treats, responding to the 'immediate' emotional and embodied needs of families. The Coastal Arts project therefore worked within a particular affective register, whereby they clearly wished to provide emotionally as well as materially for the groups they were working with. For example, one of their projects involves the use of a colourful bus to bring activities and resources into different areas. The visibility of the van was planned as part of its impact: 'something people can connect with and know when they see it in their area it's the Coastal Arts project. A bit like when you hear the tune from the ice cream van, it gives you that overwhelming feeling of happiness' (from Coastal Arts project website). As well as spreading emotions of certain kinds, Claire and Rachel also saw their own practices as rooted in caring emotions – for example they described themselves as following their own 'instincts' in designing and pursuing certain projects. Claire also spoke about the emotional toll of the work on themselves, and similarly to the women involved in the other projects, how it was difficult to have boundaries and pace their work in the face of the sense of increasing need locally: "It's really hard and really stressful, the thought of someone not being able to eat properly." This was intensified by the context of COVID-19, as discussed in Chapter 6.

Nonetheless, despite the intense emotional engagement of the women with their own work, unlike the two other projects already discussed, they were able to draw on financial and cultural and material resources around them in order to sustain themselves and their projects, as their story about how they started the project shows. Unlike, for example, the Riverlands group, the Coastal Arts project was able to package and communicate its support services in a way that was appealing and attractive to funders and agencies around them. This drew on their competences and resources within online and visual media to 'brand' their projects within this visual economy. They *were* able to successfully operate as a 'social enterprise' (unlike the projects in Stoke-on-Trent), because of their access to resources within more privileged communities and spheres, and because of their ability to communicate their projects and the needs they were meeting in a way that was appealing to decision-makers. While, in many ways, the 'sticking plaster' analogy used by Sandra could also apply to much of what Claire and Rachel were providing, they were able to galavanise community and local government support around their work. This is not to suggest that Claire and Rachel were unaware of the wider issues that underpinned the disadvantage and immediate needs which they were seeking to meet. For example, Claire spoke to me about the huge educational disadvantages and inequalities in her town, and their desire to try and tackle them. However, their inevitably small-scale projects around care, creativity and kindness clearly could not meet such aims in themselves.

Conclusion

It is not necessarily the intention of this chapter to assess the value of the projects or indeed of the individual women's engagements within and beyond their communities. They all offered powerful yet ultimately fragile forms of collective care. All the projects occupied complex spaces of care between everyday lives and gendered domestic roles; practices of paid and unpaid work; forms of governance and governmental power; and routes to personal empowerment and fulfilment. As Varley (2013) discusses, in relation to marginalised women in development contexts, there is a tendency for analysis to paint community activists as either agentic heroes, or victims of more powerful economic and political structures and agendas. In fact, their lives and citizenship practices are more ambivalent and nuanced. On the one hand, rooted in everyday caring practices and orientations, the projects showed the possibilities of a more 'capacious' approach to care (Care Collective, 2020), beyond the home and domestic sphere and familial relationships. On the other hand, the groups and individual women had access to different kinds of resources, capacities and power, and such infrastructures of support determined the trajectories of their work and empowerment. The migrant women's project was able to exist within and between the spaces of a school and the wider infrastructures of support that the education system provided. And while the Coastal Arts project was able to present the care and provisioning practices in ways that were appealing to funders and local businesses, the groups in Stoke were much more at the mercy of local authority support and governance, which fell away as austerity hit. The Coastal Arts project was also able to communicate the value of small-scale forms of support and care via the use of graphics and social media, and an appealing emotional and affective discourse of kindness and creativity (see Mould, 2018), which holds contemporary currency in policy and media spheres.

In terms of gender and empowerment, all three groups might be described as women-centred, while not explicitly aimed at women in the main. Many of the issues that they grappled with in their practices as well as within the lives of volunteers themselves could be seen as gendered, including caring for children and older generations, domestic violence, the difficulties of accessing paid work and gendered experiences of migration. The personal transformations associated with community activism appeared more profound for the first two groups of women discussed here. All case studies speak of boundaries and burnout in acting in the spaces of proximate communities, and evidence the need for forms of self-care and a recognition of own needs and capacities as part of the process of becoming an activist.

However, it was noticeable that there were no connections with the language and structures of feminist organising, or other structures and organisations concerned with women's rights. As Bassel and Emejulu argue (2017), feminism has largely not made space for Black and minority ethnic women and groups such as those involved in the migrant support project, nor, perhaps, for the White working-class women involved with the groups in Stoke-on-Trent. Furthermore, for these groups, as their activism and activities moved out of formal governance structures and into more informal and fragmented spaces, such links to wider structures of organising appeared less likely than ever. For example, as already noted, during my earlier fieldwork in Stoke, partnerships and official forums created connections between small community groups in various ways, including across divisions of ethnicity and place. These kinds of connections or infrastructures were no longer being made at the time of my second visit. This also limited the influence that the groups could have, the interventions that they could make into wider spheres of politics.

Austerity could therefore be seen as depoliticising the role of community initiatives to that of provisioning and dealing with immediate material needs in crisis mode. More optimistically, through their activism practices, all three groups could also be seen as enacting or 'prefiguring' (Ince, 2012) new modes of care and support on a neighbourhood and community level, practicing a new kind of 'meanwhile' politics (Cloke et al, 2020). Yet there remain questions about how far these fragile visions and structures of care can be scaled up within such a fragmented context. As Cohen et al (2017: 284) ask in relation to community activism under austerity more generally, there is a need to consider about how such practices can 'influence not just small-scale realities, but also national trajectories of social policy'. In considering this question, the next chapters tackle the issue of more conventionally politicised activism when services are under threat of closure.

4

Austerity politics and infrastructures of care: Children's Centre closures and activism

Introduction

This chapter moves away from considering individual trajectories of activists, and focuses on the substantive issues that are made visible during processes of austerity activism. In so doing the focus here also moves away from 'horizontal' forms of local activism that involve community connection and support, to more conventional 'resistance' or 'vertical' practices that directly address those in power, within repertoires of anti-austerity activism (Craddock, 2020). Nonetheless, in line with my sense of interwoven processes of 'resilience, resistance and re-working' (MacLeavy et al, 2021), I do not see these forms of activism as forming opposing categories, but rather as inter-related articulations of citizenship and political subjectivity (Martin et al, 2007).

In particular, as discussed in Chapter 1, I am interested in what may be made visible during processes of anti-austerity activism, in how these might be seen as politically productive interventions that can bring matters of care into politics in new ways, even when planned-for cuts go ahead. This is significant given the taken-for-granted nature of care, the ways in which it is entangled with everyday lives and experiences (Hall, 2019a). As already discussed, changes affecting care wrought by austerity, from reduced household budgets to benefit changes and service reductions, do not necessarily result in visible 'crises', but more often are coped with, managed and absorbed into everyday lives (Jupp et al, 2019).

Furthermore, the ways in which welfare services and forms of support are reduced under austerity tends to be a process rather than a dramatic event, which can also function to render changes invisible over time (Kiely, 2021). Opening hours of spaces, funding and staffing may be reduced over a considerable period of years via repeated cutbacks and reorganisations, resulting in gradual declines that may nonetheless add up to dramatic changes overall (Hitchen, 2016; Horton, 2016). Particular examples of areas of such cuts would include youth services, library services and parks (Shaw, 2019; Layton and Latham, 2021; Smith, 2021). Davidson (2019) describes this process, in relation to cuts to library services, as a gradual 'chipping away' of services which also exhaust capacities of resistance among staff and service users. However, despite this, the moment when a space providing services shuts completely is still a dramatic moment, and a juncture at which the loss of services may become public and visible. These moments of closure tend to follow emotionally and politically charged periods of consultation, local political decision-making and often public resistance and activism (Penny, 2020). This chapter will focus on such processes in relation to Sure Start Children's Centres, as producing times and spaces which shed particular light on the wider politics of austerity and care.

While some anti-austerity activism explicitly articulates wider political visions (see Penny, 2020), such politics that emerge may appear to be very localised and small-scale in scope, as is the case in the material presented here. Yet attending in detail to these localised processes, listening to what is said by service users and activists, may nonetheless render visible conflicting visions of social welfare and collective care, and that point to different futures. These conflicting visions can be seen to concern the nature of the 'infrastructures of care' (Lopes et al, 2018; Alam and Houston, 2020) that might be provided within and through aspects of the welfare state. As discussed in Chapter 1, experiences and practices of care may not be those set out in policy discourses and frameworks, but may rather spring from identifications, relationships and practices that emerge around the edges or borders of spaces and services (see Jupp, 2013b). Themes of friendship and different forms of connection, recognition and collective care are evident in what follows.

In relation to Children's Centres in particular, since 2010, it is estimated that 1,000 Children's Centres have shut (Smith et al, 2018), alongside other spaces such as youth centres, libraries and day centres (Hastings et al, 2017). Not all of these closures will have been met with public resistance and campaigning. And once a closure has taken place, the loss or lack may become hard to grasp. The impact of the loss of a youth centre or a library is difficult to quantify; people may travel further for services or not use them at all. Closures become hard to talk about, both in the short and longer term, partly because of the work of coping and getting by (Robinson and Sheldon, 2019). Everyday lives persist and continue, albeit unfolding differently to how they might have done (see Jupp, 2020). As one of my respondents put it in relation to the closure of her local Children's Centre, "It's not just what happened here before, it's what isn't going to happen in the future – the friendships that won't be formed and things like that".

Capturing the politics of closures is therefore tied up with senses of loss or perhaps futility, especially in retrospect once spaces have been shut. In both my case study areas, as I go on to discuss, Children's Centres did close, despite the campaigns. Researchers can play a role in 'witnessing' or recording such moments (Robinson and Sheldon, 2019), transient though they may be. During the campaigns I witnessed, service users, overwhelmingly women, spoke about and made visible their experiences of care and the place of the centres within them. This chapter focuses on such experiences of care and what they tell us about wider infrastructures of collective care, beginning with the policy background to Sure Start Children's Centres, and the debates about care surrounding them. The next chapter focuses on organising and activism tactics rather than the substantive issues explored here.

Sure Start Children's Centres: policy discourses and the politics of care

Children's Centre closures entailed not just a reduction in services and spaces to support families with young children, but also a shift in the politics and ethics of care as envisaged by local service providers. As set out in previous chapters, it is helpful to consider care analytically as always involving politics and ethics, alongside emotions and affect, and embodied labour and practices (Puig de la Bellacasa, 2017: 4, drawing on Fisher and Tronto, 1990). These aspects can be drawn out in taking a geographical approach to analysing particular spaces and places (Middleton and Samanani, 2021). Shifts in care arrangements under austerity therefore involve shifts in all three domains. This section sets out the shifting politics and practices of care surrounding Children's Centres as conceived within policy discourses and programmes.

Sure Start Children's Centres came into being in England and Wales in 1999, as part of the 'New' Labour government's approach to 'social investment' in the early years of children's lives (Lister, 2003b; Eisenstadt, 2011). The centres did not centrally offer childcare (although some had creches and nurseries attached). Instead they offered family support – spaces for parents and young children to spend time in and access different kinds of services (Jupp, 2013a). 'Drop-in play' spaces tended to be at the centre of what was on offer – sessions that parents could go to for free for their young children to play alongside others, and for parents to meet others. Other services on offer included health services, and parenting support of various kinds, employment and benefits advice. Initially only in certain deprived neighbourhoods, the programme was then expanded to provide 'one in every neighbourhood'. The programme had the notion of 'progressive universalism' at its centre – that is, everyone could access a Children's Centre, but different levels of need would be met via different services (Smith et al, 2018).

As should therefore be clear, the centres were intended to function as supportive spaces in a broad-based way, recognising the needs around care and support that all new parents face, potentially forming part of a localised infrastructure of care around families. However, such an approach to care was not uncontested within policy and political debates. As discussed in Chapter 2, as in other areas of New Labour policy, a community-based, holistic ethos around services clashed with a managerialist approach to targets and tightly 'evidence-based' practice (Newman, 2001). From the start, a national evaluation project was undertaken to monitor how far the centres were fulfilling certain purposes, within defined remits around education and welfare indicators, such as school-readiness among children (Belsky et al, 2007; Horton and Kraftl, 2009). The outcomes of this evaluation were not always positive, with some evidence that the most disadvantaged families were not accessing the services in early evaluations (Belsky et al, 2007). While this evidence was contested, the notion that centres were being over-used by middle-class families persisted. My earlier research (Jupp, 2013a) showed that centres tended to be used by groups of friends, groups who could exclude others. This could include exclusions based on class, although other forms of difference (ethnicity, neighbourhood, age) could also function to make others feel that they did – or did not – 'belong' in the centres.

Lying behind this earlier wave of policy discussions around Children's Centre services were questions around who 'needed' such forms of support and the role of the local state in meeting such needs. These are important questions for services to consider. However, as 'cultures of care' meet 'cultures of cuts' (Bassel and Emejulu, 2018) under austerity, such questions are being resolved in very stark ways, with many parents no longer having access to Children's Centre services. Essentially there has been a move, intensified in recent years, away from open access and universal services, to much more reduced forms of family support and 'intervention', orchestrated by service reorganisations in local authorities. Such service reorganisations have tended to involve the closures of the majority of Children's Centres, and a move to much smaller numbers of 'hubs' offering more specialist forms of support for those judged in most severe need, and involving children of all ages, not just the under-fives (Jupp, 2018). This was the case in the two local authority areas where I researched, where approximately a quarter of the centres were retained, rebranded as 'hubs', and mainly providing services for families 'referred' via other services such as social work, health visiting or schools. Indeed this notion of 'hubs' has been mobilised to justify service reductions in other areas such as libraries (Penny, 2020). This was therefore a significant reconfiguration of governance of the centres as well as rationale for their operation. This was happening without national policy change or debate, but rather emerging from the 'slow spoiling of social infrastructure' (Penny, 2020) of austerity cuts, repackaged as the restructure or reorganisation of services (Hitchen, 2019; Kiely, 2021).

Researching the politics of closures

In the two case study local authority areas, such service 'reorganisations' were being undertaken, involving closures of Children's Centres and moves towards 'hubs'. In both areas restructuring involved a move to a much smaller number of 'hubs' (approximately one quarter of the original number of centres), whose remit was to focus on the 'most vulnerable' families, or those 'in greatest need'. The body of this chapter explores how these changes were understood and experienced by both service users and staff within the centres. The research discussed here took place in 2017–18, in two local authority areas in South East England. Area A is a larger and overall affluent rural county (although with significant pockets of deprivation), while Area B is a smaller, predominantly urban post-industrial area. While there are interesting differences in how the processes of closure and campaigns unfolded in the two areas (see Chapter 6), in this chapter I focus on the data as a whole, which consisted of interviews with both parent-activists, decision-makers and professionals working with families. In Area A the research was undertaken after a number of years of consultations and campaigns, during the period that the centres were actually closing, when the campaigning phase of activism was essentially over. In Area B the research was undertaken during the process of consultation and campaigns. Having undertaken the research in Area A already, I became more emotionally and personally invested in supporting the campaign in Area B, perhaps because I had seen what was at stake in such closures. As Routledge and Derickson (2015) argue, emotions and anger can be valuable dynamics within research processes, and can lead to the production of 'situated solidarities' (see also Nagar and Geiger, 2007), and what Routledge and Derickson (2015) call 'convergence spaces', between scholarly and activism commitments. In the case of the Children's Centre campaign, this involved giving evidence to the local authority as an 'expert witness', giving media interviews and disseminating my research via a co-produced animation. When undertaking interviews I was clear with participants on my own positionality with regard to the closures, and moved away from a notion of a neutral researcher.

As the threat of closure hung over the contested spaces of the centres, powerful and heightened emotions, both positive and negative, emerged about the spaces (Stewart, 2019). More specifically, at the point of threatened closure of a service, there is clearly an overriding question circulating about the value of a service – can the closure be justified? However, this is clearly not one straightforward question and involves a series of issues about needs, values and priorities, and broader contestations over the politics of spaces and services. Researching closures tells us about what is at stake more broadly in the shifts in the design to services. While I was researching from a position of support for Children's Centre services, and solidarity with those opposing them, I also recognised that local authority officials were, in the main, seeking to manage very reduced funding from central government, in the ways that they believed could best support those who needed help most.

Shifting rationalities of care

As should already be clear, at the centre of such debates about closures were the politics, practices and feelings associated with 'needs' and 'vulnerabilities' (Brown et al, 2017; Gibbs, 2018). Austerity constrains not only spending, but also understanding of what it might be possible to expect from services, and who might be a recipient of a service 'in the current climate' (Horton, 2016). This points to a shift in the affective atmospheres (Anderson, 2009; Closs Stephens, 2016) surrounding the centres but also more broadly around the welfare state and its role in providing support and care within communities. What affective and material forms of care might now be provided to families as the services face austerity cuts?

This recalls the discussion at the start of this book about the centres (before cuts) providing 'invisible cotton wool'. In the same interview, the Children's Centre manager told me she now wondered whether what the centre had offered was a 'luxury', despite her believing passionately in the work being undertaken. The 'luxurious' elements of the centre as it might be perceived were partly around being previously open to all parents, before a move to 'targeted' services only. Beyond questions around whether all parents 'needed' services in the same way, a move to targeted services also shifts the 'place' of such centres and services within communities and within society (Jupp, 2019). Universally accessible centres acted as sites that might bring together families across difference, recognising that all families need help and collective care. The shift to 'targeted' spaces and services threatened to produce much more stigmatised spaces, focusing, as Emejulu and Bassel (2018) put it, on 'failed care'. If the state only concerns itself with certain categories of family (as classified by authorities), then the affective qualities and also the power dynamics of the spaces of service delivery will shift (McGrath and Reavey, 2016; Jupp, 2019).

Such issues therefore framed the politics that emerged during threatened and implemented closures and service reorganisations. During the consultations and campaigns against closures, the politics of care which had, to some extent, always been inherent within the programmes, became intensified and heightened as closures of centres loomed. In what follows, therefore, I trace the politics of care at stake in the closures of centres, focusing primarily on the articulations of service users and activists. These were women who came forward at different points in the campaign, some as activists, speaking at meetings and attending demonstrations, and some who responded to my call for interviewees about the value of the centres under threat of closure. As already suggested, in analysing care, Puig de la

Bellacasa (2017)'s suggestion (drawing on Fisher and Tronto, 1990) of the need to consider together ethics/politics; emotions/affect; and embodied practices/labour, is a useful starting point. One means of considering these aspects together is to focus on space and place, the geographies and places of care (Conradson, 2003; Milligan and Wiles, 2010; Power and Hall, 2018), or how dynamics of care might circulate around a particular place such as a Children's Centre (see also Jupp, 2021b). Bowlby's (2012) notion of 'caringscapes' is also useful here in considering how care practices link together different places – in particular the interconnections between the home space and spaces beyond.

The interviews discussed here focus primarily on the articulations of service users, but also referenced are interviews with professionals who worked in Children's Centres and local policy makers. Analysis is grouped together under emergent themes concerning the dynamics of care that were articulated during my interviews. As I will demonstrate, these aspects of care combined political and ethical issues with emotions and embodied practices.

Relational spaces of friendships

As my previous research has shown, Children's Centres have often been valued above all as places of friendship (Jupp, 2013a) between parents, especially mothers. During my interviews with service users, when they spoke about their story of the use of a centre, it was often the development of a friendship group which cemented their connection to a centre and enabled it to function as a space of care for them. One mother in Area B, Sarah, described to me how lonely she felt becoming a mother for the second time. Sarah had a particularly traumatic wider story as her first child had died as a teenager four years before she had a new baby. This caused her to feel very vulnerable and in need of support during her pregnancy and in the early days of looking after her new daughter. Sarah had been signed off work with antenatal depression during her pregnancy.

> 'I had my second daughter, and I still had no friends ... and I was very isolated, I actually probably felt the worst when I was pregnant than I did after I lost my first daughter, because I was so isolated, whereas when I lost her, I had gone back to work, and I had people around me all the time, just to be around people, humans, something to take your mind off – so – that was very very isolating.' (Sarah, Children's Centre service user, Area B)

Sarah eventually found a group of friends through a singing group run by the Children's Centre, the kind of activity which might clearly be seen by many as non-essential and, perhaps, 'a luxury'.

'And I went along to this group, and people smiled at me, they made space for me, they talked to me and were happy to see me, and that's where I made my friends, and that's where I met my people that I now meet up with and pop and see and message and everything like that, that group more than anything.' (Sarah, Children's Centre service user, Area B)

Sarah's account of her first visit to the singing group suggests the profound impact that the activity had on her identity as a mother – a place where she was given 'space' – literally and emotionally, and supported and enabled via the friendships and relationships formed. This ties into the discussion of the importance of the self in the previous chapter – of the need to attend to the self as part of processes of inclusion and citizenship. Such feelings of inclusion did not necessarily spring from interactions with professionals and staff at the centre, but rather from friendships formed around the spaces of the centres. As Sarah mentioned, compared to support via formal services such as counselling (which she also accessed), friendships placed her in a supportive or reciprocal relationship of support with others, rather than as a patient or service user (see also Jupp, 2012):

'I now have someone than I can just message and say – it's been rubbish – what can I do today and also its the other way round – like if they're really struggling, and I get a lot of value out of helping other people – I like being of use and of value and you do that with friends.' (Sarah, Children's Centre service user, Area B)

Supportive relationships were also described in relation to staff – this was not necessarily about formal 'interventions' or support but smaller gestures and acts of care. Ruth, another service user, who spoke to me about mental health struggles when looking after her new baby, mentioned the informal support she gained from staff:

'If you are struggling, and I struggled quite a lot, in the first, sort of nine months, because I ended up being diagnosed with post-natal depression … and the people down there, they gave me a drink, they let me hang around after session and that kind of thing, probably weren't supposed to, and if I wasn't in a fit state to go home or whatever.' (Ruth, Children's Centre service user, Area B)

As noted here, it was often the informal, non-mandated forms of support that staff 'probably weren't supposed' to offer that was mentioned by interviewees as what was valued above all within the spaces of Children's Centres. These informal interactions mentioned (such as making a cup of tea, holding a baby while you went to the toilet) could contribute to a wider feeling of care, rather than being a subject of 'intervention' in the ways increasingly envisaged with austerity policy discourses. An ex-head of a Children's Centre in Area A spoke to me about how she had envisaged the centre (prior to the cuts) as a space of support based on relationships built up over time, as well as enacted in the overall atmosphere:

> 'I think you can never get across to legislators the difference between a place where you have to jump through incredibly high levels of thresholds to get any services and then the service is sparse and time limited, compared to a Children's Centre where people walk through the door, experts in families and children under five are there on hand to gently encourage you in and keep offering a very informal, trustworthy level of support, there's no comparison between that and a service where you have to fill in a huge form with everything about you on it in order to get any level of service. And then they say, well it's an "intervention". I'm allergic to the word actually.' (Former Head of a Children's Centre, Area A)

Also apparent here is a sense of the conflicting terms under which users might access the space, either being 'gently encouraged' or mandated under the notion of 'an intervention'. These terms speak of different relationships between home spaces and spaces of service provision, within different approaches to care. Such a sense, of conflicting visions of what a Children's Centre might offer, was particularly apparent in Area A where the council overseeing cuts were explicitly driven by a particular social work agenda. The authority had been the subject of a national child sexual exploitation scandal, and were also under immense pressure to cut their costs involved with children coming into the care system. This very different rationale for working with families is apparent in this quote from a senior manager in the local authority, discussing mental health issues among mothers: "And then we're doing a big piece of work around perinatal mental health as well because that's a big issue in terms of attachment. What we find is in terms of kids requiring that statutory service, a lot of issues go back to poor attachment at a young age." It would be unfair to suggest that this official did not 'care' about the families that she wanted the service to work with, but this is clearly a very different approach to the terrain than the approach which emerged from the service user interviews. The 'problem' of mothers' mental health is a problem because of the impact on children, rather than mothers themselves, and this in itself is a problem because it might result in children requiring costly 'statutory' services. Such a rationale does not necessarily feel like a productive starting point to engage with and support mothers who are experiencing poor mental health. This is clearly an example of a shift to a focus on 'failed care' (Bassel and Emejulu, 2018) under austerity. As the accounts of service users in this section have shown, it was actually often a sense of collective support around the edges of services, rather than direct 'interventions', that might lead to service users working through mental health problems or feeling enabled to make changes in their lives. The Children's Centres could offer a kind of collective space in which service users might feel recognised and 'seen' or visible – not in a way that singled them out for 'intervention' but rather to recognise themselves, including the issues and problems they might be facing. Such a process of recognition recalls the discussion of the politics of the self in the previous chapter.

Spaces of recognition and safety

The Children's Centres were therefore narrated in interviews as spaces which played a critical role in service users' journeys through parenthood and coping with the many emotional and material challenges they faced. Such journeys were often narrated to me via forms of 'storytelling', as discussed in previous chapters, stories that often resulted in recognising users' own needs for care (Cameron, 2012; Jupp, 2020). The impulse towards 'storytelling' already noted therefore might be seen as springing at least partly from a desire to give shape to the disorientating and sometimes traumatic experience of becoming a parent. As Sarah's account of visiting the singing group in the previous section suggests, visiting a Children's Centre (and often a particular activity or session within it) could play a pivotal role within a journey to a more supported and stable experience of parenthood. Sarah saw her connection to the singing group as a turning point in her experience. In the following quote she uses spatial metaphors to highlight the sense of movement in her identity enabled by the visits to the Children Centre, such as 'avenues', and the idea of a 'small pebble', which suggests a 'rippling' or outward movement on water produced by her attendance at the sessions: "Once you start going to something like the singing group you start thinking – actually it will be alright if I go to that, and it will be alright if I go to that, and it leads out to more avenues and it starts with such a small little pebble."

The shifts that were described as enabled by such visits related to feelings of interpersonal recognition and connection, as in the previous quote from Sarah about people "making space for me" at the group. These feelings involve recognising that an individual, privatised experience taking place within the home space might in fact be echoed in others' experiences, as discussed in relation to the women becoming community activists in the previous chapter. Such recognition might stem from very small points of connection. For example, another service user, Kat, spoke about the relief in finding that "I wasn't the only mum whose child pulled their hair or wouldn't eat vegetables anymore". This was in the context of a very difficult transition to parenthood for Kat, grappling with serious mental health problems, so this sense of connection to others had a profound impact on her.

For other service users, visits to Children's Centres could provide reference points for what might be considered a 'normal' transition to parenthood, and enable a different kind of recognition around their own experience. Ruth also told me that she had struggled with mental health problems as a new parent:

> 'Everything on the surface looked fine to everybody, but I think if we hadn't been going to that kind of thing and I hadn't been seeing other parents and thinking hang on a minute, I don't think I am fine, compared to how these other mums look and are coping, this is not how I feel.' (Ruth, Children's Centre service user, Area B)

Visits to Children's Centres could therefore enable recognition among service users – and indeed staff – of particular needs and vulnerabilities. A number of my other interviewees described visits to Children's Centres as catalysts for similar feelings that "I don't think I am fine". This includes interactions relating to domestic violence, a situation where recognising abusive behaviour as 'not normal' or problematic can be experienced as a very important turning point for those being abused (see Little, 2021). As service users and staff argued, the centres (prior to cuts) being universal, open access and offering very everyday activities, such as singing, might be seen as enabling the inclusion of families in need of support who might be more wary of targeted services and 'interventions'. Needs did not necessarily have to be defined and recognised, either by professionals or service users themselves, before accessing a centre, unlike in the 'hubs' model that was being proposed.

Within this proposed new model, Children's Centre services in both areas were moving to be 'targeted' or 'referred' – so only accessible to families with identified needs who were already known to authorities such as social workers. Alice, in Area A, an activist and service user, put it like this:

> 'The great thing about Children's Centres is that they mean that families aren't invisible, so, and I think we all know invisible families, it's quite a dangerous, slippery slope. So people come along to Children's Centres for all sorts of things but it's like that sort of open door, it's all access, so that's a really, really important part of it, it's not just about referred services it's all access …

And because of that people might come just to weigh their baby or to just ask a question or they might not have time to arrange an appointment with their health visitor, whatever, or they might come to a first aid course, baby massage, whatever draws people in. And then if it's someone who's struggling you've then got well trained people as opposed to a toddler group run by volunteers, you've got well trained people that can see those signs and direct those, well get to know those people first, so they feel comfortable, it's exactly what happened with me, and then direct them towards help. So whether it's little signs like, obviously someone being introverted to the point of their children are suffering because they, they're so, struggling so much that often means there may be further problems. Or like the woman in the middle of summer that's got really, really long sleeves because she's covering up either self-abuse or someone else's abuse and things like that.' (Alice, Children's Centre service user and activist, Area A)

Alice's notion of 'invisible families' suggests families as isolated within the home space, invisible to those that might help them but also hiding needs and problems, perhaps both from oneself and from others, as in the example of long sleeves. The centres therefore act as a bridge between the private and domestic sphere and a more public and collective arena where support and recognition might be found in a range of ways (Jupp et al, 2019). The centres were also spoken about as spaces of safety (Little, 2021). In the case of issues surrounding domestic violence, a place of safety had a very material and immediate quality, as somewhere to get away from perpetrators and maybe be supported to escape. Alice told me about her own experience: "I didn't tell anyone what was going on, because that's how it is in controlling relationships. ... So they basically pulled it out of me and they helped keep me safe, I actually met my health visitor here [Children's Centre] that would actually help me escape."

An important quality for the centres therefore was a sense of open-endedness in the care that might be on offer – a space of care as a space that wasn't necessarily designed with a particular outcome in mind, a particular time frame for an 'intervention' (as in the six weeks referred to by the ex Children's Centre head), or a pre-determined sense of what needs might be met within the space. To return to the quote from Alice earlier, the needs or care that had been sought by service users might not be those that are ultimately met – so, as she says, "people might come just to weigh their baby or to just ask a question". Immediate needs and concerns often concerned the baby or young child, whereas service users' own needs as mothers might take longer to emerge or be articulated or recognised within their interactions in the centres. The open-ended and open access nature of the centres enabled the surfacing of such needs via different kinds of interpersonal interaction.

These qualities were being emphasised by research participants at a moment when it was exactly these qualities which were under threat via cuts and the move towards hubs. There was therefore a sense of a delicate ecology of support being offered by the centres that was now under threat. As one of the participants put it, "Everything works together ... you can't take one thing away or none of it will work". An enveloping or comforting quality was ascribed to the centres, the presence in the community of the buildings and relationships they framed, in themselves offering a sense of comfort (Kraftl and Adey, 2008). Sarah emphasised that just being aware of the presence of the centre was a support even when not accessing it: "It's just knowing, it's more just knowing that it's there, that I can pop and see people." As mentioned at the start of this book, the metaphor of 'cotton wool' was used to describe the operation of Children's Centres, with one particular Children's Centre lead in Area A describing the service she ran as "invisible cotton wool that wraps around the community". This very ephemeral image was striking in contrast to the 'sticking plaster' metaphor also previously mentioned. The notion of cotton wool surrounding communities suggests fitting around, an enveloping and comforting quality that fits in between and around other aspects of everyday lives.

Conclusion

As has been demonstrated, the narratives of Children's Centre service users often moved between what might be seen as 'normal' or everyday experiences of caring for young children, and what might be seen as much more dramatic or exceptional events, for example involving relationship breakdowns, severe mental health issues, domestic violence and bereavement. However, such dynamics of 'everyday' and 'crisis' situations of care were more intertwined and co-constituted than might be imagined. 'Everyday life' produced its own crises, which might be experienced as intense and dramatic, while 'crises' were managed and lived through everyday rhythms and routines (Jupp et al, 2019). A notion of 'mental health crisis' may in fact reflect the culmination of many everyday and 'normal' struggles, which tip over into how a 'mental health problem' is categorised (Pedersen and Lupton, 2018). For women becoming mothers, categorising distressing struggles with care and with the often painful shifts in identity involved as 'mental health issues' may be less helpful than recognising the collective nature of their experiences as structured by the organisation of society, care and gender roles (Thomson and Kehily, 2011), or at least the interaction of social structures with individual experiences (McGrath et al, 2008). These processes require open-ended spaces of care and support that enable different kinds of interpersonal recognition, involving mutual support as well as care (see Robinson et al, 2021).

This points to the need for everyday, informal, holistic infrastructures of support for families, of the kind at least partially offered by Children's Centres. These everyday infrastructures of care were seen to function on a local, neighbourhood basis, offering resources of accessible friendship and support. It is precisely these spaces that are under threat with austerity cuts (see Hitchen and Shaw, 2019; Penny, 2020). Within the austerity state, needs are increasingly measured and quantified, and the ways in which 'family troubles' (Ribbens McCarthy and Hooper, 2013) might be embedded within everyday lives in complex ways is overlooked.

Those who spoke out against austerity cuts, and who came forward to take part in my research, were therefore drawing attention to the value of such everyday spaces which might nonetheless 'open up worlds' (Hitchen and Shaw, 2019) for those who used them. These involve quite complex and nuanced engagements with intimate lives and invisible experiences of care, that are not straightforward to bring into the public domain. In the next chapter I move on to examine the process and practices by which anti-austerity activists sought to make their demands visible and public.

5

Small stories and political change: local activism across time and space

Introduction

The previous chapter was concerned with the competing visions of care that emerged during the processes of closures of Children's Centres, and the campaigns against such closures. As shown, these processes can be thought of as making visible and enabling the articulation of the ethics and practices of care that had been valued within the centres, at the point at which the services were under threat. The question of the value of a space such as a Children's Centre comes under intense scrutiny at the moment at which closure or service reduction is being discussed (Penny, 2020). My account so far has therefore sought to pay detailed attention to the stories and visions of care that emerged.

However, the politics of activism and, more specifically, anti-austerity activism, is clearly not simply a question of articulating an alternative vision to that being proposed by decision-makers. Key is considering *how* such a vision is articulated, the 'tactics', strategies or forms of representation deployed by those resisting change at a moment when quite complex discursive politics is in play (Hitchen, 2021). By what means and under what conditions can the voices and experiences of service users in such contexts be heard? And how far can the specificities of experience that emerge connect to wider political movements, resistance and change?

In this chapter, the modes of activism, or 'everyday dissensus' (Penny, 2020) and 'persistent interventions' (Kern and McLean, 2017) employed by the Children's Centre campaigners are discussed, to explore what they tell us about how marginalised groups might make demands on the state, within contexts of austerity and beyond. A key mode, as briefly discussed in the previous chapter, is around practices of *storytelling*, which emerged as a primary form of activism (see Cameron, 2012; Jupp, 2020). As discussed in Chapter 2, of importance is not just how stories were told, but in what contexts and spaces, and how they were listened to or received and evaluated. The chapter begins with a general discussion of the politics of storytelling, and then moves on to tracing the emergence of storytelling within the protests against Children's Centre closures. Different arenas of storytelling are considered, from council meetings to online spaces. These different arenas had the potential to connect the activists at the centre of my research with groups from elsewhere, as well as enabling local activism to speak to questions of national level politics and decision-making. The chapter therefore considers the extent to which particular and individual experience can have a transformative impact on wider political agendas (Kern and McLean, 2017). The chapter ends by considering a particular case study involving a legal challenge to Children's Centre closures, as one means by which activists might seek to 'scale up' their demands to wider arenas of justice, politics and an evaluation of needs.

Approaching the politics of storytelling

Notions of narrative and storytelling have been at the centre of much social science commentary, and indeed practice, for decades. There is not a singular definition, although McCall et al (2019: 1) suggest that, 'A story is often loosely defined as having a beginning, a middle and an end, with a protagonist (often human), an object, practice or an idea, followed by a form of transformation or conflict'. They also suggest that a story might be defined by the impulse to evoke a different reality: whereas an 'account' might simply describe or detail, the notion of a story suggests the desire to transport the reader or listener to experience events from a different perspective.

For any kind of qualitative enquiry into society, seeking out and drawing attention to the stories that people tell about their reality and experience can provide rich insights. Indeed there has been a long-standing interest in methods which enable research participants to tell 'their story' with minimal intervention from the researcher (for example Wengraf, 2001). Despite the apparent innovation associated with such methods, longer traditions of an attention to storytelling are apparent in social science traditions from anthropology (for example Maggio, 2014) to psychology and associated 'psy' disciplines (for example Stephens, 2011). These two disciplines point to different emphases on the status of a story as a cultural artefact: while anthropology might broadly see a story as reflective of individual experience within a wider cultural field, a psychological or psycho-social approach might focus more on the importance of storytelling in enabling the narration of self and identity. Within both disciplinary approaches, therefore, there is an interest in stories as linking individual and wider collective experience or arenas of sense-making. From a more politicised perspective, stories can be seen to link private and public worlds, as Hannah Arendt proposed (Benhabib, 1990), and might therefore be considered as particularly important for the activism of marginalised groups in society, traditionally excluded from formal public spheres (Derickson, 2016). For the context here, storytelling might also therefore be seen as key in bringing a politics of care to wider attention.

Cameron (2012) surveys recent research using a storytelling approach within human geography, and makes a number of important observations about the politics and possibilities of storytelling to bring about change. She notes that while social and cultural geographers have viewed stories as important 'texts' for understanding culture for some decades, more recent research approaches have explored the political potentials of storytelling as a set of practices and interventions. These potentials are linked to various qualities of storytelling including the possibilities of bringing 'small' and mundane stories and experiences into dialogue with larger structures and institutions of society and the transformative power of stories to summon up alternative visions of society. Related to both points is the emotional and affective power of stories which go beyond the verbal, textual and discursive, but rather can 'move' the listener or reader in a range of ways and involve interpersonal processes of recognition.

Cameron (2012), however, sounds a note of caution about whether stories will necessarily be heard or read in the ways intended, or whether they could end up contributing to quite different politics. I would also suggest that there is a need for caution in considering not just the listening, but the telling of stories, in terms of whose experience gets heard and prioritised (see Jupp, 2020), as discussed in Chapter 2. While the focus of storytelling may spring from a desire to include more voices and experiences within a public sphere, storytelling practices may nonetheless exclude others. Personal storytelling may also make emotional demands on the storyteller in a way that more straightforward modes of address would not. The question of whose voices and experiences get privileged within storytelling will be considered in the rest of this chapter. This relates to discussion in Chapter 3 on a politics of the self and the need to have in some ways recognised and recovered from trauma before it can be brought into the public sphere (Jupp, 2017).

More broadly, and this is not considered by Cameron, there is a question to consider about whether storytelling has now in fact become too ubiquitous in the public sphere, given the rise of digital culture and forms of populist politics that often rely on appeals to subjective and emotional experience (Davies, 2018). How do the subjective and affective experiences of storytelling relate to more conventional discursive forms of judgement and articulation? As mentioned in Chapter 2, Sabsay (2016), writing about a turn to an interest in affective and bodily 'vulnerability' in relation to citizenship, cautions of the need to continue to consider arenas of debate and judgement within democratic politics alongside more affective modes and forms of politics. The intimate and affective stories that might emerge do not absolve the need for some kind of evaluation or weighing up of claims being made, although this process will, and should always be, contentious and 'agonistic' (Mouffe, 2000; Sabsay, 2016). This idea will be returned to later in the chapter, partly through a consideration of the recourse to legal challenges within anti-austerity activism. While most legal challenges to processes of austerity have failed, legal processes nonetheless offer up alternative spheres for making visible claims, rights and needs (Hubbard and Lees, 2018).

Children's Centre activism: background

As already noted, my research traced activist responses to threatened Children's Centre closures in two local authority areas in England, that I refer to here as 'Children's Centre activism'. While I had undertaken previous research on Children's Centres (see Jupp, 2013a), it is primarily data from this research project on activism that I draw on in this chapter. As discussed in the previous chapter, in Area A I was researching after the main campaigning phase was over, just as centres were closing and the new, much reduced, structure of 'family hubs' was being implemented. I therefore relied on interview data to tell me about modes of activism during the campaign. In Area B I was very much aware of the unfolding nature of the campaign which arose during my research and that I participated in as an activist as well as researcher. I also draw on an interview with Sonia, an activist from a third area, also in South East England (Area C) in which the legal challenge discussed towards the end of the chapter took place, as well as my wider tracing of activism around Children's Centres within digital and conventional media at both a local and national level.

While, as I go on to discuss, a loosely affiliated national campaign did arise from the coming together of a number of local campaigns, in the main, campaigners in each local area were operating independently of each other. This was partly due to the different temporalities of cuts and service reorganisations in each area. In common with the fragmented dynamics of 'austerity localism' across different areas of public services (Newman, 2014; Penny, 2017; Jupp, 2020), there was no national decision or process of deciding to cut or reduce Children's Centre services. Instead there was a fragmentation of provision and of cuts as local authorities were left to try to 'square the circle' of increased need and reduced budgets. The notion of the move towards 'hubs' arose in this context. 'Family hubs' emerged as a policy idea within discussion of the expansion of Children's Centre's remits (APPG, 2016), yet paradoxically has been seized on by local authorities in the process of narrating services cuts (see Penny, 2020, for a similar analysis of library service cuts).

Such a process involved different local authority areas making decisions to close centres at different times, although mainly from 2015 onwards (Smith et al, 2018). As will be discussed, the legal or statutory framework around the provision of Children's Centres is not very clear. It would be reasonable to surmise that as some local authorities were able to close the majority of centres with impunity, then this emboldened other councils to follow suit. Research from the Sutton Trust (Smith et al, 2018) identified a 'tipping point' in closures around 2017, whereby many local authorities were apparently considering cuts as well as implementing them. Even once implemented, the process of austerity cuts was also often protracted, with different rounds of consultations and service changes often slowed down by campaigners and the various challenges they were able to mount to proposed changes. Closures were therefore processes rather than particular moments (Hitchen, 2021).

All this is to highlight the fragmented nature of campaigning against Children's Centre closures, and the difficulties for local campaigns to support each other and build solidarity across campaigns in any systematic manner. Despite this, there were many noticeable similarities in different local campaigns in terms of the modes and tactics of organising. There were therefore links to a wider repertoire of anti-austerity activism and resistance that local activists were attuned to, as well as material similarities in the situation and resources that activists found available to them (Cammaerts, 2018). There were also links to other groups and organisations. In both areas that I researched there was some support for the protestors by opposition local councillors forming coalitions with protestors. Both local authorities were controlled by Conservative (right-wing) parties, and the opposition councillors were mostly Labour (left-wing). This dynamic is not surprising given the history of the Children's Centre programme and its links to the New Labour government, as discussed in Chapter 4 (see Eisenstadt, 2011). The protestors also had some support from trade union groups at various scales. In Area A a national teaching/education union supported the activists, while in Area B a local coalition of trade union groups provided some support to the activists, for example providing tables for a street stall, and coming along to rallies.

Despite this, overall, the Children's Centre activism was not generally linked to wider anti-austerity activism and political discourse (see Chapter 2), although occasionally this emerged during meetings and protests, for example via comments from protestors about 'Tory cuts'. When such comments did emerge they were often rejected by others, complaining that opposing the closure of Children's Centres should not be seen as 'political', in keeping with dynamics of a 'post-political' moment (Penny, 2020). This might also be seen as a deliberate decision to keep the campaigns focused on the material losses of services and support, in order for them to feel inclusive to those who did not see themselves as 'political' or aligned with a particular party. In both areas it was very much service users themselves who undertook all the day-to-day organising of protests and events, and were visible and present at them.

In all areas researched, some of the service users who came forward brought particular skills and resources to activist practices, for example previous activist experience, or experience dealing with the media or council. This was not something I was able to assess systematically within the research. However, I am confident in stating that this was not the case for all service users prominent in the campaigns, the majority of whom did not seem to have experience of either campaigning or relevant professional work. Rather the spaces of campaigning offered (often fragile) connections between service users (overwhelmingly women) from different backgrounds. Such connections were sustained and enabled through the activist practices analysed in the body of this chapter. They were also sustained and enabled through private social media channels, centrally WhatsApp and Facebook messenger groups. Again these were not a focus of the research, however in both areas there were a range of (shifting and fragile) online networks which co-ordinated actions and responses behind the more public scenes set out in this chapter. More public facing Facebook and blog sites were also maintained by all the campaigns studied.

Representing care within the spaces of Children's Centre activism

One of the starting points for activism in all the areas that I researched was the use of small-scale protest events and marches, often outside council offices, especially when key decisions were taking place. Campaigners would stand together holding placards or just being present together within a public space, as seen in Figure 5.1. Such protestors often then also attended council meetings if there was a public gallery or seating area available – so perhaps standing outside the building as officials and decision-makers went in, and then going in themselves once the meeting was about to begin, as I did on a number of occasions in Area B. As service users, these campaigners were predominantly mothers of young children, and as such often brought their children and babies with them to protests, in prams or carriers. This was a practical necessity in that service users were, by definition, the primary carers for the children. However, there was certainly no attempt to discourage the presence of children who would not normally be brought along to 'political' events, or in some cases formal meetings. Huish and Little (2016), writing about the campaign that they co-ordinated in Oxfordshire against cuts to Children's Centres, mention that they specifically encouraged parents and toddlers and breastfeeding mothers to participate in the activist events organised. In Area B, a social media post asking service users to attend a council meeting scheduled for 6.30pm, a time when many young children would be eating and then getting ready for bed, encouraged service users to attend anyway, saying, 'We would ask, beg, you to bring blankies, toys, soothing bedtime things, all the paraphernalia of dinner time and turn out en masse at this meeting'. Again, this is partly a purely practical matter in that many parents of young children and babies are wedded to evening

Figure 5.1: Protestors campaigning to save Children's Centres in Buckinghamshire

Source: Angie Bond

routines, but it could also be read as a deliberate intervention into the space of a council meeting – bringing the materialities and realities of care into that time and space (Baraitser, 2009; Middleton and Samanani, 2021). In such moments, care becomes public and visible.

Indeed, the embodied presence of children and babies could shift the atmosphere and dynamics of an event and brought practices of care for young children into spaces from which they would normally be excluded or at least not visible. For example, the presence of babies and toddlers within the public galleries of formal council meetings tended to function as low level disruption to proceedings with babies crying or toddlers shouting. Their overall presence contrasted with the generally male-dominated and formally dressed local politicians and officials within the space of the meeting itself. On a number of occasions during fieldwork in Area B I witnessed extra seating and space being hastily rearranged for activists with children, their embodied presence in itself an intervention into a political space at which service users rarely had a formal voice. Indeed, the young children at the centre of discussions about Children's Centres clearly had no voice within decision-making. This added a further layer of complexity to debates about needs and vulnerabilities, as the agencies and subjectivities of young children are contested (Holt, 2013).

An extension of making the embodied presence of young children and their care form part of activist practices could be seen in various other events organised in public spaces as part of the campaigns, such as pop-up creches and picnics in visible public spaces. For example, in Area B a 'protest picnic' was held in a prominent green space near the beginning of the campaign. In Area A a 'sling flash mob' took place as part of a wider demonstration, with a group of mothers with babies in slings performing a dance to 'We are family'. Such events had a convivial and playful dynamic, which both forged bonds between protestors and also repurposed or subverted the meanings of public spaces as separate from the domestic sphere. These kinds of interventions can be seen as part of a wider repertoire of anti-austerity activism in particular, whereby the everyday impacts of the loss of services, particularly around care, are rendered visible through playful interventions in public spaces (Cammaerts, 2018). For example, as Cammaerts (2018) discusses, the 'UK Uncut' movement, campaigning on both austerity and matters of tax justice, have used playful and creative tactics to render these issues visible. This has included setting up pop-up creches and women's refuges in banks or shops that have not paid taxes in order to performatively draw attention to connections, addressing various different levels of media and representation. Sisters Uncut, campaigning specifically against cuts to domestic violence services, have adopted similar interventions, which Ishkanian and Peña Saavedra (2019) also link to 'prefigurative' approaches to activism, bringing different ways of being together into the here and now, enacted in unexpected spaces.

However, to return to the notion of storytelling, activists also used placards in particular ways at these occasions, to draw attention to their individual experiences and feelings about the services under threat. Sometimes their placards were playful and satirical (for example in Area B there were comments about particular councillors or particular spending decisions), and sometimes straightforward (such as 'Save Our Sure Starts'), but at others they were poignant and intimate, making public a particular story of the place of the Children's Centre within private and domestic lives. For example, a placard held by a child at a protest I attended outside a council meeting read 'My local children's centre gave my mum support and friendship when I was a baby'. This is a small example of the 'rendering visible' of intimate lives that debates over Children's Centres demanded. Such a placard records the benefits of the centre to lives in the past, something which is by definition hard to make visible or represent. This temporal aspect of use of the centres connects to the way that children's lives and caring needs shift profoundly over time and space, making activism and representation around them harder. Service users often had intense connections with the centres when their children were little, but then drifted away from them when children were older.

Indeed it was often remarked during the interviews that the wider public did not 'understand' Children's Centres. Sonia, the activist in Area C, mentioned that people 'needed to be educated' about Children's Centres. While there were some straightforward misunderstandings about Children's Centres in circulation (for example that they provided childcare/nurseries as opposed to family support), this sense of a lack of 'understanding' could also be related to this sense of invisibility and the difficulties of articulating benefits such as friendship and emotional support (Jupp, 2013a). Part of the job of activism, therefore, was to make the experiences of using the centres visible in time and space. Such placards could be understood as an aspect of this tactic, albeit in the first instance in a temporary and fleeting way as part of a protest event. The placards themselves nonetheless also circulated online and in conventional media such as local newspapers. Again, the circulation of personalised placards and signs at protest events might be thought of as part of a wider repertoire of contemporary activism, which connects online and offline spaces (Gerbaudo, 2012).

In Area B, activists therefore also sought to structure and capture longer stories that emerged in various ways, as part of the process of making visible the benefits of the centres. Signs reading, 'I love my Sure Start because …' were given out at various events and the completed signs were photographed for inclusion on the campaign's Facebook site. These often elicited quite short but powerful statements – Figure 5.2 shows one example. As can be seen, even in the short amount of space of the sign, a sense of narrative or story emerges, with access to the centre seen to have a transformative impact.

Figure 5.2: Photo of a placard made at a campaign event in Area B and then circulated on social media

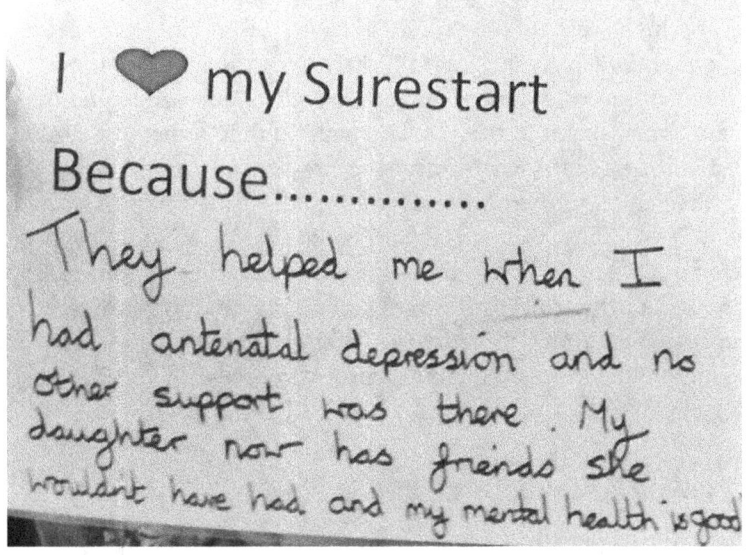

It is also worth noting the ability of this particular service user to encapsulate her complex story in a short space like this. Longer, and perhaps slightly less 'polished', stories also quickly started to be recorded on the campaign's blog site in Area B – these were sent in initially on the campaign Facebook site but organisers rapidly began to ask service users to 'send us your stories'. A 'your stories' section of the campaign blog site was set up with mostly anonymous contributions. Here is an example of one such contribution:

> I started going to XXXX centre when my daughter was about a month old through the centre we met other mums and still talk 18 months on … when my daughter was 6 months I had a bit of a break down I'm not sure it was post natal depression but I was definitely very low, on Wednesday morning while getting my daughter weighed I opened up to one of the centre's ladies – the relief to have someone to finally talk to who understood was amazing – we both shed a tear that morning and she offered and arranged counselling for me … I don't drive so having a centre in a neighbourhood has been a massive lifeline on being able to get out to a group, I feel strongly that without getting up and getting out to a group my mental health would have been badly affected, if the centres close I will deffo feel lost on what to do with our days. (Area B blog site, no page)

As is already apparent, many of the stories raised issues of maternal mental health and distress, however they might be categorised. As this story suggests, there was an awareness of categories such as 'postnatal depression', some of which were used by mothers to make sense of their feelings and experiences (Pedersen and Lupton, 2018). Of the mothers I interviewed in Area B (some of whom were active in the campaign, some of whom were not), three-quarters discussed mental health in some way. This in itself suggested the need for wider infrastructures of care around mental health, rather than treating them as individual medicalised issues (McGrath and Reavey, 2016). The point made so powerfully in this story, of accessing help for one issue while in the centre for a different reason, clearly also resonates with the stories in the previous chapter, about the open access and informal nature of the centres, enabling service users to get support around difficult and sensitive issues which were embedded in wider aspects of everyday lives.

Storytelling in meetings

The circulation of such stories online was clearly a powerful tool for the campaigners. However, in terms of the specificities of fighting service closures on a local level, probably more significant was the telling of such stories in meetings, especially where councillors and officials were present and listening. Hitchen (2021) also argues that council meetings act as key spaces and times when processes of austerity become present and visible. As already indicated, there were a series of committee, council and 'scrutiny' meetings across the two areas where various stages of official decision-making around service restructures and closures of Children's Centres occurred. These were formal, even quasi-judicial events, where the voices of the public were only heard in very specific and controlled ways. For example, service users might be called to give 'evidence' at a particular meeting or given spaces to raise concerns, but very much on the terms of the council. A time limit was normally put on members of the public speaking and they would be called forward to speak or 'give evidence' at a small table, typically at the centre of a formal meeting room with local politicians arranged in a semi-circle around them. In what follows I will discuss some examples of storytelling in meetings from both Areas A and B and what they tell us about the potentials and problematics of such a mode of activism.

Overall, it was this storytelling in formal meetings that seemed to be most powerful within the campaigns – to have the most transformational impact, in Cameron (2012)'s terms, on the decision-makers present. Indeed, stories told in such contexts also possessed the other qualities Cameron (2012) draws attention to, in terms of bringing 'small stories' into larger political debates, and in terms of being emotional and affective, inviting forms of interpersonal recognition. For all the restrictions imposed on those telling their stories in these meetings, the officials present were obliged to listen and engage. It could be argued that gaining this kind of attention for such stories across media platforms is very difficult – to oblige someone to listen and engage with personal and sensitive material in a sustained way, given the volume of stories and experiences circulating within digital culture – as I go on to discuss further in the next section of this chapter.

Alice in Area A (a prominent activist in the campaign in that area) told me about a number of other mothers who had used their stories within meetings in this way as part of the campaign. She also spoke about a teenage child who had witnessed the impact the support from a Children's Centre had had on her mother, indeed who had escaped an abusive relationship because of this support. Based on events in her past, this older child was able to have a voice in the campaign in a way that younger children could not. Alice recounted a council meeting where this teenager had spoken to powerful effect:

'But yeah, so she'd made this amazing speech, half the Tories were in tears, which is, you don't see that much, and they actually had a break, they actually went out for a break, which is the first time it's happened since 1990 something or whatever. And they ended up coming together with almost like a coalition budget with £2 million extra to children's centres, like I said that was the day that all the councillors were sat there, leafing through our paperwork instead of the council paperwork on that day, so yeah.' (Alice, Children's Centre Service user and activist, Area A)

This sense of the powerful and disruptive emotional impact of service users' stories also arose in Area B at a meeting of the 'Scrutiny Committee' with responsibility for children and young people's services. The committee involved local politicians, who were discussing the proposals by the council to close the majority of the Children's Centres. Kat was the only service user who had come forward to speak. As already mentioned, the room was laid out in a very formal fashion with 'witnesses' called to speak from a small desk and chair in the middle of the room.

Kat had written out her story and she read it out from paper that she held. As she read she became increasingly visibly upset, and had to stop reading a couple of times while another service user came over and comforted her. The telling of her story had a powerful emotive effect on many of those present, as was apparent in subsequent discussions at the meeting when it was referred to a number of times. In the first part of her account she spoke about her own traumatic childhood with an alcoholic mother and then her own struggles with mental health after the birth of her daughter:

'As a guilt-racked mum, I pushed myself to attend my local Children's Centre. It was here that my recovery started (although it is still ongoing). It is a safe space to take my son, down the road, no commitment, no money, where you would think it was just somewhere my son could play.

In fact it was the complete opposite, it was a safe space for me to get a little bit of respite.

A place where the staff went out of their way to catch up with me.

A place where I could meet other mums and discover I wasn't the only mum whose child pulled their hair or wouldn't eat vegetables anymore.

A place where I took a postnatal wellbeing course, the first step to tackling my depression.

A place where me and my son took a cooking course.

A place where, in my darkest hour, I was in the arms of a playworker sobbing because I felt I was a complete failure.

And finally, a place where I decided to give back. I trained as a Breastfeeding Peer Supporter and now give support to other local mums myself.' (Kat, Children's Centre service user and activist, Statement to Scrutiny Committee, Area B)

As can be seen, her story is quite beautifully and carefully constructed, from the repetition of 'a place ...' to the sense of transformation and resolution that emerges. It therefore obviously has a performative and rhetorical element to it in its attempts to express both the large and small benefits of the centres – from profound emotional support to cookery courses. As already noted, her telling of the story elicited powerful reactions among the councillors and officials present, many of whom were visibly moved, and her story was clearly an important intervention in the debate. While the centre closures did go ahead in this and the other area, a number of 'concessions' were made by decision-makers during this process, including keeping more centres open across the region. Although this was not admitted directly, it seemed that this meeting represented a turning point and played a role in changing some decision-makers' minds.

However, the story was also very raw, and involved Kat's own vulnerability. For Kat herself, whom I got to know and stayed in touch with after the campaign, the emotional exposure involved in speaking at this and other meetings was personally difficult. One of the councillors, speaking in favour of the closures, said, in a clear reference to Kat's story, "it's all very well being emotional, we need to look at the facts", by which he clearly meant the monetary economics of the situation. Kat told me, in a later interview, how upset she felt about some of the feedback she had received, indicating that she did not feel understood, that her experience was not acknowledged. "It does feel like – 'oh those mums, they can't have everything', people just don't understand what value they have to your lives." She also wrote in a subsequent blog post that after the meeting a councillor had given her an awkward handshake and said she was glad "that she had got her life back together". Kat commented that, "she obviously hadn't listened at all". This anecdote demonstrates that the storytelling had unsettled councillors, but their reaction was not what Kat intended. This highlights the vulnerabilities involved in telling personal and emotional stories, the demands that it makes of storytellers, and the dangers that the stories might not be heard in the ways intended (Cameron, 2012). After the meeting Kat withdrew from the campaign for some time, although she later returned to it, and indeed became involved in local politics as a Labour Party councillor candidate. Her trajectory shows the ways that local activism may not follow a linear path or progression to 'empowerment' but rather might be entwined within the life course in complex ways, as the stories in Chapter 3 also show.

To return to Area A, Alice told me about an occasion when number of the activists went to speak to a different council body. She and another activist had both left abusive and violent relationships because of the support they had found at Children's Centres, as this quote refers to:

'When I went to speak to them, the line was, which made me so angry I had to leave because I was going to throw a chair, "if you help people they will never help themselves". And I was just, well essentially "we're not in Victorian times" so, and this was after myself, my friend that I said about … her situation [referring to situation at home with domestic violence], she was, there was armed police when she left her situation, it was pretty bad. And obviously you know my situation and then someone else who'd had really bad PND with three young children, we all stood up and made heartfelt speeches each and then that was what they said.' (Alice, Children's Centre service user and activist, Area A)

The three women had clearly made themselves vulnerable by telling their stories in this forum and they were essentially humiliated in response.

Storytelling beyond the local

As should be clear, then, storytelling both emerged organically as service users sought to highlight the importance of the centres for them, and was orchestrated in various performative ways by campaigners. This was in order to address the feeling mentioned by Kat in the previous section, that "people just don't understand, what value they have to your lives", although listening and understanding was of course not guaranteed. In the first instance, articulating this importance was clearly a localised question about resisting the closure of the centres that service users relied on. Nonetheless the closure of the centres was more than a local issue. As discussed at the opening of this chapter, closures of centres happened across many English local authorities from 2015 onwards (Smith et al, 2018). The fact that the same processes were happening elsewhere was referred to by decision-makers, particularly in Area B where plans for closures came after other authorities had already followed a similar path, such as Area A. A council officer at a public meeting in Area B reported that "all local authorities are going for 'hubs'". While the 'hubs model', as it was referred to, meant different things in different places (see Smith et al, 2018), it was discussed as the strategy that all local authorities were adopting and therefore a reasonable path to be adopted.

As already noted, however, this was not a national or co-ordinated policy decision. From 2010, but particularly from 2015 onwards, there was essentially a vacuum at the level of central government in terms of what should happen around Children's Centre services (Jupp, 2018). Although there had been the parliamentary working group that produced a paper on 'family hubs' (APPG, 2016), this was never adopted as official government policy. Indeed, while this paper was referred to enthusiastically by councils seeking to bolster the rationale for their plans, the vision within the paper was concerned with augmenting what was offered by centres, and therefore quite different to that adopted by councils under austerity as moving to 'hubs' meant shutting centres. If there was a central government strategy, it was to let councils 'square the circle' of funding and make their own decisions about Children's Centres, within the 'austerity localism' approach outlined (Penny, 2017, 2020). Central government indeed stopped keeping records of numbers of Children's Centres across the country, and questions asked in parliament about closures were often responded to somewhat unclearly (for example see https://questions-statements.parliament.uk/written-questions/detail/2020-01-22/6707). Investment in childcare (as opposed to family support) was often centred in wider debates (Jupp, 2018). There was therefore a kind of 'dissonant' effect, both locally and nationally, whereby claims of investment and service improvement masked the material impacts of closures and service reductions (Kiely, 2021).

In the face of this collective silence or blindness to the fate of Children's Centres within central government, a more ambitious task for local activists was therefore to raise the profile more broadly of the value of the centres and to try to engage national politicians and the media in these matters. The strategy of putting these stories online, already discussed, clearly offered one means by which stories might reach a wider audience. As indicated, Facebook was a platform that was used by activists in the various local campaigns, and during 2017/18, a number of local activists formed a new national network of activists, operating primarily through Facebook, which sought to provide a platform across local campaigns. Sonia, the activist in Area C, was, and remains, instrumental in this network, which has functioned primarily as a space for different local campaigns to share petitions, announcements and news. The site also links the issue of Children's Centre closures to other issues and campaigns around children, services and austerity cuts, for example around Special Educational Needs. Sonia told me that some of the plans for the network hadn't worked out, for example, a national march.

There was clearly a difficulty in sustaining momentum for a cross-local campaign, given the fragmented nature of changes taking place within different timescales and the energy involved in fighting cuts on a local level. My own research showed that local campaigns produced waves of involvement and collective energy which then petered out as closures went ahead locally. However, one activist practice that was successfully undertaken across different local campaigns involved collecting 'stories' from across different campaigns and editing them into images for the site. An example is given at Figure 5.3. Many of the stories had a particular focus or theme,

Figure 5.3: Post from National Children's Centres campaign Facebook site

highlighted in the use of subtitles and underlined sections, as shown. For example, the theme of community and getting 'settled' in an area as a migrant mother was highlighted in a number of stories (echoing the issues raised within Chapter 3), as were issues of mental health, domestic violence, isolation and wellbeing. The example in Figure 5.3 also demonstrates the place that involvement in the campaign itself might play in processes of recovery from trauma and feelings of empowerment. The stories were all presented in the format shown in Figure 5.3, with different colours, which in itself brought the 'small stories' from different local contexts into a shared wider context.

Strategies to expand local activism to a national level also involved lobbying of MPs and national government via various means, as well as using national media to spread awareness of the closure of centres as a national issue. Sonia, leading the campaign in Area C, had a background in press and marketing and was unusual in entering a local campaign with a clear sense that the decision-making around her local centres ultimately rested on wider national decision-making: "I knew there were different stakeholders who were involved with all this, and I knew that I had to find ways to get to all of them." To this end, Sonia secured meetings with politicians, but she also formed alliances with sympathetic national journalists and with think tanks such as the Sutton Trust who were concerned about the closure of Children's Centres and undertook research and lobbying of their own (see Smith et al, 2018). For example, she and other activists in Area C gave press interviews from the perspective of service users as part of articles and reports generated by both national media outlets and think tanks.

Via such means, Sonia was able to generate exceptional media and political focus both on her local authority area and the wider issue. Her own professional background and personal tenacity, and the cultural and social capital involved (as well as class position), clearly gave her resources that many other activists did not possess, and drew decision-makers in to listen, like the women involved in the Coastal Arts project. This is not to say that the process was easy or straightforward for her. Indeed she told me that she had thrown herself into the campaign after the death of her mother, and her feelings about her own loss of a support network after the birth of her son. This ties into the points made in Chapter 4 about the lifecourse and motivations for activism.

As already noted, to a lesser extent, campaigns in both Areas A and B did also involve individuals with relevant professional backgrounds that they were able to mobilise in the campaign, including an individual with press and PR experience in Area B and academic researchers and those with policy expertise in Area A. Such involvement could bring wider networks and resources into the campaigns in general, although on a very localised level could mean that certain centres received more attention than others. In both

Areas A and B, centres in middle-class or at least demographically mixed areas were more visible within the campaigns, although the local campaigns as a whole always made the case for retaining centres across their areas. The former centre manager in Area A, discussed in the previous chapter, mentioned that the service users in her (economically deprived area) had not particularly spoken out against the closure, "they maybe weren't noisy about it, but you could see how upset people were". This raises questions about the resources needed for activism, perhaps particularly activism that involves a level of exposure and vulnerability around needs as a family. 'Going public' with family problems may feel much more risky for working-class and marginalised women who are far more likely to be the subject of 'interventions' around family life (Ribbens McCarthy and Hooper, 2013; Bywaters et al, 2018). Furthermore, as already mentioned, there is the issue of narrating or giving shape to personal experience which is far harder if issues are ongoing or unresolved.

All this speaks to issues of visibility and voice in relation to experiences that take place in the private, domestic sphere and where marginalised women in particular face stigma and vulnerability in speaking out. Despite the gathering of stories on placards and online, the experiences involved are also quite hard to convey via written text, which is perhaps why the stories told in person at meetings seemed particularly powerful. In person, the stories were embodied and the storytellers themselves were visible in a way that they weren't in examples online. From my own perspective as a researcher who also wished to contribute to a national debate on the future of Children's Centres, I decided to explore the potentials of animation to tell my participants' stories (Dwyer and Davies, 2010). Working with digital arts students from my university we worked together on a four-minute animation using audio interview transcripts as a starting point. As well as offering anonymity to storytellers, I was interested in how visual representation could literally render visible feelings and experiences that would not be captured by text. In line with my interest in 'small stories' (Cameron, 2012) and the less dramatic aspects of care that might be offered by centres, I also wanted to include aspects of the experience of Children's Centres that were more 'ordinary', which might be sidelined within debates, but were nonetheless powerful and meaningful within everyday lives, and could be rendered visible through a visual medium.

In the end the pressures of time and space on such an animation (both in terms of resources and the 'attention economy' which it would form part of) resulted in having to work with much smaller snippets of data than I had at first imagined, which did not allow me to tell 'stories' in their entirety but rather small extracts from these stories. Video animation is a complex and time-consuming medium to produce. There are obviously also possibilities for more expansive forms of personal storytelling via text-based drawn

Figure 5.4: Images from Save Our Sure Starts animation. The images accompany service users speaking about the repetitious nature of their domestic life (a) and about the support offered at the Children's Centre (b). The animation can be watched in full at https://www.youtube.com/watch?v=tKb1NWVNFlw

Source: Eleana Gabriel and Yee Hui Wong, School of Engineering and Digital Arts, University of Kent

comics and zines, as in the work of Hall (2019c) and Taylor (2020) both also exploring the impacts of austerity on intimate and everyday lives. Nonetheless those small parts of interview data we were able to animate did, I believe, take viewers into the worlds of storytellers, and were affective and emotional, as I witnessed when showing the animation to audiences in a range of contexts. Figure 5.4 shows some stills from moments in the animation.

Evaluating stories in court

So far in this chapter, storytelling in a number of settings has been discussed as central to a range of interventions and practices undertaken by Children's Centre activists. This final section takes the activists' demands and experiences into a different sphere – that of legal process in court. This concerns Area C, in which Sonia had successfully campaigned alongside other activists within both local and national spheres, as previously mentioned, to halt the closures of centres. The court case, as explained further in this section, related to how the consultation around closures (which the local authority had been obliged to undertake) had been carried out (see also Penny, 2020). In fact there was also a court case in Area A at a certain stage in the campaign, but it did not reach a full judicial review in the High Court as in Area C.

The practice of seeking legal challenge or protection via the law has been used by anti-austerity activists in a range of contexts, including matters of housing (Watt, 2016; Hubbard and Lees, 2018) and benefit caps and reductions (Fenton-Glynn, 2015). Indeed legal proceedings have had some impact in a number of areas of welfare reform and cuts, through providing challenges to practices adopted by local authorities under austerity, for example in how families impacted by the cap in benefits are treated with regards to becoming homeless (Fenton-Glynn, 2015). As Hubbard and Lees discuss, while legal systems might be understood as ultimately 'state-centric institutions' (2018: 10) that are unlikely to challenge dominant policy paradigms, they might also offer up sites for differential politics.

As examples around housing and benefits caps show (Fenton-Glynn, 2015), as austerity pressures bear down on local authorities in terms of the resources available to them, the legal or statutory obligations that they work within become harder to meet, for example obligations to provide suitable or adequate housing. Therefore they are operating at the edge of these obligations, in ways that open up their actions to legal challenge. As I will go on to discuss in relation to Children's Centres in particular, legal frameworks around public services may relate to an era of welfare state provision in which both the pressures of austerity and the current level of need around services were not envisaged. In many ways it could be argued that the resort to legal challenges represents a failure of democratic process – or perhaps part of a 'post-political' dynamic (Swyngedouw, 2007). Such processes bring the law into effectively making policy, in this case ruling on values around welfare and care that might properly be dealt with through other forms of politics.

In the rest of this section I discuss the matters at stake in this case, and what the process tells us about how far a politics of care and everyday life might be negotiated and evaluated within a legal sphere. I attended the hearing as an observer. In common with the local council meetings, the occasion of the court case involved a number of local campaigners attending, bringing placards and taking photos outside the court building. There was a sense of anxiety and anticipation among the campaigners, as the case felt like both the culmination of several years of campaigning, and the end of the road in terms of where their demands might go.

The case for judicial review in Area C was brought by an anonymous mother on behalf of her child, a service user who did not disclose her identity. The case was brought against the local authority making the decision to close Children's Centres. The full details of the family's situation and story were not made public. The court was told, however, that she was a single mother with five children, of whom the claimant was the youngest. She accessed a particular Children's Centre, that was earmarked for closure, on an almost daily basis for a wide range of forms of support. In common with other activists, it was the 'open access' approach at the centre that she particularly valued, and which was under threat in the restructuring. Because of her lack of a car and her daily routine involved with taking older children to school, the centre due to close was her only option for accessing support.

Although these were the only details in the public domain, in common with other arenas of storytelling and protest, at the centre of this family's situation were questions of need, of everyday life, the material realities of care and the desire for open-ended spaces and forms of support as discussed in the previous chapter. These therefore involve matters of the politics and ethics of care (Puig de la Bellacasa, 2017), and what the local welfare state should provide. However, the judicial review did not relate to the closure of the centre in general; the politics and ethics of care are hard to define in legal terms, and the legislation surrounding Children's Centres does not address these in any direct way.

Indeed the relevant legislation (HM Government, 2006) was produced at a time when Children's Centres were a universal service, rather than the contested entity that they have since become (Jupp, 2018). The relevant law seeks to protect their provision in a broad brush way (obliging local authorities to provide 'sufficient Children's Centre services to meet local need') and to ensure that local residents had a say in any changes to provision so that a consultation was required if a centre was to be closed. Councils are also obliged to ensure that 'the most vulnerable families' are not adversely impacted by changes. However, it would be reasonable to surmise that at the time of making the law it was not envisaged that there would be a need to protect the very existence of Children's Centres, and therefore there is a lack of specificity in many aspects of the legal framework, as the analysis that follows demonstrates.

Instead the legal challenge hung on the way in which the council had undertaken the process of consultation and decision-making around the closure of centres. This is therefore a matter of procedure rather than the substance of the new reduced service, although these are obviously intertwined to some extent. The case brought by the claimant rested on the following (in relation primarily to the Childcare Act 2006, within which legislation concerning Children's Centres is found):

- firstly, that the consultation was unfair because it was presented and proceeded on the a priori assumption that Children's Centres would close (with no option for retaining the status quo in the consultation documents), and also these closures were not made clear in consultation documents;

- secondly, that it did not address the duty that councils have 'to provide sufficient Children's Centres to meet local need' in the way it carried out the consultation; and furthermore that there was not sufficient regard for equalities matters.

The court case, during which barristers presented the case of the claimant and of the local authority before a judge, therefore brought the politics of Children's Centre closures into the legal sphere in new ways. The legislation surrounding Children's Centres in the Childcare Act had not been tested this way previously before in court. Had the case been successful, it would have potentially changed the course of closures not just in that particular local authority area, but many others as well. In the absence of a national policy debate on Children's Centres, the court case could therefore be seen to stand in for some of the matters at stake. In particular it tested what was meant by 'sufficient Children's Centres to meet local need', bringing questions of defining needs and responsibilities for care to meet those needs into the legal sphere. Nonetheless bringing this debate into a legal context inevitably involved a narrowing of how these questions of needs were discussed, and also the kind of voices and narratives that shaped them.

The presentation of arguments in court by the barrister acting for the claimant and mother focused on the consultation process with local residents, and how the council assessed local need and presented options to residents through the consultation documents and process. The discussions in court therefore shed light on the dynamic previously discussed, whereby the closures or reductions of services were not directly addressed or necessarily even acknowledged by service providers. Instead the language of 'service improvement' and restructuring masked the material changes at stake (Jupp, 2018; Hitchen, 2019; Penny, 2020). While the barrister presenting stopped short of claiming that the consultation documents were duplicitous, she suggested that it would have been hard for consultees to ascertain the reality of the process of closures that was proposed. This opened up some interesting questions about what a consultation was for, and how it should be conducted, with the barrister making the argument that "Consultation should be a profound dialogue between the government and the governed about reality"; in other words, that consultation processes should not be superficial or disingenuous processes that do not clearly present the material matters and questions at hand. As Hitchen (2019) argues in relation to cuts to library services, the sense of the 'cut as transformation', or what Kiely (2021) calls a 'camouflaging' of austerity, is linked to the politics of 'austerity localism' (Newman, 2014; Penny, 2017) whereby local politicians seek to remain electable, while also making potentially very unpopular cuts. Therefore cuts and service closures end up being narrated as positive improvements to services.

In the case of this consultation, and indeed others that I am aware of, the consultation masked the changes to Children's Centres by presenting the closures as part of something called a new 'Early Help Strategy', rather than anything in particular to do with Children's Centres. The Children's Centres were also to be renamed as 'Family Centres' as part of these changes (see Jupp, 2018). As the barrister pointed out, neither 'Early Help' nor 'Family Centres' represent a defined term or set of services in the way that 'Children's Centres' do. Therefore discussion during the court case touched on whether they amounted to the same service. In so doing, some of the shifting rationalities and politics of care discussed in the previous chapter were brought into legal discussions. 'Early Help' is a term which has come to replace 'early intervention' within children's services and can be seen as linked to the emergent paradigms of care discussed in the previous chapter (Webb and Bywaters, 2018). It is associated with social work practices and targeted 'interventions' aimed at certain 'vulnerable' categories of family deemed to be in need, before they might reach more formal social work interventions. It is not linked to any particular age of children, although there is a notion that 'catching problems early' can save more costly and complex problems later in the life of a family (Gillies et al, 2017). This is clearly not a negative service to be providing; however it is not the same service as Children's Centres which are meant to function as universal, open-access spaces, for families with children aged under five, that begin from an assumption that all families have needs and require caring and supportive spaces where they can gain support from each other as well as professionals.

By shifting the discourse of policy and services away from Children's Centres to Early Help, the sense of what 'needs' the centres were designed to address therefore also shifted. Discussion during the court case focused on whether the local authority had considered their duty to 'provide sufficient local Children's Centres to meet local need'. Of course, the question of what constitutes a need in this context is contested, and related to different ethical and political aspects of care, the subtleties of which could not really be debated within a court room.

Overall, the challenge to the actions of the local authority was not successful. The judge found that 'the Council carried out a fair Consultation before it made the Decision; it took the responses properly into account, and it complied with all its relevant statutory duties'(The full judgment is available at http://www.bailii.org/ew/cases/EWHC/Admin/2019/1817.html.) The details of the judgement suggest that while the closure of Children's Centres was not made as explicit as it might have been, the broader changes to Early Help proposed made it clear that not all centres would be operating. Furthermore that while considering providing 'sufficient centres to meet local need' may not have been addressed explicitly in the document, it was addressed implicitly in the whole design of the proposed new service which would focus on 'the most vulnerable families in greatest need'. There is a general sense in the text of the judgement that the judge recognises the difficult position that local authorities are in with reduced budgets. Therefore not providing an option for 'no change' or no closures was reasonable given that they stated that, 'it was not a sustainable way for it to keep providing its early help services to meet the needs of children and families effectively within the reduced budget available'. The wording is interesting here, as the discursive shift from Children's Centre services to 'Early Help services' is clear, with no mention of 'Children's Centre services'.

Indeed, a similar language and approach to consultation was used within Area B, whereby the purposes and remit of Children's Centres were discursively merged with 'Early Help', a term that was never clarified or delineated during the consultation processes. Based on the judgement in this court case, it appears that local authorities will no longer be obliged to retain something called 'Children's Centres' at all, and that they can still claim to be following the legislation that surrounds them.

To return to the story of needs and care at the centre of the case, as stated at the outset, the court process could not, and did not, allow for discussion and exploration of the wider shifting rationalities of care and of children's services that were at stake in the cuts. As mentioned, the legal framework had not envisaged a time when Children's Centres would not exist at all, and perhaps for this reason did not provide sufficiently robust statutes that could protect the services as originally designed when they were under threat. Nor could the court case really foreground the experience and story of the claimant and his family, because the aspects of care they valued were not defined in law and could not therefore be the subject of a legal challenge. Nonetheless, in the absence of a wider political debate around care, needs and the disappearance of Children's Centres, the case at least rendered some of these issues public, and opened up the possibility of new forms of resistance.

Conclusion

Overall, following and observing the court case underlined this lack of debate about Children's Centre services within the sphere of government and politics. Apart from the localised spaces of the campaigns considered, questions of ethics, politics and affective and practical matters of care around the Centres have been sidelined and silenced. This reflects a broader lack of debate or evaluation around welfare services as they have shrunk under austerity, sidelining these debates within very local struggles as discussed.

The lack of such a sphere of broader debate and evaluation means that, more generally, the 'stories' that service users came forward to tell so powerfully within different spaces of the campaigns risk being ignored or drowned out by other voices. Even those seeking to defend Children's

Centres from a policy perspective have tended to attempt to monetise and prove the value of Children's Centres in purely instrumental terms (for example Cattan et al, 2019). Many think tanks and policy researchers have produced well intentioned reports on these terms, setting out to 'prove' the value of the centres (for example Smith et al, 2018). However, as the original evaluations have shown throughout (Belsky et al, 2007), it is difficult to show cause and effect with such services. Treating them as if it were possible to provide data on links between centre use and childhood outcomes, as if there were no other factors impacting on children's lives, was always essentially doomed to failure.

Again, what is needed is a politics and political discourse within which matters of care can become revalued (Tronto, 2015; Care Collective, 2020). One should no more seek to 'prove' the value of a Children's Centre than one would a school or other spaces and services, which, while undoubtedly contested and under pressure, remain institutions and spaces which are still collectively valued within a broader vision of the welfare state. A much more robust vision of localised infrastructures of care is needed, which includes spaces such as Children's Centres that might provide the 'invisible cotton wool' and comfort around people's lives. This might involve services and formal support but also the friendships and solidarity which might develop beyond services. The next chapter considers how informal forms of care and solidarity arose during the COVID-19 pandemic.

6

Provisioning in times of crisis

Introduction

This chapter continues themes of the previous chapters, around a politics of everyday life, including local action, domestic life, care and questions of austerity and the responsibilities and reach of the state. However, it places them within a different context, the 2020 global COVID-19 pandemic, or more specifically the initial phases of the pandemic, March–September 2020. There are too many aspects of society which have been thrown into sharp relief by the crisis to consider here in much detail – questions of class, work and inequality, race and vulnerability, disability and much more besides (Rose-Redwood et al, 2020; Andrews et al, 2021). Social science will continue to make sense of the pandemic for decades to come, and so the discussion here can only be partial and provisional, especially given that it is still ongoing at the time of writing. In what follows I focus on the nature of local action during the early stages of the pandemic. What were the politics, ethics, affects and practices of care that emerged at this moment of immense strain on society? What infrastructural forms did these take? And what do they reveal about the possibilities and problematics of a localised politics of care?

If austerity as discussed in preceding chapters can be understood as 'slow violence' (Pain, 2019) or 'crisis ordinary' (Berlant, 2008; Brickell, 2020a), then the COVID-19 crisis was (and is, at the time of writing), a much more visible and immediate crisis, which has impacted on almost every sphere of human life and interaction in a dramatic way. The need to render it visible as a crisis itself is not an issue. However, while at the centre of the pandemic is a new medical and bodily set of problems, the wider social, political and economic problems caused, or rather interwoven with, this medical crisis are clearly not new nor caused directly by the virus. Rather they are being illuminated and intensified in new ways.

In this chapter I draw on some autoethnographic reflections as well as more conventional research methods. As discussed elsewhere (Bowlby and Jupp, 2021), I am interested in Puig de la Bellacasa (2017)'s idea of thinking with metaphors of 'touch', to consider the idea that the COVID-19 crisis has involved a kind of pressing down onto aspects of society, a pressure which enables us to see aspects that were already there more clearly. I thought about this metaphor in an embodied way when

Figure 6.1: Leaf-printing, April 2020, made during home-schooling with my daughter, Caitlin

doing leaf-printing with my young daughter during homeschooling (see Figure 6.1). Making the images illuminated aspects of the leaves' structures, but it also made visible the variety of leaves in our garden at a time when there was little access to spaces beyond the home. The practices of pressure involved also mirrored my feelings of strain as our home became a place of education as well as work, and of care for children during a time of widespread feelings of crisis and anxiety. In this I acknowledge my immense privilege in relation to my economic and material circumstances during the pandemic.

As well as some autoethnographic reflections, the body of research discussed in this chapter, as set out in the Introduction, draws on interviews with community organisations and volunteers. Interviews were undertaken in autumn 2020. In particular I discuss the Coastal Arts project run by two women, Claire and Rachel, which is discussed in more detail in Chapter 3. The chapter also draws on additional research undertaken into a 'mutual aid' local network in a market town in South East England, which I call the town mutual aid network. The research involved three interviews with local co-ordinators, Dave, Marian and Frances, as well as my own involvement in this network over eight months, as a 'mutual aider' supporting neighbours, from which I draw autoethnographic reflections (although this was clearly not undertaken as research).

Perhaps because I already knew them slightly as co-volunteers, or because I had been doing the volunteering work we were discussing, I decided to do these mutual aider interviews using a different style compared to previous research. I brought my own research questions and concerns more explicitly into the research encounter, explaining my reflections and analysis around mutual aid at points in the interview and asking them to respond. It was an attempt at a more co-productive style of research interview, rather than an extractive model (Way et al, 2015). I therefore brought my 'researcher' self more fully into the research encounter, rather than being either a neutral interviewer or an activist/volunteer split off from my researcher identity (Derickson and Routledge, 2015). This style is not necessarily appropriate for all interviews or research though. Furthermore, there is an argument for the value in holding open the critical space for research outside of the spaces of activism, irrespective of the researcher's own commitments to activist causes (Brown and Pickerill, 2009).

In general, it is worth noting that unlike many events or contexts studied by social scientists, the COVID-19 pandemic has been experienced in some way by everyone including obviously researchers themselves. This experiential proximity might be seen as both a source of insights into the crisis, but also perhaps risks overly colouring our own analysis. Like other phenomena encountered primarily in the home space (such as parenting and care), the intensity of our own experiences of the pandemic could overwhelm other insights. The fragmented and unequal nature of experiences of the pandemic is in itself a wider challenge for analysis. I try to remain alert to these tensions in the discussion that follows. I begin by discussing the changing geographies of 'home' and 'community' as sites of care during the pandemic, before moving on to consider how new infrastructures of local action emerged in this context and some reflections on the impacts, potentials and problematics of this action. Many of the themes and questions from previous chapters will be picked up here as well.

Home space and atmospheres of crisis

In terms of the meanings of home, as I discuss elsewhere (Bowlby and Jupp, 2021), the home space, often somewhat hidden in public discourse, has come to the centre of media and public discussions during the pandemic (see also Jupp et al, 2019; Brickell, 2020a). The dominant feature of 'lockdown' or mass quarantining has been the command to 'Stay Home and Save Lives' or 'Stay Safe and Stay Home' (BBC News, 2020a). The notion of 'household' has also gained huge policy and media focus, as the unit within which citizens have been allowed to socialise and spend time without so-called 'social distancing' (Bowlby and Jupp, 2021). There is no doubt that home and household have thus become increasingly dominant sites of everyday lives and experiences, as education, work and social life have been reconfigured to take place within them, often, supposedly at least, facilitated by digital technology – although this has not been straightforward or equitable (Chung et al, 2020).

Indeed, as this suggests, the seemingly simple or straightforward instructions involved in 'staying home', working and learning from home within a household, actually masks many more complex and problematic experiences of home and household which remain hidden and largely undiscussed because of public/private divides (Brickell, 2020a). Such hidden aspects of home include questions of mobility and immobility (Dobusch and Kreissl, 2020). Marginalised sections of the population are not able to 'stay home' – either because of working in what Sophie Lewis (2020) has termed 'sacrifice zones' – from health and social care workers, to Amazon delivery drivers, supermarket workers and more – or because of lack of access to safe housing for myriad reasons. The meanings and impacts involved in staying home are also clearly vastly different depending on access to housing, family and household composition, sexuality, disability and much more (Dasgupta, 2020). Home may simply not be the safe place that has been figured in such instructions, and nor has it necessarily ever been. As demonstrated in the discussion of mothers' experiences of looking after babies at home in Chapter 4, home can be a place that feels oppressive, isolating and even dangerous.

Relatedly, another aspect of home and household which has come into focus for many during the pandemic has been the difficulties for even the most well-resourced household to exist as an independent and self-sustaining unit. Social and governmental networks and spaces of care and support, or infrastructures, were largely shut down during the pandemic. For many commentators, the difficulties involved around care in particular has highlighted the limitations of the notion of the nuclear family and household as a way of thinking about and organising care in society (Chatzidakis et al 2020; Kay, 2020; Lewis, 2020). Again, as the experiences discussed in Chapters 4 and 5 demonstrate, spaces of care beyond the home, such as Children's Centres, can be vital in supporting care within it (see also Jupp, 2019). Lockdown has revealed, in a very stark way, how family or household lives are only really made liveable and possible by resources, practices and spaces of care and self-care outside the home and immediate household. These might be everyday practices such as a walk to the post office or market for someone living alone that enables them to interact with others, informal childcare sharing arrangements with other families, or more formal kinds of support and services. In the UK, in June 2020, three months into lockdown, regulations were changed to allow adults living alone or with children to form a 'support bubble' with another household, in recognition of the particular difficulties they faced in coping with lockdown as a single household (BBC News, 2020b). Nonetheless, the length of time it took for this change to be made suggests the lack of understanding among policy makers of the diversity of family and household life beyond an idealised nuclear family model (Kay, 2020). Many sections of society felt largely forgotten or invisible during the pandemic, as media and policy discussions and decisions seemed to ignore their struggles around care and self-care (for example people with intellectual disabilities; see Adams, 2020). This is of course not a new feeling for many marginalised groups in society. Perhaps the more remarkable aspect of this was the number of individuals and families who found themselves in this unfamiliar position, from middle-class parents (such as myself) struggling with the almost impossible task of homeschooling children alongside full-time work, to business owners suddenly reliant on welfare state benefits and payments in new ways.

Indeed, in a very material and immediate way, at the start of the lockdown in the UK, the command to 'stay at home' placed some households in an impossible situation, especially those who were told that they were particularly vulnerable to the virus and should, in the policy term used, 'shield', and not leave home at all (BBC, 2020a). Access to food, medication and other essential supplies and services for such households who could not go out at all did not appear to have been considered at the time this command was made. Other households undoubtedly decided to 'shield' themselves even if they were not formally designated within this category, or experienced crises in relation to everyday lives for a range of reasons linked to the pandemic, as the previous discussion indicates. At this early stage there was a feeling of total crisis in the infrastructures of society to cope with the health and care emergencies unfolding.

It was within this context of crisis that new forms of local neighbourhood action emerged, and indeed continue to emerge, as the pandemic shifts and new forms of restrictions and regulations unfold or are relaxed. However, there was a particular intensity about the early months of pandemic restrictions in the UK (March–July 2020) that can be thought of as producing particular collective emotional atmospheres or affects (Anderson, 2009; Denning, 2021), as all my interviewees reported. Emotions discussed included anxiety, feeling overwhelmed and worried about others. Dave from the mutual aid project told me:

> 'A lot of people were really scared, and there were a lot of people who were vulnerable, or older, or living on their own, already isolated. There was a lot of fear in the air ... it was horrible to think of so many other people not knowing where to turn to ... a lot of people were essentially becoming prisoners in their own homes.' (Dave, Mutual aid project co-ordinator, Market Town)

This sense of "fear in the air" (alongside the airborne virus itself) refers to that notion of collective atmosphere, both felt and projected onto others. This intense atmosphere also however contained within it strongly felt emotions of solidarity and connection with neighbours, that were different from feelings that might normally circulate within a community. Marian, one of the other mutual aid co-ordinators, spoke about her feelings during one of the 'clap for carers' events, which became a weekly moment when neighbours would stand on their doorsteps to clap or play instruments (Wood and Skeggs, 2020):

> 'When it first started we were all kind of like clapping on our doorsteps and I would stand out there and just think, "oh, my street, I love my street, I love my neighbours", and I would think "wouldn't it be lovely if we had a big street party" and stuff like that ... and now [referring to current phase of pandemic] I've just forgotten about that.' (Marian, Mutual aid project co-ordinator, Market Town)

These intense collective emotions were experienced in a temporary way, and it is notable in this and other interviews that there is a dynamic of sense-making in relation to the emotions experienced in the past. Marian seems unsure what has now happened to these feelings. They reveal an almost visceral desire for connection with others, arising in this context when physical togetherness had become impossible, when caring for others largely meant staying away from them. There was therefore a particular intensity and paradoxical quality in such yearnings for connection. As Marian's quote shows, this intensity also had a galvanising quality in terms of acting as a catalyst for local action (in this example, the idea of a street party in the future after the pandemic is over). In the shorter term, such feelings could translate into rapid local action to support those in need and vulnerable. Indeed, alongside acknowledging aspects of the crisis which were a continuation and intensification of existing socio-economic conditions and issues, it is also important to acknowledge this sense of the crisis producing exceptional spaces and times, where different kinds of local actions and connections around care were opened up. In the next section I consider the overall structures of local care and practices that emerged, and how these structures can be understood politically.

New infrastructures of local care?

As already noted, feelings of solidarity and neighbourly support were widespread at the start of the pandemic across the UK. The kinds of local action these feelings produced could take different forms. At the most everyday and informal level, media reports showed people started doing things with and for neighbours that they wouldn't have done previously, ranging from errands to more unusual activities such as distanced dancing, sing-alongs and music in the street or front garden (Solnit, 2020). Furthermore, these events were often captured on social media, thus potentially acquiring new meanings and audiences as they circulated (Metro online, 2020). Social distancing regulations made coming together in space and time particularly difficult, while at the same time producing this renewed engagement with the locality of the neighbourhood, at least for some households who were able to go out. In some areas at least, new forms of creativity appeared within local public realms – from rainbow pictures displayed in windows to hop-scotch chalked on the pavement for local children (Russell and Stenning, 2020). It is hard to know how widespread such practices were. Claire from the Coastal Arts project (previously discussed in Chapter 3), who lived in a wealthy neighbourhood, remarked on the differences in experiences of lockdown and local action in different parts of the town, related to class and location:

> 'Where I live is a very affluent village and we all did so many lovely things for kids ... I had a "communication chicken" [a ceramic chicken that notes could be left under in her drive, as Claire explained afterwards] outside my gate, so the mums would message me and someone would write a note and leave it under the chicken and I would write back ... and there was another lady making ribbon trails, there were all these nice things going on that weren't happening in our poorer communities ... I mean you can't be tying ribbons on a tree when you're worried about feeding your children.' (Claire, Community arts worker, Coastal Town)

It is noticeable here the centrality of children to concerns about the pandemic and care, within a recognition of the unequal experience of lockdown in different families, linked to class and socio-economic status above all.

As well as this kind of (uneven) informal and everyday activity, at a much more formal level, both the NHS and local authorities recruited volunteers to help with aspects of the crisis, although there was a considerable lag time with these formal schemes, meaning any vulnerable people reliant on them would have been in great difficulty.

Mutual aid networks, and the network which the Coastal Arts project became part of, might be thought of as sitting in between these two forms of support (see Preston, 2020; Spade, 2020; Springer, 2020), drawing on very localised existing connections on streets, but also collectively participating in something more formalised that provided coverage across a wider area. Individuals involved with mutual aid might also be doing very everyday forms of 'helping out' locally, and participating in formal volunteer schemes, so there was not necessarily a clear distinction between such practices. Across the UK as a whole, approximately 4,000 'mutual aid' schemes arose in the context of the pandemic (see https://covidmutualaid.org/), although there was no blueprint for how they operated, meaning some, for example, were more affiliated to other local organisations or structures, while others were freestanding. Unusual organisational models and structures therefore arose.

The primary purpose of both my case study organisations was to provide everyday support to others in relation to food, medication and offer open-ended forms of support for dealing with the social and emotional impacts of lockdown. The town mutual aid scheme, which is one of my case studies, involved recruiting a network of volunteers to offer support to neighbours. Within a market town of around 20,000 inhabitants, upwards of 150 volunteers were recruited to provide neighbourhood support within the space of a few weeks. The rapid development of this network can be seen as particularly remarkable, and as Dave pointed out, the network was established much faster than new infrastructures and volunteering initiatives run by the state. Claire from the Coastal Arts project told me that she had been overwhelmed initially, and said she cried, "and was just a nightmare for about two days, but then we sat down and thought, right, this is what we need to do", with regards to how they were going to continue supporting the different groups in their town now that being together physically was impossible. Claire also talks about how the rapid development of their new ways of working was "adrenaline fuelled", and those working on the mutual aid project too described the intense early atmosphere of the pandemic as having a galvanising impact. In both of these case study areas, there is no doubt that digital spaces and connections played a key role in creating these new networks. Feelings of concern and of the need for action circulated on social media sites in the first instance. The town mutual aid project arose on Facebook, and both Facebook and WhatsApp groups played a key role in establishing and sustaining practices. The connections generated, both between volunteers and among those being helped via volunteers, might be thought of as examples of 'stranger intimacies' (Koch and Miles, 2020) that are a broader feature of new digitally mediated socialities.

These new intimacies were about new connections between those who already knew each other too. Indeed in the town where the Coastal Arts project was located, while there was not a 'mutual aid' scheme that bore that name, a new alliance of charities, community groups, church groups and volunteers quickly formed, which enabled them to act quickly and responsively. As Claire put it, "we all really pulled together". Claire also spoke about being able to access funding quickly, and to be given relative autonomy in how funding was spent. Again this suggests the circulation of new feelings of concern and a more instinctive apprehension of 'needs'. This was very different to the usual bureaucratic processes and demands for certain outcomes that they would be accountable for in terms of accessing funding. The Coastal Arts project started to provide what they called 'Creative Care packages', delivering them personally to individual households and families that they worked with, such as young carers and isolated older people. As mentioned in relation to the project more generally in Chapter 3, much of the impulse behind their work stems from the notion of providing some of the resources which Claire and Rachel feel they have, to other parts of their town. So the project enabled some of the creative community action mentioned earlier (such as the 'communication chicken') to be spread beyond the particular privileged middle-class environment of the village where they lived. The care packages included food, drink and 'treats', but also 'wellbeing' resources such as art materials and creative activities. Similar to the 'communication chicken', Claire told me that they acted as "little carrier pigeons", carrying messages and making connections between individuals who would normally meet face to face through the organisation's activities. It was clear that Claire felt that the organisation had gained new purpose and clarity of mission through the work during lockdown, and had formed new connections with other local organisations.

The town mutual aid co-ordinators were not formally linked to any other organisation and were aware that they were participating in the development of a new organisational form – a network that was not formally constituted, but that nonetheless sought to provide oversight and accountability and support for the volunteers recruited. All of the co-ordinators I interviewed had quite extensive knowledge and experiences of the voluntary sector, working for a range of environmental and social non-governmental organisations (NGOs). They were therefore able to draw on such resources, skills and capital to form the network. While class was not explicitly discussed during my interview, it would be reasonable to classify the co-ordinators as middle class. It should however be noted that the co-ordinators reported that the volunteer mutual aiders were diverse in background.

This meant that there were connections between the mutual aid activity and pre-existing forms of community activity. Between the co-ordinators they had a detailed understanding of the matters of risk, vulnerability and accountability that arose when recruiting neighbourhood volunteers. These matters were clearly more complex than ever in the context of social distancing and airborne disease, and the network also drew on resources informally circulated from other mutual aid groups being set up elsewhere at the time (via a Facebook group in particular). Specific challenges included protecting the health and vulnerability of neighbours, and how to handle money when undertaking shopping errands. The group provided extensive guidance to volunteers and initiated a semi-formal process of volunteers needing to read and sign various forms in order to become 'mutual aiders'. Trust in the volunteers and the process of volunteers gaining trust from those they were supporting was a major concern. Dave told me: "We were quite paranoid about someone in authority saying, 'you can't do this' so we wanted to really make sure that there was really plenty of mutual oversight and ways for people to call up and check if it was legit."

In relation to this point in particular, the network partnered with a well-known local charity who had access to the network's records of volunteers so that anyone phoning could check that the volunteers had formally signed up with the scheme. Dave reported that even this matter was complex because of the demands of data protection legislation.

As all these points show, the mutual aid network therefore occupied a hybrid space between informal neighbourly help and a formalised NGO or charity. On an affective level, the notion of trust and care rooted in informal community and familial bonds was clearly important: 'mutual aiders' were assigned to provide support to close neighbours (in their street or a next-door street) only, and this was an important part of the vision. As Dave explained: "We wanted to create natural trust and reassurance, which I think is the best kind, you know, rather than DBS checks, you know that kind of neighbour-to-neighbour, that familiarity."

At the same time, Dave was clear that the idea was to create an organisation that provided systematic support and oversight, rather than simply connect up neighbours that might have helped each other anyway. He told me that he completely rejected a particular discourse of 'kindness' as a motivation or catalyst for local action, referring to some of the discourses of emotions that currently circulate within policy and media spheres, as discussed in Chapter 2. Indeed such a discourse did circulate around mutual aid projects, and around the Coastal Arts project as discussed in Chapter 3. Dave told me, "I've always hated this 'random acts of kindness' idea, I've always hated that phenomena, because I thought it was very cutesy, and because it has no social or political conscience whatsoever ... helping each other shouldn't be down to 'randomness' or philanthropy or some individual deciding that."

As these quotes show, Dave's involvement in local action was narrated quite differently from many others involved in local action discussed in this book, and indeed others involved with the mutual aid scheme. He occupied much more of an identity as a political 'activist' and had considerable experience in more conventional forms of organising and activism, such as anti-arms trade activism. He therefore entered the mutual aid project from a much more consciously 'politicised' perspective, with less reference to events in his own lifecourse compared to those discussed in Chapter 3 – although the fact that he had been furloughed from work was a significant factor in giving him time to work on the mutual aid scheme.

Dave was engaged with anarchist and radical ideas, especially around food provisioning and distribution, and told me that he saw the mutual aid project as a chance to put these ideas into practice, in what he called a "softly anarchist" way. One aspect of this, that underlines the idea and history of 'mutual aid' in general (Springer, 2020), was that the project was about collective support and solidarity and was therefore different, not only to the 'random kindness' idea discussed in the previous paragraph, but also to a 'charitable' or 'recipient' approach to support. Instructions to mutual aiders emphasised the idea that 'we might all need help at some point, so those providing mutual aid one week might be receiving it the next'. As Dave pointed out, this was quite different to, for example, a foodbank model, with a clear division between volunteers and recipients and a gatekeeping and conditional element to accessing food there (via a system of referrals and vouchers). Furthermore, also important to the philosophy of the scheme was a lack of hierarchy in decision-making – there were six area co-ordinators, but they all told me that their purpose was to assist with collective oversight rather than directing volunteers. Volunteers working within the same road or small locality were encouraged to form 'cells' that could work together. I was part of a group of five volunteers who communicated with each other to divide up tasks and asked each

Figure 6.2: The organisation of the town mutual aid scheme

other for advice etc. Figure 6.2 shows the map that Marian used to map mutual aiders in her area.

Therefore the mutual aid scheme had an explicit aim to make a new kind of organisation, and, for some of those involved at least, a much more implicit aim to make a new kind of world, within a framework of prefigurative politics (Ince, 2012; Cooper et al, 2019). As already noted, this makes the project unusual compared to other projects discussed in this book – although this is not to say that other projects did not have 'political' ambitions to make changes in society. Rather this project was connected to such a discourse politically. Just as 'lockdown', 'shielding' and 'social distancing' became meaningful new terms during the pandemic, so too did 'mutual aid'. Indeed, it may be that the pandemic has an impact on local action, not necessarily in changing the work that volunteers or community organisations do, but in reframing practices and organisations, linking them to organisational forms and discourses. Dave understood the possibilities of prefigurative politics as linked to the initial stage of the COVID-19 crisis, which he saw as having a productive energy as well as being a time of suffering:

> 'At the beginning, as well as being scary, there was an enormous amount of possibility opening up, what had been considered immoveable, unchangeable rules of how society worked, what government can and can't intervene in were absolutely blown apart – and it was very exciting ... and it was always going to be a long-term thing, although we feel leaden now, something did explode about how we organise society and perceptions of what can and can't be done, who counts as key workers, what the government can do to intervene. ... It turns out that they can intervene and they can pay our wages ... those bits of shrapnel are still up in the air, and we'll find out in the years to come which bits land and what's to come ... I don't feel that the reshifting of possibilities is finished yet ... it's still there to be shaped.' (Dave, Mutual aid project co-ordinator, Market Town)

As can be seen in this quote, there was a strong temporal element in his response, with the pandemic figured as a kind of explosion into time, shifting the past, present and future. The quote also evidences shifting affective energies, including the idea of 'feeling leaden now'. This response was in the context of a discussion about whether the energy around mutual aid shifted over time and whether it would be sustained beyond the short term of crisis, a theme I discuss further in the next section as part of a reflection on more practical and personal experiences of doing mutual aid.

The everyday practices and caring labour of mutual aid

The following text is taken from the leaflet which the mutual aid scheme distributed to all residents of the town where it was based. The work of being a 'mutual aider' began with this act.

> **Hello! If you're self-isolating you're not alone**
> Are you unable (or worried) to leave home because of Coronavirus (COVID-19)? Do you need someone to run errands, pick up a prescription, point you to other help, etc? We can help!
> We are a co-ordinated group of residents getting together to support our neighbours at this difficult time. We don't want anything in return – we'll just be available if you need help, big or small, while isolated.
> **I live locally and my own details are:**
> Full name:
> I live in (road):
> My phone number is:
> If you are in isolation, I can help with any of the following, just call or text me:
> ☐ Picking up shopping   ☐ Posting mail
> ☐ Going to the library   ☐ A friendly phone call
> ☐ Urgent supplies incl. prescriptions
> ☐ Other (eg help accessing additional support)
> **For hygiene & safety, deliveries will be to the doorstep (we'll keep 2m distance and won't cross the threshold). We'll take every precaution to ensure we only spread kindness! And we washed our hands before delivering this!**

As already mentioned, considerable time and care was expended on explaining to volunteers how to stay safe and minimise risk when leafleting, for example storing the leaflets in a resealable plastic envelope to minimise handling. As well as involving this set of practical issues, the leafleting was an act of care, and could have quite a powerful emotional impact. Marian mentioned this to me when explaining why she got involved with the scheme:

> 'I really liked the idea ... I was particularly taken by that simple act of writing your name on a piece of paper and putting it through a neighbour's door and saying "I'm here if you need me", it was so simple but so effective, the person getting it would feel, even if there wasn't a need for practical support, they would feel that there was somebody there, that if they needed someone there was someone there.' (Marian, Mutual aid project co-ordinator, Market Town)

Marian's sense of the affective impact of this leaflet was borne out by my own experiences of receiving this leaflet while self-isolating with my family. As discussed earlier in this chapter, the removal of all other networks and resources of care and education around our household was a shock and I felt truly overwhelmed. Receiving this leaflet from a neighbour was very affecting, even though I did not ask for help from the local volunteer. This comforting feeling of being aware of structures, even if they are not being used, relates to points made in previous chapters about the comforting presence of Children's Centres within communities, and a broader sense of the importance of these affective qualities of welfare services and other infrastructures of care. Because of these feelings I became involved with the network once we had stopped isolating.

At the time of distributing my own leaflets the restrictions were at their most extreme, the streets were completely empty of pedestrians and cars, and even doing something as simple as putting a leaflet through a neighbour's door felt like quite a radical act. And indeed, while 'care for vulnerable people' did fall into one of the categories for being allowed to leave one's home at the time of this leafleting, at a more fundamental level it felt like resistance against the notion, discussed earlier in the chapter, that we should all 'stay home' and act as independent and self-sustaining households. Once I had distributed my own leaflet, I received phone calls from people wanting to tell me how happy they were to receive it – not asking for practical help but wanting to acknowledge the feeling of care which came from receiving it. The co-ordinators I interviewed told me that this was a common experience. Therefore the network produced these affective senses of care for neighbours, alongside more practical forms of support, beyond the individual household.

Such care therefore strengthened and intensified the kinds of practices discussed elsewhere in the book, especially in Chapter 3, of neighbourly connections that could provide everyday support between households over time (not just within the context of a pandemic). As Dave told me: "It was trying to build, build on and create these organic connections that weren't there before … that was the goal at the back of our minds, can this kind of strengthen the fabric … at a neighbourhood level."

Nonetheless, the context of the pandemic can be seen to throw up some particular challenges and difficulties for sustained community action. In many ways these concern the very reasons why the mutual aid network sprang up in the first place, in terms of the immediate and pressing nature of the crisis being encountered, and the intensities of 'vulnerability' involved. My own experience was that the practice of mutual aid became more difficult over time, as I go on to discuss. This is of course not necessarily the case for everyone, and an issue with mutual aid as it operated was that, despite the small 'cells' previously mentioned, the work primarily took place via individualised relationships, so it is hard to generalise from any one set of experiences. Because of the pandemic situation there were also no opportunities to meet in person with other mutual aiders. While the Facebook and WhatsApp groups provided practical signposting it was hard to build supportive connections and relationships in that way.

In terms of what others did, from my interviews, some mutual aiders did a range of tasks for a number of neighbours, from chatting on the phone or on the doorstep from time to time, posting letters, shopping, picking up prescriptions and so on. My own experience began like that, but contact with most neighbours slowed quite quickly and my mutual aid work consisted mainly of food shopping. The experience of materially providing food for other households threw me into quite an intense relationship with neighbours whom I did not know previously. The work of shopping did not just entail the actual buying of food: there was the work of receiving shopping lists which we would often then discuss with regards to the details and specificities of what they wanted, either in person or on the phone; the handing over of debit cards and store cards, to be used 'contactless' or then requiring a PIN to be handed over too as the lists got longer. The shopping itself often entailed a lengthy queue outside a supermarket and the complexity of juggling multiple sets of shopping; and then delivering the shopping to them.

These were not simply practical tasks – there was an intimacy and emotional element in suddenly becoming responsible for other households being able to access basic sustenance; and to become privy to their everyday consumption habits and practices. These aspects of our lives would normally be firmly in the private realm; especially the trust and delicacy of handling money, credit cards and receipts. I often felt anxious while doing the shopping, for example, convinced that I would lose the credit card or receipts and that trust between us would break down. My anxiety also stemmed, I am sure, from the intensity of undertaking these tasks from within the context of a pandemic. I became an important conduit of experience for those who were 'shielding' and not leaving their homes. This speaks to the fragmented nature of pandemic experience.. As well as being 'shielded' therefore from some aspects of the pandemic, they had also lost autonomy and freedom as well as wider social interaction.

I should make clear that I also benefited from being a 'mutual aider' and it gave me some sense of control and contribution, in a situation in which so much felt out of control. I am offering these insights not because my own experience was particularly difficult, certainly not within the wider context of the pandemic. Rather I am interested in the potentialities but also limitations of this broader model of collective care and neighbourhood support, which the pandemic both 'turbo-charged' but also placed under strain. In relation to my earlier point about the categorisation of vulnerability, this sense of a bifurcation of experiences and identities (between those classed as 'vulnerable' and not) within the pandemic became more intense as time went on. Myself and my family returned to a level of social contact and mobility (for example travelling to see friends) in a way that others within the 'shielding' and 'vulnerable' categories could not. This therefore undermined a notion of 'mutual aid' in terms of a more collective and solidaristic set of practices in response to shared conditions. Shared conditions were perhaps experienced at the start of the pandemic, and then became more fragmented and inequitable over time, leading to the feelings of guilt, discomfort and stigma which characterises food insecurity more generally (Strong, 2020).

This then created a different context within which to seek to manage the ongoing needs and dependencies involved in the mutual aid scheme. As we reached the end of August, I withdrew from everyday involvement in support, helping those I had been shopping for to find other ways to access food. I felt at the time that this was probably right for them too, to be able to access food independently, given the feelings of guilt mentioned. There was also a sense of relief on my part in letting go of this burden of care, or responsibility, alongside the care I was undertaking for my children, parents and other friends and family. In many ways as time went on, I came to recognise how far I was struggling too, to understand my own care needs, a notion discussed in previous chapters.

Indeed, while mutual aid can be read as a utopian experiment in prefigurative collective care (Care Collective, 2020), it could also feel like another (gendered) burden of unpaid labour, extending beyond the household in ways that increased rather than spread the burden of care for some individuals. There is no comprehensive data on this, but the mutual aid co-ordinators I spoke to reported that there were more women than men involved in the scheme. There is evidence (WBG, 2020a, 2020b) that women in particular have been unequally impacted by the pandemic in a whole range of ways, taking on proportionately more childcare and emotional and practical support for others within households, alongside losing more income and indeed employment overall. In common with the women discussed in Chapter 3, the context of the pandemic, and heightened and intense social need, made it harder than ever to maintain boundaries around the self in ways that enabled self-care as well as care for others (see Chapter 1). This could lead to stress and burnout in trying to navigate what might be reasonable to contribute to forms of collective care and action. In the context of the work of the Coastal Arts project, Claire spoke to me about the difficulties they now found in their new way of working, issues of boundaries that had been resolved in their previous ways of practising: "As a human being, you just want to do everything you possibly can ... we had come to a point in the old world where we knew where our boundaries were … but this … it's like all the boundaries have gone … when do we say no, we're not doing that?"

Claire spoke to me about various examples of people needing help and support, and her not knowing how to draw a line around her caring capacities: "That was really hard and stressful because the thought of someone not being able to eat properly, not being able to wash their clothes … the real basics of life … it's brought it into focus, how delicate people's hand to mouth existence is."

Again she compared her own cupboard, which she said always had spare food in, to those she supported who were already living very precariously with regards to food: "They don't have any capacity for extra." Working in this context had led to a sense of burnout for her and her colleagues though, which had involved a process of reflection and of stepping back from that "manic, adrenaline-fuelled community focused thing at the beginning … it's not sustainable."

Indeed, as discussed earlier, senses of time, of temporality, shifted in quite dramatic ways over the course of the pandemic (Bailey et al, 2020). As already noted, the early months, of roughly March–June 2020, produced an intense, and what Claire from the Coastal Arts project referred to as an "adrenaline-fuelled", experience. New experiences of time within this took different forms. For some, such as Dave already mentioned, the furlough scheme from work provided new resources of time in straightforward ways. For others, even where the pandemic produced new pressures on time, the sense of normal routines and indeed society breaking apart and being dislocated in profound ways, opened up spaces and times for local action that would not normally be there. For example, Marian told me that she really did not have the time to commit to the mutual aid scheme, but that nonetheless at the beginning she was working nearly full-time on it. This intense early lockdown time, and its particular atmospheres and affects, later shifted, for example via those on furlough going back to work, and both mutual aiders and their beneficiaries adapting to the very strange ongoing new 'normal'. As those I interviewed told me, there were feeling of exhaustion and feeling 'leaden' as grappling with the ongoing realities and restrictions associated with COVID-19 continued. What then had been the meaning and significance of this earlier wave of local activity and collective care?

Conclusion

As discussed in relation to 'storytelling' and narration more widely across the chapters, it is hard to trace a story or narrative arc when the story is unfinished. This seems to be the collective case in relation to the pandemic, still ongoing at the time of writing. The initial drama of the first lockdown has subsided, leaving ongoing fear, uncertainty and anxiety for some, but mixed into aspects of 'normality' and a fragmentation of experience. In this situation, as my interviews show, there is a need for both individual and collective sense-making. The narratives that emerge are important because they have the power to shape how we organise our lives into the future (Care Collective, 2020).

So what kind of 'infrastructure of care' did the mutual aid model provide, and what could be learnt from it beyond the pandemic? Despite the strengths of the mutual aid model, including its speed and nimble-ness in responding to crisis, and its ability to draw upon what Dave called the "natural trust between neighbours", there are huge questions and issues that become apparent if this model were to seek to provide support for communities longer term. Some of these I experienced viscerally and personally when providing mutual aid: the burden and intensity of providing care for those beyond my household, and the difficulties of drawing a line or boundaries when personal feelings and relationships were at stake. The support provided was unequal and fragmented, dependent on different resources within communities, as well as individual interpersonal circumstances and orientations. Volunteers at least were mostly connected to the mutual aid network via social media, so this excluded others. And while the experiments in collective care that arose could provide emergency support, their distanced and fragmented nature could never fully stand in for some of the embodied and material practices of care that were not possible during lockdowns (MacLeavy, 2021). This in itself is important in considering futures of care when technologically mediated structures are emergent (MacLeavy, 2021).

These difficulties nonetheless show how this experience (and indeed that of the pandemic more broadly) has brought home the nature of care as work (Care Collective, 2020). The question then is how such work should be organised in society (MacLeavy, 2021), as discussed in the opening chapters of this book. Social welfare, in theory at least, promises a professionalisation of care which takes care out of the realm of the familial and the intimate, and the inequalities and inconsistencies this leads to (Fink, 2004). However, it is the failure of this promise that is the subject of Fraser's (2016) critique of the welfare state and care discussed in the opening chapter. And as discussed in preceding chapters, austerity and state rollback has placed this model under immense strain, with much basic provisioning being moved to the voluntary and community sector (for example Cloke et al, 2017), albeit in a less dramatic way than occurred during the pandemic.

What then is the shape of welfare services and the wider state that might emerge post-pandemic? There is the possibility going forward that the pandemic could lead to more, not less, state involvement in everyday lives (Bowlby and Jupp, 2021). As Dave pointed out, the COVID-19 pandemic created immense and sudden social, political and economic change, and it saw the welfare state intervene into people's lives as never before, through paying wages through furlough schemes in particular. As the 'shrapnel', as he put it, lands, it remains very much an open question whether the crisis will lead to a re-drawing of boundaries between the welfare state and community action, an expansion or retraction of what will be provided by the state or left to an inevitably uneven patchwork of community action. What is more certain is that material and embodied need, poverty and insecurity will increase in society, in the longer term, far beyond the short-term crisis of lockdown. Mutual aid will may be part of the solution to this but can clearly never be a sustainable means to meet such needs in society.

However, the mutual aid networks may have other more subtle impacts, even if they do not continue to operate on an ongoing basis. There is a value in considering further the ethics and politics they enacted, and taking this seriously as an intervention (Springer, 2020). The work of mutual aid and other organisations enabled and enacted a vision of lockdown as involving far more than the nuclear family and household, and of times and spaces of care and support. The broader 'politics of lockdown' across the world have tended to see left-wing progressive governments arguing for stricter and more far-reaching lockdowns as opposed to more libertarian and laissez-faire approaches on the right (for example Murphy, 2021). What has perhaps been missing from progressive visions has been the importance of more inclusive practices of care and attention to different groups in society and their experiences and vulnerabilities during lockdown. The work of mutual aiders and others have sought, at least in partial and fragmented ways, to enact this vision.

On a more localised and practical level, the work during lockdown both via the mutual aid scheme and via the Coastal Arts project did undoubtedly create new connections and relationships, which are hard to measure or quantify especially as the crisis is ongoing. However they are likely to shift existing local infrastructures of care in ongoing ways. The projects revealed a capacity for self-initiated community action using new forms of organising, partly using social media, and the new kinds of connection between strangers, or 'stranger intimacies' (Koch and Miles, 2020) potentially generated. They might also be seen to shift some of the affective atmospheres around communities, including the possibilities for rapid social and political action. For example, following lockdown when there was a UK government plan to stop serving free school meals to children in the school holidays (Inews, 2020), residents in the mutual aid scheme town began to make plans to set up a community canteen to step in instead, via discussion on a local Facebook group. Unlike some of the more divisive political discourses that often circulated on local social media (discussed in the next chapter) no one raised the issue of whether such children were genuinely in need or overly dependent. There was an overall acceptance of the level of need in the community, and the fact that the community itself could and would provide if and when social welfare failed. This more active and politicised community infrastructure might therefore be a longer-term impact of mutual aid during lockdown.

Conclusions: a politics of everyday life?

Towards a politics of everyday life

This book has presented the voices and experiences of local activists and community actors of different kinds, working in diverse settings, and with different orientations towards their local action and activism. The case studies have sought to evaluate the potentials and problematics of such sites and practices of activism. Such evaluations include the lives of activists and those they work with, but also in relation to wider spheres of politics, representation and governance. In this way I have traced the outlines of a politics of everyday life, always 'in the middle of things' (Tronto, 2015: 4) and enmeshed in other dynamics. As previously discussed, some of the practices here would not normally be included within studies of social movements or activism (see Martin et al, 2007; Jupp, 2012). By bringing them together I have aimed to demonstrate the slippery boundaries between what might normally be seen as 'volunteering', community action and political activism. All the projects can be seen as interventions into matters of politics, involving citizenship and empowerment, and questions of care and collective infrastructures. In particular I have considered together the case study of anti-austerity activism around Children's Centres in Chapters 4 and 5, involving practices likely to be understood as activism, alongside case studies of different forms of local action, provisioning and material support (in Chapters 3 and 6) more likely to be understood as 'volunteering' or 'community action'.

In this final chapter I draw together some wider conceptual conclusions about such political significance or politics of everyday life. I do this through considering this politics as operating across three different registers of experience: firstly, personal experiences of political subjectivity and citizenship; secondly, the sphere of the local or community as a site of action and intervention; and lastly, experiences of and encounters with the state, on a local or national level. Matters of care cut across the different registers or spheres, as well as experiences of crises, be it crisis on a personal, local or wider national (or global) level (Jupp et al, 2019). While I thus focus on the projects as productive of citizenship practices and a politics of everyday life, this of course does not detract from a critique of the conditions of crisis that frame them. In the body of this chapter I consider each of these three sites in turn (citizenship, local community and the welfare state), pulling together some conclusions from the empirical material, and pointing to their wider significance and the further questions raised. Before considering these themes, however, I offer some personal reflections on methods and the challenges of researching alongside community actors and activists, especially within marginalised communities and populations, and under the conditions of crisis that austerity and now COVID-19 have produced.

Reflecting on methods: listening to the voice of local activists

For the projects discussed in the various chapters, I used different methods (see discussion in Chapter 2) including various forms of ethnography, individual interviews and discussion groups. The first round of the Stoke-on-Trent project (discussed in Chapter 3) formed my research for my PhD and took place 15 years ago (Jupp, 2006). Reading fieldwork notes again, after all this time, was a strange experience. I was struck by how much space was devoted to my own feelings of discomfort and my often awkward negotiations of relationships and engagement in the field. My embodied presence as someone very obviously different from the groups I was working with, including in relation to class, location and mobility, created multiple moments of discomfort and unease (Longhurst et al, 2008; Hall, 2014). At the start I was concerned about being accepted and included into the groups, getting to know and gaining trust from people who were fairly bemused by my presence. However, gradually, with one of the groups at least, I become in a way too much included, depended upon to support their activities, at a time when they were always short of resources and support, and constantly asked to help out more, in ways that I could not fulfil given that fieldwork time in Stoke was limited. Disengaging and 'leaving the field' (Hall, 2014) was also a rather agonising process that I felt ethically and personally conflicted by. While I had offered my time and support to the groups in multiple ways, I ultimately felt that I was extracting knowledge and experience from them.

It also struck me that to a varying degree I have continued to feel such discomfort across all projects. Such awkwardness springs partly from the interpersonal challenges of negotiating relationships and research practices that is common to all fieldwork (Rose, 1997; Moss, 2002). As Rose (1997) points out, there are limitations to how far a reflexive awareness of positionality and power actually resolves the myriad intersubjective tensions at the centre of a research process. However, it also springs from the particular ethical problematics of researching, of extracting knowledge and data, from situations of precarity and material deprivation, in which knowledge and capacities are needed for more urgent and immediate questions and matters than those addressed in spheres of academic knowledge (Hall, 2017). During my PhD fieldwork, I moved from a position as a somewhat detached researcher undertaking interviews and discussions groups, to a researcher-volunteer, working with and for the community groups on activities from arts and crafts, play sessions, theatre trips and Christmas parties. In many ways, this trajectory has occurred during all my projects: for the Children's Centre projects (discussed in Chapters 4 and 5) I moved to become an activist on the Children's Centre campaign myself, speaking to the media and giving evidence to local authority committees and consultations, as well as attending campaign events. The research on COVID-19 and community responses (in Chapter 6) sprung from my own involvement in the mutual aid network. Indeed I conducted the interviews with co-ordinators as reflective dialogues between the two of us (see Way et al, 2015) whereby I spoke about my own experiences and reflections on them as part of a process of collaborative analysis, along the lines of the themes discussed in that chapter.

While this has been a complex process at every turn, involving ethical and epistemological questions about my own roles, positionalities and knowledge production, I have to conclude that I am most comfortable taking up a 'scholar-activist' position (Askins, 2009; Derickson and Routledge, 2015; Routledge and Derickson, 2015), whatever that might mean within these various contexts. This is not to say that my own research contributes to activism in a direct way, as I feel aware of the need to hold onto a critical space of reflection on activism through the process of academic knowledge production. Rather I see activism practices as occurring alongside academic research – as a parallel rather than indistinguishable process (Askins, 2009). Through acting as a volunteer or activist I am contributing my labour to causes I believe in – and simultaneously producing forms of academic knowledge that are not necessarily immediately useful to those causes or groups (Derickson and Routledge, 2015). This is not necessarily a comfortable process and nor is it possible to resolve the tensions raised. However, even more now compared to when I started the research 15 years ago, small community groups and projects are dealing with very material and pressing issues of food, shelter and suffering within communities, and as researchers (and as human beings) we need to help them attend to these issues in the here-and-now, while we are co-present with them.

Despite this sense that the academic research might not contribute directly and in an immediate way to any of the projects and matters that activists were concerned with, on a different ethical and epistemological level, I hope that the book has shown my profound commitment to listening and taking seriously the experiences and perspectives of my research participants (Back, 2007; Bassel, 2013). Reading interview transcripts and notes, in some cases years after a research project, as well as listening to the recordings of more recent research conversations and interviews, was a joyful experience in many ways. In an embodied way, this process meant that I could see and hear these rich encounters again and feel again the energy of these exceptional people (Okely, 2007). Indeed, as well as listening to what these voices are telling us in a straightforward sense, I hope that the preceding chapters also demonstrate the importance of listening on a more profound level, in terms of taking seriously the values and visions that emerge from their practices (Back, 2007). The community activists may have felt themselves to largely just be coping, or 'getting by' and improvising in how they coped in crisis conditions (Jupp, 2012). Nonetheless, I believe that their practices also be seen as enacting visions of better societies, of what citizenship might mean, of how communities can function and of how the state might support a more caring society, in a prefigurative way (Ince, 2012; Cooper et al, 2019). In the rest of this Conclusion I discuss these themes in turn, bringing the visions emerging from my research participants into dialogue with academic knowledge and the discourses of contemporary politics.

Local activism and a politics of care: routes to citizenship and empowerment?

Much of my research approach and material has focused on capturing the life histories or stories of those undertaking local action and activism of different kinds. In adopting this focus I am interested in the (intertwined) personal and political trajectories of such action, and how participants chose to place it within their own narratives. In terms of what these political trajectories might consist of, as discussed in Chapter 2, I see this as an 'entangled' politics, involving modes of 'resilience' and 'reworking' as much as 'resistance', as MacLeavy et al (2021) propose. As discussed elsewhere, I would also add the notion of 'recognition' to this analysis, in terms of the importance of the self and interpersonal processes in experiencing citizenship (see Derickson, 2016; Robinson et al, 2021).

As discussed in Chapter 3 in particular, nearly all my research participants narrated their movement into forms of activism and local action via reference to their own, often gendered, lifecourses, and most of my research participants were women. Relevant aspects of their lives included centrally having children, losing a job, needing to find different forms of work and labour, and caring for wider family including older relatives. Such changes could create new relationships and connections within a local area or spark different ways to understand self and community. In particular, as some of the case studies show, becoming a parent for the first time clearly brought about such changes at quite a profound level of sense of self (Thomson and Kehily, 2011). While having a baby might be assumed to lead women to become more focused on their home space and domestic matters, a number of the women discussed in this book demonstrate the opposite movement.

For example, the women at the centre of the migrant mothers support network in Chapter 3 narrated journeys out of motherhood into engagement with a wider community and support networks around other migrant families. The Children's Centre activists in Chapters 4 and 5 became involved in campaigning and articulating alternative visions of local care and support. It would of course be a mistake to overlook the hugely unequal and fragmented nature of contemporary childhoods and parenting practices (Katz, 2018). However, these examples show how becoming a parent can potentially lead to a new commitment to collective spaces and practices of care, and a focus on relationships and resources outside the home. The kind of caring capacities that might be produced through parenthood were also capacities that could catalyse forms of local activism and connection (Jupp, 2012, 2017). This route into political subjectivity and citizenship is not necessarily well recognised, and mothers' collective actions and connections are in particular often marginalised and trivialised (see Erel et al, 2018). However, for women and indeed men, struggling to access spheres of paid work, or marginalised from other arenas of public life, practices and capacities of care could potentially lead to forms of personal empowerment and the enactment of citizenship at whatever level. These were clearly not individual experiences but intermeshed with connections with others, via friendships in particular (see Jupp, 2012). Again, friendships, particularly between mothers, are often seen as trivial matters, yet they play an important role in structuring experience and subjectivities (Bunnell et al, 2012), especially under conditions of crisis (Hall, 2019b). While I focus here on parenting as it was at the centre of a number of case studies, other forms of care might also have this 'capacious' quality in extending outwards from the home (Care Collective, 2020).

As can be seen in the testimony of a number of research participants, especially in Chapter 4, involvement in local activism has therefore led to broader senses of empowerment, and the desire (as in the words of Umay from the migrant parents' project) to 'start exploring my own life'. This included collectively resisting the forms of disempowerment they are subject to, on the basis of ethnicity, gender, class, location and other axes of difference, including in their cases the 'hostile environment' currently surrounding immigration in the UK (Burrell and Schweyher, 2019). Their identities and common experiences as 'migrant mothers' enabled them to forge solidarity and friendship across different migrant groups and communities.

Nonetheless, in the case of the migrant parents' project, it was not necessarily clear how such women might develop their own practices of citizenship and political empowerment into wider spheres, beyond the spaces of the project. Indeed, I remember the project co-ordinator telling me that the women clearly had a desire to take their activism and senses of empowerment to a wider level, but she was not sure what that might mean in practice. While there is no doubt that the women saw themselves as concerned with empowerment around their intersectional gendered identities, there were no connections between their project and broader spaces of women's organising. This suggests some of the limitations of contemporary feminist activism, that it has not been inclusive enough in its practices and organisation, and does not include spaces for women marginalised on the basis of race and class, as Black feminist scholarship in particular has pointed out (Okolosie, 2014; Bassel and Emejulu, 2017).

Beyond engagement with feminist activism, in relation to more formal spheres of politics, progressive political parties often bemoan the lack of diversity and representation in politics and the loss of activists entering politics from working-class backgrounds in particular (for example Shaheen, 2020). However, the sphere of community organising and activism rarely seems to provide a route to involvement in formal politics, at least in a UK context. The US has a more powerful tradition of 'community organising', especially among Black communities, with such practices potentially included in broader understandings of political action (Helgeson, 2014). However, an exception in relation to the case studies presented here was Kat, discussed in Chapter 5, who stood as a local councillor following her involvement in the Children's Centre campaign. Interestingly, she was someone who was undoubtedly 'burnt out' at an earlier stage in the Children's Centre campaign, having spoken out about her own struggles with mental health and motherhood at a meeting. Her example indeed suggests how movement in and out of activism and citizenship across the lifecourse is rarely straightforward, and trajectories may be interrupted or unexpected (Woolvin and Hardill, 2013).

Indeed, beyond formal arenas of politics, and empowerment via in-person forms of organising and activism, digital spaces clearly offer new arenas and forms of connection (Gerbaudo, 2012; Chambers, 2013). To return to the migrant women's project, discussed in Chapter 3, the women involved in that had begun to use Facebook and other social media to speak out around particular issues such as women's health, and potentially to connect to wider groups. The mutual aid group discussed in Chapter 6 was enabled by online connections both locally and further afield, and social media was also used by the Children's Centre campaigners to join up local campaigns to wider national debates. As explored in relation to the Children's Centre campaigners, small-scale, localised stories from service users could be brought together online to show commonalities and connections across individual experiences, as well as communicating the affective and embodied experiences of the storytellers (Cameron, 2012). Nonetheless, the capacity to tell such stories, and to have them listened to, was not necessarily equally available, a point Phipps (2016) makes in discussing 'experiential capital' in contemporary feminism. I return to the point about inequalities within a politics of care later in this section.

Overall, while varying offline and online practices of local citizenship may therefore offer routes to broader forms of empowerment, undertaking forms of local action based on care may also be experienced as burdensome and exhausting. The practices discussed in the books are rooted in caring capacities, subjectivities and experiences, within contexts of worsening material need. As Bassel and Emejulu write (2018), care has a kind of irreducible ambivalence, 'a double-edged sword' of both potential empowerment and oppression. While care may provide transformation, connection and empowerment, care is also labour, and is a burden (Care Collective, 2020), as many of the activists interviewed in this book attest. Most, although not all, of the activists in this book were working within their own communities and populations. In these cases there was a kind of experiential and material proximity which seemed to increase potential for burnout.

The vast majority of activists interviewed across all the various projects spoke about burnout, and the difficulties of maintaining boundaries in their community work. For example, Sandra and Jill in Chapter 3 spoke about being "always on call" and "always available" to the other residents in their neighbourhoods that they were seeking to support. The women from the Coastal Arts project, discussed in both Chapter 3 and the Conclusion, spoke about the impossibility of maintaining boundaries within the crisis conditions of the communities they worked in under the pandemic. Such burnout concerns not so much the material labour of activism, but the emotional burden of responsibilities and care involved (Brown and Pickerill, 2009). This involves the emotional and mental labour entailed in holding someone in mind and being attentive and empathetic to their experiences, whether it be shopping for a neighbour via mutual aid, or encouraging other service users to speak out in relation to Children's Centre cuts.

Relatedly to matters of burnout and the exhausting nature of caring labour, 'mental health issues', however they might be framed, were also raised repeatedly in my discussions with activists across the various projects. Mental health issues were sometimes talked about as a spur to activism, in relation to a need to connect with others locally and recover from personal crises, as in the examples of Sandra and Jill in Stoke-on-Trent. Mental health was also talked about as a more substantive issue that might be a focus for local action, in relation to the care and support that was needed for those experiencing mental distress. This was the case for the Children's Centre activists discussed in Chapters 5 and 6, drawing attention to the need for particular support for mothers around the ante- and postnatal periods of having a baby. Such needs would also apply to others experiencing particular burdens of individual care around elderly relatives or adults with disabilities or long-term conditions.

Indeed, the experience of mental distress, however it might be narrated, seemed to be widespread among the activists and communities within my case studies. The notion of mental health as an individual problem or issue is clearly hard to sustain (Pedersen and Lupton, 2018) and points to the need to consider mental and emotional distress as collective and structural sets of issues, for example in relation to gender, poverty and ethnicity (Parr, 2011). Mental health issues can therefore be potentially ameliorated by attending to these, as well as collective support systems and spaces (McGrath and Reavey, 2018). In considering the kinds of caring local spaces and infrastructures which are suggested by the projects in this book, there is a clear desire for support around mental and emotional distress, enabling connections between those suffering in an isolated way. Again, it is interesting that what might be considered a very personal and individualised experience of mental distress and suffering leads to a desire for collective and community support at various levels (Kiely, 2021). Crucially, both the crisis of austerity (see Stenning and Hall, 2018; Hitchen and Shaw, 2019) and the crisis of the COVID-19 pandemic can be seen as crises of mental health, the true scale of which has largely remained hidden.

Considering matters of burnout and mental distress relates to the notion of 'self-care' as an aspect of caring practices. The notion of 'self-care' is not a trivial point, although it is often presented within a discourse of certain versions of neoliberal femininity (Gill and Orgad, 2018). A more politicised notion of self-care potentially represents quite a profound challenge to dominant understandings of what care and 'good care' consists of (Lorde, 1988; Ahmed, 2014). While good care is often conceptualised as a dyadic relationship between carer and another being cared for, inserting a notion of self-care into this suggests a more complex circulation of empathetic and caring impulses and practices. As discussed in the opening chapters, Raghuram (2016) shows how a consideration of self-care within discourses of care can draw attention to intersectional inequalities among those giving as well as receiving care. Focusing on care-giving among racialised women, Raghuram argues that such groups' own care needs are often erased within discourses of care, nor recognised by the care-givers themselves. Indeed the difficulties of such a process of recognition of one's own needs was articulated most clearly by the migrant women's group discussed in Chapter 3. This in itself points to the need for a politics of recognition as part of processes of resistance to or reworking of structures of power.

These questions of self-care and recognition return us to matters of inequalities in the politics of care. Clearly, resolving the burdensome nature of care is not simply a question of individual boundaries and self-care, however that might be understood. Such a burden is not equally shared in society, and we know that care labour of varying kinds is unequally distributed within society, centrally across gender, but also race and class (Care Collective, 2020). Therefore community movements and projects, as discussed throughout the book, have the potential to increase burdens of care on already burdened sections of society. As well as potentially drawing on caring capacities, processes of empowerment and citizenship should also give women the right *not* to be burdened by care, or at least to attend to this unequal burdening across gender, race and class (Care Collective, 2020).

Alongside inequalities in who provides care, there are also inequalities in who is seen as worthy of care within widely held discourses of who may be deserving of care or not, or just who may be felt to be somehow 'easier' to care for (Held, 1995; Wood et al, 2020), including within the kind of local community projects discussed. A politics of care needs to attend critically to such normative and moralistic dimensions of discourses of care, and dynamics of stigma (Tyler, 2020). Many of the most marginalised groups in society, for example those suffering with drug and alcohol dependence, are less likely to be the focus of widespread community action and care as opposed to, for example, young children. For example, despite the relative lack of success of the Children's Centre campaign discussed, there was no equivalent campaign around cuts to adult social care, involving many of the most vulnerable people in society (Levitas, 2012). Both these points about different forms of inequality in relation to care (in who does the caring and who is cared for and about), suggest the need to challenge norms in society, through representation and forms of critical evaluation of needs and action. However, they also perhaps point to some of the limits of community and local activism, and the need for wider forms of collective resourcing and politics and arenas of care. As Tronto (2010) argues, caring practices require democratic and agonistic spaces via which a politics of care can be debated. This links to the points made in the opening section about affective modes of politics, and the need for a more discursive evaluation of claims, as Sabsay (2016) argues, to guard against the dominance of those with most 'experiential capital' (Phipps, 2016). Both these points potentially suggest the importance of wider collective structures such as those around the welfare state in enacting a wider politics of care. Questions of the state will be discussed in the final section of this conclusion. First, though, I discuss notions of the local scale as arenas for citizenship and activism, via questions of 'community'.

Community and the atmospheres and spaces of local action

All the case studies discussed in the book involve citizenship practices and actions around the scale of the 'local' or 'community'. As discussed in the opening chapters, these spheres of politics and indeed social life have been the subject of extensive critique within social sciences (for example Joseph, 2002) because they have been seen as sites of conservative or normative politics, which do not engage sufficiently with matters of difference nor indeed constitute properly 'political' action. However, as the case studies have sought to show in the round, local spheres are a primary site of engagement and connection for many everyday lives, and indeed for citizenship practices for those who may have little access to more conventionally 'political' spaces. As Gibson-Graham (2003; see also Jupp, 2012) argues, 'the local' is the site via which capacities for political action and intervention might be 'cultivated'. A politics of care, enacted through local provisioning or neighbourhood support, can only really begin from such local connections. Nonetheless, it would be wrong to deny the ambivalences and complexities of this scale. In this section I draw together conclusions from across the case studies about the affordances and problematics of such a scale, and with a focus on how this might be changing due to social, economic and technological shifts.

Like 'care', the concept of community has within it a set of ambivalences which are relevant to consider when evaluating community as a sphere of action (for example Neal et al, 2021). Community seems to frame both belonging, inclusion and warmth, but also exclusion, division and hostility. For example, looking back at my first round of fieldwork notes in Stoke-on-Trent, Sandra and Jill, who generally gave very positive accounts of their areas, also spoke to me frequently about conflict in their neighbourhoods, especially between young people and older people. This revolved around concerns over 'anti-social behaviour' and older people feeling fearful of groups of teenagers, as well as teenagers themselves feeling alienated and stigmatised. The interview data also contains more subtle ambivalences, for example Sandra saying that "everybody knows everybody around here", but then later complaining about people "keeping themselves to themselves" and not contributing to collective life. These different versions of community speak to its constructed nature, with multiple 'imaginings' of community (Anderson, 2006) perhaps co-existing together. Such imaginings might also be thought of as 'affective atmospheres' (Anderson, 2009; Denning, 2021), collectively sensed and experienced feelings relating to a locality, involving feelings such as belonging and connection, or exclusion and division. As discussed in Chapter 6, such (shifting) atmospheres could also frame motivations towards and experiences of local action. Under the COVID-19 pandemic, such atmospheres seemed to shift quite rapidly during different stages of 'lockdown' and the spreading of the virus.

Such ambivalent atmospheres were produced not just via face-to-face interactions or material experiences of place, but also via media representations and discussions at different scales. In earlier fieldwork in Stoke, I also analysed the local newspaper as a site of different and contested versions of community (Jupp, 2006). Moving forward to my more recent data, such ambivalences were more likely to be discussed in relation to social media platforms. In a number of recent interviews across these case studies, when asking participants how they would describe their communities, social media platforms, especially Facebook, featured in the first responses that they gave. Local Facebook groups can be seen as offering up one representation or performance of community, thus shaping particular 'affective atmospheres' (Anderson, 2009). These groups were often experienced in very negative ways. Online racism, intolerance and hostility were mentioned in particular. Marian, interviewed in Chapter 6 about the town mutual aid scheme, told me how upset she had been by some discussions on a large local Facebook group, specifically relating to an environmental campaign that she was involved in: "That was all really upsetting, and then people say, 'Oh, it's so friendly in [name of town]', you wouldn't expect this kind of aggression and abuse."

This is an interesting quote because Marian herself was someone who spoke about the friendliness of the town, in general, and also during the pandemic (in relation to the mutual aid scheme). Yet alongside the uprising of kindness and support she had witnessed, she also believed that hostility and division was on the rise during the pandemic. She told me:

> 'That's [that is, hostile and aggressive arguments online] carried on during covid, when people are already feeling quite scared and vulnerable ... one factor may be people being at home more during covid, you kind of spend more time on social media. ... And people are maybe feeling more under threat and aggressive.' (Marian, Mutual aid co-ordinator, Market Town)

This is really quite a strikingly different vision of community relations to that portrayed in the rest of the interview when she was talking about the mutual aid scheme. Of course, the people involved are not necessarily the same, but it would also seem reasonable to suggest that the Facebook group and the mutual aid group brought people together in quite different ways, under different affective conditions. It is not as straightforward as contrasting face-to-face local community with online community, as the mutual aid project in many ways was also an online project, reliant on Facebook and WhatsApp to connect mutual aiders and those needing support. However, there was no doubt that social media was serving quite a different purpose here.

The Facebook groups and mutual aid scheme thus produced different kinds of subjectivities and practices of community, as well as different affective atmospheres around what it meant to be part of that community. Indeed, I witnessed the ways in which the mutual aid scheme produced feelings of comfort and connection, not just for those taking part an active in it either as volunteers or recipients, but those who followed the project online and were aware of its practices. Similar to the feelings of comfort that were noted in Chapter 4 around the presence of a Children's Centre in a community, even if not being accessed, the presence of mutual aid and community support projects could produce positive feelings and affects for a wider group. Indeed such feelings, that care would be available if needed, might be thought of as part of the localised infrastructures of care enacted or articulated via a number of the projects.

As well as the acts of material support involved, the embodied acts of care involved in mutual aid were potentially able to produce feelings and practices of connection across people with quite different politics and values. Indeed Dave, the mutual aid co-ordinator interviewed in Chapter 6, mentioned this as a particular challenge with regards to local community activism, as opposed to the more conventional activism involving ideologically like-minded people that he was normally engaged in. There was not necessarily a shared vision or set of values across those involved in the mutual aid project. At a time of division and difference within national politics (for example as expressed in the Brexit referendum), crossing such divides could feel uncomfortable (Neal et al, 2021). In some ways then, this sense that local politics involves working with people across difference works against some of the usual assumptions about the homogeneity of a politics of the local. Nonetheless, it is hard to assess how far differences with regard to race, class and other axes of difference were being negotiated on this and other projects in ways which generated solidarity, and how far there were attempts to dismiss, gloss over or set aside these differences.

Partly what is being grappled with here are questions about how 'community' is lived and experienced within an increasingly digital age (Dobson et al, 2018), as involving both face-to-face and online interactions. As the discussions of Facebook mentioned attest, community was now constituted in digital spaces as much as in public spaces and via face-to-face interactions. The popularity of 'local' social media sites within a global digital platform paradoxically attests to the ongoing importance of local place. As literature in geography and anthropology has explored (for example Massey, 1993; Eade, 2003; Dyck, 2005), the local and the global are not necessarily binary opposites, but are articulated through each other in shifting ways.

Such articulations are being remade at the present moment because of the crisis of COVID-19 (Rose-Redwood et al, 2020) and the restrictions on mobility arising, as well as the need to continue to restrict our own mobility and energy consumption because of the climate crisis. As already discussed in Chapter 6, these imperatives to restrict mobility will be experienced in uneven and unequal ways, with only some of those working able to 'work from home' (Bowlby and Jupp, 2021). And indeed working from home, either during COVID-19 lockdown, or more long-term, depends on the mobility of others such as couriers and delivery drivers to continue to be mobile and deliver services and goods to the home. Nonetheless, overall, it is clear that mobility, work, local place and digital culture are shifting and may continue to shift. A shift away from commuting and office-based work may frame new connections with local living environments and communities for at least some workers, although such a privilege is clearly not equally distributed because of the unequal nature of work (Dorow et al, 2017). Therefore we may be entering a time when, paradoxically, social and intimate lives may be increasingly lived out at local scales (including via local online platforms) and the pleasures of local conviviality and mutual connection may enable new collective local identities and practices (Parry, 2020). Indeed as Koch and Miles (2020) argue, we can see the development of new kinds of connection between strangers, 'stranger intimacies', whereby intentional connections with strangers are sought out, enabled by digital platforms. They discuss both dating and 'hook-up' apps as well as platforms enabling accommodation sharing as representing new forms of urban sociality, within which strangers are no longer encountered randomly within public spaces but intentionally within private and domestic spheres. Such dynamics can be thought of as applying not just to urban spaces though, but to the towns and semi-urban locations at the centre of the book's case studies.

Furthermore, as the example of mutual aid shows, social media and instant messaging provide opportunities for community and local action to adopt the strategies and indeed organisational forms of much wider scales of activism (for example McLean et al, 2019). Rather than seeking to form organisations at whatever scale, these tactics allow local activists to move straight to action of various kinds, to mobilise significant numbers and quickly create new connections and practices. Digital culture, of course, also allows for the 'stretching' or 'scaling up' of local action, as in the example of Children's Centres, enabling both wider campaigns and wider practices of citizenship for those involved. This potentially means that individuals who might be isolated in their engagement with a local issue can feel part of a wider movement, without necessarily needing to gain widespread support locally.

However, across all the forms of local action discussed in this book, from neighbourhood projects to anti-austerity activism, migrant networks and mutual aid, it is striking that none of them did really connect with wider struggles (Fincher and Panelli, 2001), although the Children's Centre campaigns in particular sought to do this, as discussed in Chapter 5. There are a number of reasons for this, including the fact that local action is clearly motivated by proximity, by particular issues that may look and feel very close at hand, tied in with the particular affective atmospheres of place. For example, even if the local Children's Centre would be more likely to be saved by lobbying at a national level, getting involved in a national campaign is quite a different proposition to seeking to save a local one. And campaigning for migrant rights in general is different to seeking to support families locally. As well as the practices being different, the senses of political subjectivity or citizenship are also different, as well as the scales and sites of engagement, as referred to earlier.

Another limitation for the 'scaling up' of local action to wider politics involves a more general affective dimension about the fragmented and hidden nature of a politics of care. Despite the potential for social media to produce wider awareness of local projects, most local action based on home and community spaces and practices also has an inherent invisibility, even for those potentially within such movements (Jupp, 2017). For example, mutual aid takes place through individual relationships between neighbours, and while social media connects mutual aiders to some extent, the practices involved in these interactions are not visible to each other. Other practices discussed in this book have some elements of collectivity, for example the residents' groups in Stoke (discussed in Chapter 3) running meetings and sessions for different groups, but are nonetheless largely based on interpersonal relationships and practices of care. This has a number of impacts, but one of them is perhaps a difficulty in seeing such a set of practices as 'political' (Martin et al, 2007; Jupp, 2012). For the Children's Centre activists in Chapters 4 and 5, the issue was rendering political, and significant, the matters of care and support at the centre of the services they wished to protect.

Everyday, personal forms of helping and care may seem to sit more easily with a language of emotions, reciprocity and 'kindness' rather than politics. Indeed, as discussed, the Coastal Arts project introduced in Chapter 3 worked within this discourse, a discourse that has recently gained a level of media and policy traction, arguably as part of a wider turn to more emotional 'governance' (Jupp et al, 2016). As this case study shows, there is a kind of affective and visual economy around the language and communication of emotions in these ways, especially online, that can make such community projects particularly appealing to funders and wider agencies.

However, as Dave from the mutual aid project argues, there is a critique that 'kindness', however 'radical' (Bregman, 2020), has "no social or political conscience", and indeed this could be seen as part of its appeal within contemporary governance. Similar to framing mental distress as a personal and subjective issue, as discussed in the previous section, a focus on emotions and kindness as the hallmarks of community projects potentially depoliticises them. It also problematises the notion of more systematic provision, rights and entitlements for those in need. Indeed, more specifically, Dave was talking about the idea of 'random acts of kindness' as opposed to a more systematic or somehow regulated (in the case of mutual aid, self-regulated) set of practices.

While there is clearly an importance and instinctive appeal in discourses of kindness and empathy, there are questions about how far these instincts can take the place of more formal political structures (Pedwell, 2014). A central issue in this debate about the politics of kindness on a local level would be how 'needs' are evaluated and potentially met. Within a notion of 'random acts of kindness' being encouraged locally, there would be no attempt to meet collective needs, but a series of individual acts without any kind of collective overview. Within a 'mutual aid' model or infrastructure, of the kind that Dave was discussing, there would be a collective apprehension and resourcing of need, through forms of common property and practice. In theory, needs would be met without a clear division between those holding (and gatekeeping) resources and those with needs, as a state or charity model frames. However, the mutual aid model, and my experience as reflected on in Chapter 6, raises issues about the ability of community activism to provide independently of the state. While the case studies have demonstrated the affordances and potentials of the local as a site of political action, there needs to be also a wider consideration of the economic and political structures which might shape relations between local sites. The final section of this chapter considers this terrain.

Local action, the place of the state and infrastructures of care

This focus on the role and future of the welfare state returns us to the questions with which this book started, about the shifting shape of the local state under austerity, and the messy and entangled practices of local action and activism that emerge as the welfare state retreats. The case studies presented in this book therefore take place within the 'shadows' (Wolch, 1989) of the welfare state. Power et al (2021) propose the notion of 'shadow care infrastructures' to trace ambivalent practices and politics of survival and resistance in this context. These practices can also be seen through the lens of 'meantime' provisioning that from a critical perspective should never become permanent features of local support, yet do also produce fleeting experiences of a hopeful new politics (Cloke et al, 2017, 2020). Indeed while viewing such projects as 'over-shadowed' by the powerful structures of governmental, economic and political change, it might also be possible to approach questions of the state in relation to these projects from a different perspective. At moments throughout the book I have sought to centre these practices and spaces as articulations and experiments in collective care. The notion of 'prefiguration' (Ince, 2012; Cooper et al, 2019) can help to explore what is being enacted and articulated within such local experiments, and what wider political and economic structures might learn from them. In the final part of this chapter I draw together some conclusions on this issue.

One set of issues here concerns spaces and scales of action, as well as temporalities, and the processes via which material needs, support and care might be met or given or not. In many ways, the mutual aid experiment discussed, within the context of the COVID-19 pandemic, makes more apparent and stark tensions which are clearly present within other forms of local action, in providing food and essentials via very small-scale structures of volunteer labour (Cohen et al, 2017). The structures and organisational forms of mutual aid arose mostly organically, and in a fragmented and differentiated way dependent on aspects of localities and indeed individuals and specific existing organisations (Springer, 2020). The fluid and organic nature of mutual aid networks meant they were able to mobilise very quickly, and to draw on and draw in existing neighbourly connections and caring relationalities, as Chapter 6 shows. This seems important in considering what a local infrastructure of care could and should look like. However, mutual aid would not and could not claim to be meeting needs within an area in a systematic way. Structures of the welfare state, in theory, enable this more systematic provision to meet citizens' needs, but also crucially enable some kind of evaluation of those needs. This is not simply a question of scale, but of democratic structures which, again in theory at least, enable a recognition and a weighing up of claims and rights (Tronto, 2010). If there was a turn to embracing even more localised collective forms of provisioning, many people would find it even harder or impossible to articulate their needs and demands, may lack the 'experiential capital' (Phipps, 2016) to be able to 'tell their story', or may not be in a position to participate in forms of mutual and collective provisioning. The welfare state, at least in principle, is able to do that in a way that small-scale local experiments cannot.

Of course, in practice, this notion of the welfare state is currently hugely problematic. As set out at the opening, Fraser (2016) has shown how citizenship and entitlement within neoliberal welfare states has still largely depended on paid work, with needs, claims and rights around the unpaid work of care and social reproduction largely ignored, or superficially 'fixed'. Where there are rights and claims that are being evaluated, there are huge inequalities around how different groups encounter the state, are recognised, listened to and judged, along axes of class, race, ability, location, gender and more (for example Garthwaite, 2015). State 'care' has often amounted to systematic abuse and violence, as the histories of the welfare state attest (Fink, 2004). And austerity has stripped back many of the structures and frameworks which seek to provide systematic support to citizens, so that 'austerity localism' (Penny, 2017) results in a much more fragmented and inequitable 'safety net' of support and care in any case (Clayton et al, 2016).

How, then, to remake understandings of state structures of social welfare and care? Indeed, while there is a history of progressive thought involving a rejection of the state, as Rai (2019) points, out, both anti-austerity movements and many feminist and post-colonial struggles have not rejected the notion of the state, have indeed called for further protection and infrastructure from it. And as Rai (2019) also argues, different ideological and institutional frameworks of the state do have different impacts and affects on citizens, so we cannot lump different state formations together from a critical perspective. 'The state' in itself involves different spaces, structures, rationalities and commitments (Clarke, 2005). As a number of case studies in this book have shown, it may be important to attend in particular to identifications and interactions on the edges of services and formal structures, that can support a progressive politics of everyday life. Cooper and colleagues (2019) argue we should explore diverse welfare systems that might enable – rather than either constrain or demand – diverse forms of local and civic action.

Placing care and caring at the centre of political and economic thinking may help enable new ways of imagining the state and its wider political and economic framings. Tronto (2010) calls for attention to 'caring institutions', in order to potentially enable a meshing of care and justice (for example Fisher and Tronto, 1990; Tronto, 2015). Caring institutions also potentially enable citizens to become empowered, as Honig (2017) argues, to encounter the state and public services and spaces as the enabling or holding environment (drawing on Winnicottian ideas) within which political subjectivities can grow. As the projects in this book have shown, local action and community projects can generate conviviality, political energy and transformation. Yet there is always a mutual entanglement with wider state structures. As Honig (2017) also argues, 'public things' become properly public when occupied by citizens and civil society, and in so doing inhabiting and holding structures of power to account, and challenging their inequalities.

As argued throughout this book, one way to think about welfare state and civil society structures together is to consider multifaceted 'infrastructures' of care (Alam and Houston, 2020; Power and Mee, 2020), which might include the resources and structures of the state, but also other forms of commoning and collectivity. Such infrastructures would include buildings, spaces, relationships, discourses and resources. These resources and the provision of these resources matter, yet they might be inhabited, experienced and remade in diverse ways. Indeed these infrastructures therefore involve material resources, but also have more affective and intangible qualities around feelings of being supported, comforted and cared for. As a number of research participants in this book have shown, both welfare state provision and community projects have a profound value in terms of presence within localities, generating affective atmospheres of care. An infrastructural approach to care can therefore emphasise the importance of care as a set of atmospheres and relationships beyond the home and household, whist also valuing the subjectivities and practices which emerge from it (Jupp, 2017). It also allows us to view stories, experiences and feelings as collective as well as individual, and to consider how affect, embodiment and emotion might be brought into politics in progressive ways. Such a politics remains emergent at the current moment, but through a focus on local activism in times of crisis, this book has sought to provide glimpses of such alternative structures.

Appendix: overview of research projects

Dates	Project title/focus	Key participants and organisations involved	Methods used	Chapters discussed in
2004–5	PhD project on local activism in Stoke-on-Trent	Two residents' groups in deprived post-industrial neighbourhoods, Riverlands and Southfields, especially two group chairs, Sandra and Jill	Extended ethnography as a volunteer-participant with the groups; interviews and discussion groups	Chapter 3
2013	Revisiting Stoke-on-Trent neighbourhoods in relation to austerity and localism	As above, plus interviews with local authority officials and stakeholders	Stakeholder interviews; joint depth interview with Sandra and Jill, group discussions with wider groups and two ethnographic visits	Chapter 3
2014	Migrant mothers and activism	Social enterprise in North London running parenting support for migrant families in primary schools; interviewees including Ana, Nadifa, Umay	Half-day workshop attended by 20 women; four in-depth 'life story' interviews	Chapter 3
2017–18	Children's Centre closures and activism	Two main case study local authority areas in South East England – Areas A and B, plus one interview and one court case observation in Area C	In Area A – in-depth interviews with activists, Children's Centre workers and local authority officers; in Area B – activist-ethnography involving attending meetings tracking social and conventional media; in-depth interviews with service users; Area C – interview with one activist, observed one court case (11 interviews in total)	Chapters 4 and 5

Appendix

Dates	Project title/focus	Key participants and organisations involved	Methods used	Chapters discussed in
2019–20	Coastal Arts project and austerity (as part of wider project on women and voluntary sector under austerity); follow-up interview on voluntary action during COVID-19	Project co-ordinators – Claire and Rachel	Two in-depth interviews and email exchanges	Chapters 3 and 7
2020	Mutual aid during the pandemic	Market town mutual aid scheme; including interviews with co-ordinators Dave and Marian	Auto-ethnography of my involvement March–September 2020; three in-depth interviews with co-ordinators	Conclusion

References

Abraham, M. (ed) (2010) *Contours of citizenship: Women, diversity and practices of citizenship*. Farnham: Ashgate.

Adams, D. (2020) How coronavirus could affect the wellbeing of people with intellectual disabilities. *The Conversation*, 17 March, available at https://theconversation.com/how-coronavirus-could-affect-the-wellbeing-of-people-with-intellectual-disabilities-133540

Ahmed, M.H. (2020) Black and Minority Ethnic (BAME) alliance against COVID-19: One step forward. *Journal of Racial and Ethnic Health Disparities*, 7(5): 822–8.

Ahmed, S. (2014) Self care as warfare. Blog post, 25 August, available at https://feministkilljoys.com/2014/08/25/selfcare-as-warfare/

Alam, A. and Houston, D. (2020) Rethinking care as alternate infrastructure. *Cities*, 100: 102662. https://doi.org/10.1016/j.cities.2020.102662

All Party Parliamentary Group on Children's Centres (APPG) (2016) Family Hubs: The future of Children's Centres. July, available at https://www.basw.co.uk/system/files/resources/basw_82938-8_0.pdf

Anderson, B. (2006) *Imagined communities: Reflections on the origin and spread of nationalism*. London: Verso.

Anderson, B. (2009) Affective atmospheres. *Emotion, Space and Society*, 2(2): 77–81.

Andrews, G.J., Crooks, V.A., Pearce, J.R. and Messina, J.P. (eds) (2021) *COVID-19 and similar futures: Pandemic geographies*. London: Springer Nature.

Arthurs, D. (2020) Kind ways people are helping their neighbours during the coronavirus outbreak. *Metro*, 19 March, available at https://metro.co.uk/2020/03/19/nice-things-people-neighbours-coronavirus-outbreak-12423657/

Askins, K. (2009) 'That's just what I do': Placing emotion in academic activism. *Emotion, Space and Society*, 2(1): 4–13.

Askins, K. (2014) A quiet politics of being together: Miriam and Rose. *Area*, 46(4): 353–4.

Askins, K. (2016) Emotional citizenry: Everyday geographies of befriending, belonging and intercultural encounter. *Transactions of the Institute of British Geographers*, 41(4): 515–27.

Back, L. (2007) *The art of listening*. Oxford: Berg.

Bailey, S., Bastian, M., Coleman, R., Grabham, E., Lyon, D. and Pierides, D. (2020) A day at a time: A research agenda to grasp the everyday experience of time in the COVID-19 pandemic. *Discover Society*, 15 September, available at https://discoversociety.org/2020/09/15/a-day-at-a-time-a-research-agenda-to-grasp-the-everyday-experience-of-time-in-the-covid-19-pandemic/

References

Bambra, C., Riordan, R., Ford, J. and Matthews, F. (2020) The COVID-19 pandemic and health inequalities. *Journal of Epidemiology and Community Health*, 74(11): 964–8.

Baraitser, L. (2009) Mothers who make things public. *Feminist Review*, 93(1): 8–26.

Barnes, M. and Prior, D. (eds) (2009) *Subversive citizens: Power, agency and resistance in public services.* Bristol: Policy Press.

Bassel, L. (2013) Speaking and listening: The 2011 English riots. *Sociological Research Online*, 18(4): 111–21.

Bassel, L. and Emejulu, A. (2017) *Minority women and austerity: Survival and resistance in France and Britain.* Bristol: Policy Press.

Bassel, L. and Emejulu, A. (2018) Caring subjects: Migrant women and the third sector in England and Scotland. *Ethnic and Racial Studies*, 41(1): 36–54.

BBC News (2020a) Prime Minister Boris Johnson's lockdown statement. 23 March, available at https://www.youtube.com/watch?v=vJycNmK7KPk

BBC News (2020b) PM Boris Johnson: Single adults can form support bubbles. 10 June, available at https://www.youtube.com/watch?v=vJycNmK7KPk

Bell, S.E. and Braun, Y.A. (2010) Coal, identity, and the gendering of environmental justice activism in central Appalachia. *Gender & Society*, 24(6): 794–813.

Belsky, J., Melhuish, E.C. and Barnes, J. (eds) (2007) *The national evaluation of Sure Start: Does area-based early intervention work?* Bristol: Policy Press.

Benhabib, S. (1990) Hannah Arendt and the redemptive power of narrative. *Social Research*, 57(1): 167–96.

Berlant, L. (2008) *The female complaint: The unfinished business of sentimentality in American culture.* Durham, NC: Duke University Press.

Berlant, L. (2009) The intimate public sphere. In Radway, J.A., Gaines, K., Shank, B., and Von Eschen, P. (eds) *American studies: an anthology.* New Jersey: John Wiley & Sons: 109–18.

Bezanson, K. and Luxton, M. (2006) *Social reproduction: Feminist political economy challenges neo-liberalism.* Montreal: McGill-Queen's University Press.

Bock, J.J. and Cohen, S. (2017) Conclusion: Citizenship, community and solidarity at the end of the welfare state. In Cohen, S. Fuhr, C., and Bock, J. (eds) *Austerity, community action, and the future of citizenship.* Bristol: Policy Press: 277–87.

Bosco, F.J. (2006) The Madres de Plaza de Mayo and three decades of human rights' activism: Embeddedness, emotions, and social movements. *Annals of the Association of American Geographers*, 96(2): 342–65.

Bowlby, S. (2012) Recognising the time–space dimensions of care: Caringscapes and carescapes. *Environment and Planning A*, 44(9): 2101–18.

Bowlby, S. and Jupp, E. (2021) Home, inequalities and care: Perspectives from within a pandemic. *International Journal of Housing Policy*, 21(3): 423–32.

Bowlby, S. and McKie, L. (2019) Care and caring: An ecological framework. *Area*, 51(3): 532–9.

Boyer, K., Dermott, E., James, A. and MacLeavy, J. (2017) Regendering care in the aftermath of recession? *Dialogues in Human Geography*, 7(1): 56–73.

Bregman, R. (2020) *Humankind: A hopeful history*. London: Bloomsbury.

Brickell, K. (2020a) Stay home, stay safe? A political geography of home in COVID-times. *Geography Directions*, July, available at https://blog.geographydirections.com/2020/07/08/stay-home-stay-safe-a-politicalgeography-of-home-in-covid-times/

Brickell, K. (2020b) *Home SOS: Gender, violence, and survival in crisis ordinary Cambodia*. Chichester: John Wiley & Sons.

Briggs, A. (2021) 'Period poverty' in Stoke-on-Trent, UK: New insights into gendered poverty and the lived experiences of austerity. *Journal of Poverty and Social Justice*, 29(1): 85–102.

Brown, G. and Pickerill, J. (2009) Space for emotion in the spaces of activism. *Emotion, Space and Society*, 2(1): 24–35.

Brown, K., Ecclestone, K. and Emmel, N. (2017) The many faces of vulnerability. *Social Policy and Society*, 16(3): 497–510.

Brown, W. (2003) Women's studies unbound: Revolution, mourning, politics. *Parallax*, 9(2): 3–16.

Brown, W. (2009) *Edgework: Critical essays on knowledge and politics*. Princeton, NJ: Princeton University Press.

Bunnell, T., Yea, S., Peake, L., Skelton, T. and Smith, M. (2012) Geographies of friendships. *Progress in Human Geography*, 36(4): 490–507.

Burrell, K. and Schweyher, M. (2019) Conditional citizens and hostile environments: Polish migrants in pre-Brexit Britain. *Geoforum*, 106: 193–201.

Butler, J. (2014) Bodily vulnerability, coalitions, and street politics. In Sabadell-Nieto, J., and Segarra, M. (eds) *Differences in Common*. Leiden: Brill Rodopi: 97–119.

Butler, J., Gambetti, Z. and Sabsay, L. (eds) (2016) *Vulnerability in resistance*. Durham, NC: Duke University Press.

Butler, P. (2016) Trussell Trust to deliver more emergency food parcels than ever before. *The Guardian*, 8 November, available at https://www.theguardian.com/society/2016/nov/08/trussell-trust-to-deliver-more-emergency-food-parcels-than-ever-before

Bywaters, P., Brady, G., Bunting, L., Daniel, B., Featherstone, B., Jones, C., Morris, K., Scourfield, J., Spark. T. and Webb, C. (2018) Inequalities in English child protection practice under austerity: A universal challenge? *Child & Family Social Work*, 23(1): 53–61.

Cahill, C. (2007) The personal is political: Developing new subjectivities through participatory action research. *Gender, Place and Culture*, 14(3): 267–92.

Cameron, E. (2012) New geographies of story and storytelling. *Progress in Human Geography*, 36(5): 573–92.

Cammaerts, B. (2018) *The circulation of anti-austerity protest*. London: Palgrave Macmillan.

Cappellini, B., Marilli, A. and Parsons, E. (2014) The hidden work of coping: Gender and the micro-politics of household consumption in times of austerity. *Journal of Marketing Management*, 30(15–16): 1597–624.

Care Collective (2020) *The care manifesto: The politics of interdependence*. London: Verso.

Cattan, S., Conti, G., Farquharson, C. and Ginja, R. (2019) *The health effects of Sure Start*. London: Institute for Fiscal Studies.

Centre for Cities (2019) A decade of austerity. Report, available at https://www.centreforcities.org/reader/cities-outlook-2019/a-decade-of-austerity/

Chambers, D. (2013) *Social media and personal relationships: Online intimacies and networked friendship*. New York: Springer.

Chatzidakis, A., Hakim, J., Littler, J., Rottenberg, C. and Segal, L. (2020) From carewashing to radical care: The discursive explosions of care during COVID-19. *Feminist Media Studies*, 20(6): 889–95.

Chung, C.K.L., Xu, J. and Zhang, M. (2020) Geographies of COVID-19: How space and virus shape each other. *Asian Geographer*, 37(2): 99–116.

Clarke, J. (2005) Welfare states as nation states: Some conceptual reflections. *Social Policy and Society*, 4(4): 407–15.

Clarke, J. (2020) Populism: The view from anthropology. *Soundings: A Journal of Politics and Culture*, 75: 172–5.

Clarke, J. and Newman, J. (2012) The alchemy of austerity. *Critical Social Policy*, 32(3): 299–319.

Clayton, J., Donovan, C. and Merchant, J. (2016). Distancing and limited resourcefulness: Third sector service provision under austerity localism in the north east of England. *Urban Studies*, 53(4): 723–40.

Cloke, P., May, J. and Williams, A. (2017) The geographies of food banks in the meantime. *Progress in Human Geography*, 41(6): 703–26.

Cloke, P., May, J. and Williams, A. (2020) Postsecularities of care: In-common ethics and politics of the meantime(s). *Cities*, 100: 102667.

Closs Stephens, A. (2016). The affective atmospheres of nationalism. *Cultural Geographies*, 23(2): 181–98.

Coddington, K. and Micieli-Voutsinas, J. (2017) On trauma, geography, and mobility: Towards geographies of trauma. *Emotion, Space and Society*, 24: 52–6.

Cohen, S., Fuhr, C. and Bock, J. (eds) (2017) *Austerity, community action, and the future of citizenship*. Bristol: Policy Press.

Conradson, D. (2003) Geographies of care: Spaces, practices, experiences. *Social & Cultural Geography*, 4(4): 451–4.

Cooper, D. (2017) Prefiguring the state. *Antipode*, 49(2): 335–56.

Cooper, D., Dhawan, N. and Newman, J. (eds) (2019) *Reimagining the state: Theoretical challenges and transformative possibilities.* Oxford: Routledge.

Cox, R. (2011) Competitive mothering and delegated care: Class relationships in nanny and au pair employment. *Studies in the Maternal*, 3(2).

Craddock, E. (2020) *Living against austerity: A feminist investigation of doing activism and being activist.* Bristol: Bristol University Press.

Dabrowski, V. (2020) 'Neoliberal feminism': Legitimising the gendered moral project of austerity. *The Sociological Review*, 69(1): 90–106.

Dasgupta, R. (2020) Coronavirus lockdown: LGBTQ people face hostility and loneliness. *The Conversation*, 16 April, available at https://theconversation.com/coronavirus-lockdown-lgbtq-people-face-hostility-and-loneliness-135974

Davidoff, L. (2003) Gender and the 'great divide': Public and private in British gender history. *Journal of Women's History*, 15(1): 11–27.

Davidson, E. (2019) Continuity and change: The voices of Scottish librarians. *Scottish Affairs*, 28(4): 395–13.

Davies, W. (2018) *Nervous states: How feeling took over the world.* New York: Random House.

Denning, S. (2021) Three foodbanks in a decade of austerity: Foodbank affective atmospheres. *Antipode*. https://doi.org/10.1111/anti.12716

Derickson, K.D. (2016) On the politics of recognition in critical urban scholarship. *Urban Geography*, 37(6): 824–9.

Derickson, K.D. and Routledge, P. (2015) Resourcing scholar-activism: Collaboration, transformation, and the production of knowledge. *The Professional Geographer*, 67(1): 1–7.

DeVerteuil, G., Power, A. and Trudeau, D. (2020) The relational geographies of the voluntary sector: Disentangling the ballast of strangers. *Progress in Human Geography*, 44(5): 919–37.

Dobson, A.S., Robards, B. and Carah, N. (eds) (2018) *Digital intimate publics and social media.* New York: Springer.

Dobusch, L. and Kreissl, K. (2020) Privilege and burden of im-/mobility governance: On the reinforcement of inequalities during a pandemic lockdown. *Gender, Work & Organization*, 27(5): 709–16.

Dorow, S., Roseman, S.R. and Cresswell, T. (2017) Re-working mobilities: Emergent geographies of employment-related mobility. *Geography Compass*, 11(12): e12350.

Dowling, E. (2018) Confronting capital's care fix: Care through the lens of democracy. *Equality, Diversity and Inclusion: An International Journal*, 37(4): 332–46.

Dwyer, C. and Davies, G. (2010) Qualitative methods III: Animating archives, artful interventions and online environments. *Progress in Human Geography*, 34(1): 88–97.

Dyck, I. (2005) Feminist geography, the 'everyday', and local–global relations: Hidden spaces of place-making. *Canadian Geographer/Le Géographe canadien*, 49(3): 233–43.

Eade, J. (ed) (2003) *Living the global city: Globalization as local process*. Oxford: Routledge.

Eisenstadt, N. (2011) *Providing a sure start: How government discovered early childhood*. Bristol: Policy Press.

Elliott, K. (2016) Caring masculinities: Theorizing an emerging concept. *Men and Masculinities*, 19(3): 240–59.

Emejulu, A. and Bassel, L. (2018) Austerity and the politics of becoming. *JCMS: Journal of Common Market Studies*, 56: 109–19.

Emejulu, A. and Bassel, L. (2020) The politics of exhaustion. *City*, 24(1–2): 400–6.

Erel, U. (2011) Reframing migrant mothers as citizens. *Citizenship Studies*, 15(6–7): 695–709.

Erel, U. (2013) Kurdish migrant mothers in London enacting citizenship. *Citizenship Studies*, 17(8): 970–84.

Erel, U., Reynolds, T. and Kaptani, E. (2018) Migrant mothers' creative interventions into racialized citizenship. *Ethnic and Racial Studies*, 41(1): 55–72.

Evans, M. (2015) Feminism and the implications of austerity. *Feminist Review*, 109(1): 146–55.

Farnsworth, K. and Irving, Z. (eds) (2015) *Social policy in times of austerity: Global economic crisis and the new politics of welfare*. Bristol: Policy Press.

Featherstone, B., Gupta, A., Morris, K. and Warner, J. (2018) Let's stop feeding the risk monster: Towards a social model of 'child protection'. *Families, Relationships and Societies*, 7(1): 7–22.

Featherstone, D., Ince, A., Mackinnon, D., Strauss, K. and Cumbers, A. (2012) Progressive localism and the construction of political alternatives. *Transactions of the Institute of British Geographers*, 37(2): 177–82.

Fenton-Glynn, C. (2015) Austerity and the benefit cap: In whose best interests? *Journal of Social Welfare and Family Law*, 37(4): 467–9.

Fincher, R. and Panelli, R. (2001) Making space: Women's urban and rural activism and the Australian state. *Gender, Place and Culture: A Journal of Feminist Geography*, 8(2): 129–48.

Fink, J. (2004) *Care: Personal lives and social policy*. Bristol: Policy Press.

Fisher, B. and Tronto, J. (1990) Toward a feminist theory of caring. In Abel, E. and Nelson, M. (eds) *Circles of Care: Work and Identity in Women's Lives*. New York: SUNY Press: 35–62.

Foundational Economy Collective (2018) *Foundational economy: The infrastructure of everyday life*. Manchester: Manchester University Press.

Franklin, J. (2019) Home economics: Home and care in neoliberal policy. In Jupp, E., Bowlby, S., Franklin, J. and Hall, S.M. (eds) *The new politics of home: Housing, gender and care in times of crisis*. Bristol: Policy Press: 13–38.

Fraser, N. (1990) Rethinking the public sphere: A contribution to the critique of actually existing democracy. *Social Text*, 25/26: 56–80.

Fraser, N. (2013) *Fortunes of feminism: From state-managed capitalism to neoliberal crisis*. London: Verso.

Fraser, N. (2016) Contradictions of capital and care. *New Left Review*, 100(99): 117.

Garthwaite, K. (2014) Fear of the brown envelope: Exploring welfare reform with long-term sickness benefits recipients. *Social Policy & Administration*, 48(7): 782–98.

Garthwaite, K. (2015) 'Keeping meself to meself': How social networks can influence narratives of stigma and identity for long-term sickness benefits recipients. *Social Policy & Administration*, 49(2): 199–212.

Garthwaite, K. (2016) *Hunger pains: Life inside foodbank Britain*. Bristol: Policy Press.

Gerbaudo, P. (2012) *Tweets and the streets: Social media and contemporary activism*. London: Pluto Press.

Gibbs, J. (2018) The politics of vulnerability: affect, relationality, and resistance in UK austerity. Doctoral dissertation, London School of Economics and Political Science.

Gibson-Graham, J.K. (2003) An ethics of the local. *Rethinking Marxism*, 15(1): 49–74.

Giddens, A. (2013) *The third way and its critics*. Chichester: John Wiley & Sons.

Gilchrist, A. (2003) Community development in the UK: Possibilities and paradoxes. *Community Development Journal*, 38(1): 16–25.

Gill, R. and Orgad, S. (2018) The amazing bounce-backable woman: Resilience and the psychological turn in neoliberalism. *Sociological Research Online*, 23(2): 477–95.

Gillies, V., Edwards, R. and Horsley, N. (2017) *Challenging the politics of early intervention: Who's saving children and why*. Bristol: Policy Press.

Gilligan, C. (1993) *In a different voice: Psychological theory and women's development*. Cambridge, MA: Harvard University Press.

Gould, D.B. (2009) *Moving politics: Emotion and ACT UP's fight against AIDS*. Chicago, IL: University of Chicago Press.

Gray, M. and Barford, A. (2018) The depths of the cuts: The uneven geography of local government austerity. *Cambridge Journal of Regions, Economy and Society*, 11(3): 541–63.

Greco, M. and Stenner, P. (eds) (2013) *Emotions: A social science reader*. Oxford: Routledge.

Greer Murphy, A. (2017) Austerity in the United Kingdom: The intersections of spatial and gendered inequalities. *Area*, 49(1): 122–4.

Griggs, S. and Roberts, M. (2012) From neighbourhood governance to neighbourhood management: A 'roll-out' neo-liberal design for devolved governance in the United Kingdom? *Local Government Studies*, 38(2): 183–210.

Guardian (2005) Tony Blair's conference speech 2005. 27 September, available at https://www.theguardian.com/uk/2005/sep/27/labourconference.speeches

Gunaratnam, Y. and Lewis, G. (2001) Racialising emotional labour and emotionalising racialised labour: Anger, fear and shame in social welfare. *Journal of Social Work Practice*, 15(2): 131–48.

Hall, S.M. (2014) Ethics of ethnography with families: A geographical perspective. *Environment and Planning A*, 46(9): 2175–94.

Hall, S.M. (2017) Personal, relational and intimate geographies of austerity: Ethical and empirical considerations. *Area*, 49(3): 303–10.

Hall, S.M. (2019a) Relational biographies in times of austerity: Family, home and care. In . In Jupp, E, Bowlby, S, Franklin, J and Hall, S.M. (eds) *The New Politics of Home: Housing, Gender and Care in Times of Crisis*, Bristol: Policy Press: 63–86.

Hall, S.M. (2019b) Everyday austerity: Towards relational geographies of family, friendship and intimacy. *Progress in Human Geography*, 43(5): 769–89.

Hall, S.M. (2019c) *Everyday life in austerity: Family, friends and intimate relations.* London: Palgrave Macmillan.

Hall, S.M. (2020a) The personal is political: Feminist geographies of/in austerity. *Geoforum*, 110: 242–51.

Hall, S.M. (2020b) 'It died once at playgroup, I didn't know what to do': Towards vital, vibrant, material geographies of the mobile phone in austerity. *Social & Cultural Geography*: 1–18. doi: 10.1080/14649365.2020.1843698

Hall, S.M. (2020c) Social reproduction as social infrastructure. *Soundings: A Journal of Politics and Culture*, 76(1): 82–94.

Hastings, A., Bailey, N., Bramley, G. and Gannon, M. (2017) Austerity urbanism in England: The 'regressive redistribution' of local government services and the impact on the poor and marginalised. *Environment and Planning A*, 49(9): 2007–24.

Held, V. (1995) The meshing of care and justice. *Hypatia*, 10(2): 128–32.

Helgeson, J. (2014) *Crucibles of Black empowerment: Chicago's neighborhood politics from the New Deal to Harold Washington.* Chicago, IL: University of Chicago Press.

Henry, C. (2018) The abstraction of care: What work counts? *Antipode*, 50(2): 340–58.

Hitchen, E. (2016) Living and feeling the austere. *New Formations*, 87: 102–18.

Hitchen, E. (2019) Pessimism, paranoia, melancholia: The affective life of austerity. Doctoral dissertation, Durham University.

Hitchen, E. (2021) The affective life of austerity: Uncanny atmospheres and paranoid temporalities. *Social & Cultural Geography*, 22(3): 295–318.

Hitchen, E. and Raynor, R. (2020) Encountering austerity in everyday life: Intensities, localities, materialities. *Geoforum*, 110: 186–90.

Hitchen, E. and Shaw, I. (2019) Intervention: Shrinking worlds: austerity and depression. *AntipodeFoundation.org*, 7, available at https://antipodeonline.org/2019/03/07/shrinking-worlds-austerity-and-depression/

HM Government (2006) Childcare Act 2006, available at https://www.legislation.gov.uk/ukpga/2006/21

Holmes, H. (2019) Unpicking contemporary thrift: Getting on and getting by in everyday life. *The Sociological Review*, 67(1): 126–42.

Holt, L. (2013) Exploring the emergence of the subject in power: Infant geographies. *Environment and Planning D: Society and Space*, 31(4): 645–63.

Honig, B. (2017) *Public things: Democracy in disrepair*. New York: Fordham University Press.

Horton, J. (2016) Anticipating service withdrawal: Young people in spaces of neoliberalisation, austerity and economic crisis. *Transactions of the Institute of British Geographers*, 41(4): 349–62.

Horton, J. and Kraftl, P. (2009) What (else) matters? Policy contexts, emotional geographies. *Environment and Planning A*, 41(12): 2984–3002.

Howard, A.L. (2014) *More than shelter: Activism and community in San Francisco public housing*. Minnesota: University of Minnesota Press.

Hubbard, P. and Lees, L. (2018) The right to community? Legal geographies of resistance on London's gentrification frontiers. *City*, 22(1): 8–25.

Hughes, S.M. (2020) On resistance in human geography. *Progress in Human Geography*, 44(6): 1141–60.

Huish, J. and Little, G. (2016) Together we are strong. In Regn, L. and Unterrainer, T. (eds) *Standing up for education*. Nottingham: Spokesman Books: 90–107.

Imrie, R. and Raco, M. (eds) (2003) *Urban renaissance? New Labour, community and urban policy*. Bristol: Policy Press.

Ince, A. (2012) In the shell of the old: Anarchist geographies of territorialisation. *Antipode*, 44(5): 1645–66.

Ince, A. and Hall, S.M. (eds) (2017) *Sharing economies in times of crisis: Practices, politics and possibilities*. Oxford: Routledge.

Ishkanian, A. and Peña Saavedra, A. (2019) The politics and practices of intersectional prefiguration in social movements: The case of Sisters Uncut. *The Sociological Review*, 67(5): 985–1001.

Isin, E.F. (2017) Enacting international citizenship. In Basaran, T., Bigo, D., Guittet, E.P. and Walker, R.B. (eds) *International political sociology: Transversal lines*. Abingdon: Routledge: 185–204.

Isin, E.F. and Nielsen, G.M. (eds) (2013) *Acts of citizenship*. London: Zed Books.

Jensen, T. (2013) Austerity parenting. *Soundings*, 55: 61–71.

Jordan, A. (2020) Masculinizing care? Gender, ethics of care, and fathers' rights groups. *Men and Masculinities*, 23(1): 20–41.

Joseph, M. (2002) *Against the romance of community*. Minnesota: University of Minnesota Press.

Jupp, E. (2006) Making public space: Community groups and local participation in Stoke-on-Trent. Doctoral dissertation, Open University.

Jupp, E. (2007) Participation, local knowledge and empowerment: Researching public space with young people. *Environment and Planning A*, 39(12): 2832–44.

Jupp, E. (2008) The feeling of participation: Everyday spaces and urban change. *Geoforum*, 39(1): 331–43.

Jupp, E. (2012) Rethinking local activism: 'Cultivating the capacities' of neighbourhood organising. *Urban Studies*, 49(14): 3027–44.

Jupp, E. (2013a) Enacting parenting policy? The hybrid spaces of Sure Start Children's Centres. *Children's Geographies*, 11(2): 173–87.

Jupp, E. (2013b) 'I feel more at home here than in my own community': Approaching the emotional geographies of neighbourhood policy. *Critical Social Policy*, 33(3): 532–53.

Jupp, E. (2017) Home space, gender and activism: The visible and the invisible in austere times. *Critical Social Policy*, 37(3): 348–66.

Jupp, E. (2018) Children's Centres are disappearing. *The Conversation*, 11 April, available at https://theconversation.com/childrens-centres-are-disappearing-heres-what-it-means-for-the-under-fives-and-their-parents-94792

Jupp, E. (2019) Spaces of care beyond the home: Austerity and children's services. In Jupp, E., Bowlby, S., Franklin, J. and Hall, S.M. (eds) *The New Politics of Home: Housing, Gender and Care in Times of Crisis*. Bristol: Policy Press: 87–106.

Jupp, E. (2020) Care, austerity and citizenship story-telling as protest in anti-austerity activism in the UK. In Hall, S., Horton, P. and Pimlott-Wilson, H. (eds) *Austerity across Europe*. Abingdon: Routledge: 181–94.

Jupp, E. (2021a) The time-spaces of austerity urbanism: Narratives of 'localism' and UK neighbourhood policy. *Urban Studies*, 58(5): 977–92.

Jupp, E. (2021b) Emotions, affect and social policy: Austerity and Children's Centres in the UK. *Critical Policy Studies*. https://doi.org/10.1080/19460171.2021.1883451

Jupp, E., Pykett, J. and Smith, F.M. (eds) (2016) *Emotional states: Sites and spaces of affective governance*. Abingdon: Taylor & Francis.

Jupp, E., Bowlby, S., Franklin, J. and Hall, S.M. (2019) *The new politics of home: Housing, gender and care in times of crisis*. Bristol: Policy Press.

Katz, C. (2017) Revisiting minor theory. *Environment and Planning D: Society and Space*, 35(4): 596–9.

Katz, C. (2018) The angel of geography: Superman, Tiger Mother, aspiration management, and the child as waste. *Progress in Human Geography*, 42(5): 723–40.

Kay, J.B. (2020) 'Stay the fuck at home!': Feminism, family and the private home in a time of coronavirus. *Feminist Media Studies*, 20(6): 883–8.

Kern, L. and McLean, H. (2017) Undecidability and the urban: Feminist pathways through urban political economy. *ACME: An International Journal for Critical Geographies*, 16(3): 405–26.

Kiely, E. (2021) Stasis disguised as motion: Waiting, endurance and the camouflaging of austerity in mental health services. *Transactions of the Institute of British Geographers*, 46(3): 717–31.

Knight, D.M. and Stewart, C. (2016) Ethnographies of austerity: Temporality, crisis and affect in Southern Europe. *History and Anthropology*, 27(1): 1–18.

Koch, R. and Miles, S. (2020) Inviting the stranger in: Intimacy, digital technology and new geographies of encounter. *Progress in Human Geography*. https://doi.org/10.1177/0309132520961881

Kofman, E. (2012) Rethinking care through social reproduction: Articulating circuits of migration. *Social Politics*, 19(1): 142–62.

Kraftl, P. and Adey, P. (2008) Architecture/affect/inhabitation: Geographies of being-in buildings. *Annals of the Association of American Geographers*, 98(1): 213–31.

Laslett, B. and Brenner, J. (1989) Gender and social reproduction: Historical perspectives. *Annual Review of Sociology*, 15(1): 381–404.

Lawless, P. (2006) Area-based urban interventions: Rationale and outcomes. The New Deal for Communities programme in England. *Urban Studies*, 43(11): 1991–2011.

Lawrence, J. (2019) *Me, me, me? Individualism and the search for community in post-war England*. Oxford: Oxford University Press.

Lawson, V. (2007) Geographies of care and responsibility. *Annals of the Association of American Geographers*, 97(1): 1–11.

Layton, J. and Latham, A. (2021) Social infrastructure and public life: Notes on Finsbury Park, London. *Urban Geography*: 1–22. https://doi.org/10.1080/02723638.2021.1934631

Levitas, R. (2012) The just's umbrella: Austerity and the big society in coalition policy and beyond. *Critical Social Policy*, 32(3): 320–42.

Lewis, S. (2020) What COVID-19 reveals about the family. *Politics/Theory/Other* podcast, available at https://soundcloud.com/poltheoryother/102-what-covid-19-reveals-about-the-family-w-sophie-lewis

Lister, R. (1998) From equality to social inclusion: New Labour and the welfare state. *Critical Social Policy*, 18(55): 215–25.

Lister, R. (2003a) What is citizenship? In Lister, R. and Campling, J. (eds) *Citizenship: Feminist perspectives*. London: Palgrave: 13–42.

Lister, R. (2003b) Investing in the citizen-workers of the future: Transformations in citizenship and the state under New Labour. *Social Policy & Administration*, 37(5): 427–43.

Lister, R. (2007) Inclusive citizenship: Realizing the potential. *Citizenship Studies*, 11(1): 49–61.

Lister, R., Williams, F., Anttonen, A., Gerhard, U. and Bussemaker, J. (2007) *Gendering citizenship in Western Europe: New challenges for citizenship research in a cross-national context*. Bristol: Policy Press.

Little, J. (2021) Caring for survivors of domestic abuse: Love, violence and safe space. *Social & Cultural Geography*. https://doi.org/10.1080/14649365.2021.1921243

Lonergan, G. (2015) Migrant women and social reproduction under austerity. *Feminist Review*, 109(1): 124–45.

Longhurst, R., Ho, E. and Johnston, L. (2008) Using 'the body' as an 'instrument of research': Kimch'i and pavlova. *Area*, 40(2): 208–17.

Lopes, A.M., Healy, S., Power, E., Crabtree, L. and Gibson, K. (2018) Infrastructures of care. *Human Ecology Review*, 24(2): 41–60.

Lorde, A. (1988) *A burst of light: Essays*. Ithaca, NY: Firebrand Books.

Lowndes, V. and McCaughie, K. (2013) Weathering the perfect storm? Austerity and institutional resilience in local government. *Policy & Politics*, 41(4): 533–49.

Lowndes, V. and Pratchett, L. (2012) Local governance under the coalition government: Austerity, localism and the 'Big Society'. *Local Government Studies*, 38(1): 21–40.

Lupton, R. (2003) *Poverty street: The dynamics of neighbourhood decline and renewal*. Bristol: Policy Press.

MacLeavy, J. (2011) A 'new politics' of austerity, workfare and gender? The UK coalition government's welfare reform proposals. *Cambridge Journal of Regions, Economy and Society*, 4(3): 355–67.

MacLeavy, J. (2021) Care work, gender inequality and technological advancement in the age of COVID-19. *Gender, Work & Organization*, 28(1): 138–54.

MacLeavy, J. and Manley, D. (2018) (Re) discovering the lost middle: Intergenerational inheritances and economic inequality in urban and regional research. *Regional Studies*, 52(10): 1435–46.

MacLeavy, J., Fannin, M. and Larner, W. (2021) Feminism and futurity: Geographies of resistance, resilience and reworking. *Progress in Human Geography*. doi: 03091325211003327

Maggio, R. (2014) The anthropology of storytelling and the storytelling of anthropology. *Journal of Comparative Research in Anthropology and Sociology*, 5(2): 89–106.

Marshall, T.H. (1964) *Class, citizenship and social development*. New York: Doubleday.

Martin, D.G., Hanson, S. and Fontaine, D. (2007) What counts as activism? The role of individuals in creating change. *Women's Studies Quarterly*, 35(3/4): 78–94.

Massey, D. (1993) Power-geometry and a progressive sense of place. In Bird, J., Curtis, B., Putnam, T., Robertson, G. and Tuckner, L. (eds) *Mapping the futures: Local cultures, global change*. Abingdon: Routledge: 59–69.

McCall, B., Shallcross, L., Wilson, M., Fuller, C. and Hayward, A. (2019) Storytelling as a research tool and intervention around public health perceptions and behaviour: A protocol for a systematic narrative review. *BMJ Open*. doi: 10.1136/bmjopen-2019-030597

McDowell, L. (2015). Roepke lecture in economic geography – the lives of others: Body work, the production of difference, and labor geographies. *Economic Geography*, 91(1): 1–23.

McDowell, L., Bonner-Thompson, C. and Harris, A. (2020) On the margins: Young men's mundane experiences of austerity in English coastal towns. *Social & Cultural Geography*, 52(5): 916–32.

McGrath, L. and Reavey, P. (2016) 'Zip me up, and cool me down': Molar narratives and molecular intensities in 'helicopter' mental health services. *Health & Place*, 38: 61–9.

McGrath, L. and Reavey, P. (eds) (2018) *The handbook of mental health and space: Community and clinical applications*. Abingdon: Routledge.

McGrath, L., Reavey, P. and Brown, S.D. (2008) The scenes and spaces of anxiety: Embodied expressions of distress in public and private fora. *Emotion, Space and Society*, 1(1): 56–64.

McLean, J., Maalsen, S. and Prebble, S. (2019) A feminist perspective on digital geographies: Activism, affect and emotion, and gendered human-technology relations in Australia. *Gender, Place & Culture*, 26(5): 740–61.

Meegan, R. and Mitchell, A. (2001) 'It's not community round here, it's neighbourhood': Neighbourhood change and cohesion in urban regeneration policies. *Urban Studies*, 38(12): 2167–94.

Middleton, J. and Samanani, F. (2021) Accounting for care within human geography. *Transactions of the Institute of British Geographers*, 46(1): 29–43.

Milbourne, L. and Cushman, M. (2015) Complying, transforming or resisting in the new austerity? Realigning social welfare and independent action among English voluntary organisations. *Journal of Social Policy*, 44(3): 463–85.

Milligan, C. and Wiles, J. (2010) Landscapes of care. *Progress in Human Geography*, 34(6): 736–54.

Morrow, O. and Parker, B. (2020) Care, commoning and collectivity: From grand domestic revolution to urban transformation. *Urban Geography*, 41(4): 607–24.

Morse, N. and Munro, E. (2018) Museums' community engagement schemes, austerity and practices of care in two local museum services. *Social & Cultural Geography*, 19(3): 357–78.

Moss, P. (2002) Taking on, thinking about, and doing feminist research in geography. In Moss, P., Falconer Al-Hindi, K. and Kawabata, H. (eds) *Feminist geography in practice: Research and methods*. Hoboken, NJ: Wiley-Blackwell: 1–17.

Mouffe, C. (2000) *The democratic paradox*. London: Verso.

Mould, O. (2018) *Against creativity*. London: Verso.

Muehlebach, A. (2011) On affective labor in post-Fordist Italy. *Cultural Anthropology*, 26(1): 59–82.

Murphy, S. (2021) Keir Starmer calls for immediate lockdown in England. *The Guardian*, 3 January, available at https://www.theguardian.com/politics/2021/jan/03/keir-starmer-calls-for-immediate-lockdown-in-england-as-covid-cases-soar

Nagar, R. and Geiger, S. (2007) Reflexivity, positionality and identity in feminist fieldwork revisited. In *Politics and practice in economic geography*. Thousand Oaks: Sage: 267–78.

Neal, S., Gawlewicz, A., Heley, J. and Jones, R.D. (2021) Rural Brexit? The ambivalent politics of rural community, migration and dependency. *Journal of Rural Studies*, 82: 176–83.

Needham, C. (2014) Personalization: From day centres to community hubs? *Critical Social Policy*, 34(1): 90–108.

Newman, J. (2001) *Modernizing governance: New Labour, policy and society*. London: Sage.

Newman, J. (2012) *Working the spaces of power: Activism, neoliberalism and gendered labour*. London: A&C Black.

Newman, J. (2014) Landscapes of antagonism: Local governance, neoliberalism and austerity. *Urban Studies*, 51(15): 3290–305.

Noddings, N. (1984) *A feminine approach to ethics and moral education*. Berkeley, CA: University of California Press.

Nowicki, M. (2021) Is anyone home? Appropriating and re-narrativisating the post-criminalisation squatting scene in England and Wales. *Environment and Planning C: Politics and Space*, 39(4): 838–55.

Nussbaum, M.C. (2013) *Political emotions*. Cambridge, MA: Harvard University Press.

Okely, J. (2007) Fieldwork embodied. *The Sociological Review*, 55(1): 65–79.

Okolosie, L. (2014) Beyond 'talking' and 'owning' intersectionality. *Feminist Review*, 108(1): 90–6.

Ormerod, E. (2021) The place of politics and the politics of place: Housing, the Labour Party and the local state in England. *Political Geography*, 85: 102308.

Ortega-Alcázar, I. and Wilkinson, E. (2020) 'I felt trapped': Young women's experiences of shared housing in austerity Britain. *Social & Cultural Geography*: 1–16. https://doi.org/10.1080/14649365.2020.1829688

Pain, R. (2019) Chronic urban trauma: The slow violence of housing dispossession. *Urban Studies*, 56(2): 385–400.

Parr, H. (2011) *Mental health and social space: Towards inclusionary geographies?* Chichester: John Wiley & Sons.

Parry, K. (2020) The great get together as an experiment in convivial politics. *European Journal of Communication*, 35(6): 543–64.

Pateman, C. (2016) Sexual contract. *The Wiley Blackwell Encyclopedia of Gender and Sexuality Studies*: 1–3. doi: 10.1002/9781118663219

Paterson, M. (2009) Haptic geographies: Ethnography, haptic knowledges and sensuous dispositions. *Progress in Human Geography*, 33(6): 766–88.

Pedersen, S. and Lupton, D. (2018) 'What are you feeling right now?': Communities of maternal feeling on Mumsnet. *Emotion, Space and Society*, 26: 57–63.

Pedwell, C. (2014) *Affective relations: The transnational politics of empathy*. New York: Springer.

Penny, J. (2017) Between coercion and consent: The politics of 'cooperative governance' at a time of 'austerity localism' in London. *Urban Geography*, 38(9): 1352–73.

Penny, J. (2020) 'Defend the Ten': Everyday dissensus against the slow spoiling of Lambeth's libraries. *Environment and Planning D: Society and Space*, 38(5): 923–40.

Petts, R.J., Carlson, D.L. and Pepin, J.R. (2021) A gendered pandemic: Childcare, homeschooling, and parents' employment during COVID-19. *Gender, Work & Organization*, 28: 515–34.

Phipps, A. (2016) Whose personal is more political? Experience in contemporary feminist politics. *Feminist Theory*, 17(3): 303–21.

Pottinger, L. (2017) Planting the seeds of a quiet activism. *Area*, 49(2): 215–22.

Power, A. and Hall, E. (2018) Placing care in times of austerity. *Social & Cultural Geography*, 19(3): 303–13.

Power, E.R. and Mee, K.J. (2020) Housing: An infrastructure of care. *Housing Studies*, 35(3): 484–505.

Power, E.R., Weisel, I. and Mee, K. (2021) Shadow care infrastructures: Sustaining life in post-welfare cities. Working paper, presentation at Interpretive Policy Analysis conference, June.

Pratt, G. (1997) Stereotypes and ambivalence: The construction of domestic workers in Vancouver, British Columbia. *Gender, Place and Culture: A Journal of Feminist Geography*, 4(2): 159–78.

Preston, J. (2020) Classed practices: Pandemic preparedness in the UK. In Preston, J and Firth, R (eds) *Coronavirus, class and mutual aid in the United Kingdom*. Cham: Palgrave Macmillan: 29–55.

Prügl, E. (2020) Untenable dichotomies: De-gendering political economy. *Review of International Political Economy*, 28(2): 295–306.

Puig de la Bellacasa, M.P. (2017) *Matters of care: Speculative ethics in more than human worlds* (Vol. 41). Minnesota: University of Minnesota Press.

Pykett, J. (2015) *Brain culture: Shaping policy through neuroscience*. Bristol: Policy Press.

Raghuram, P. (2004) The difference that skills make: Gender, family migration strategies and regulated labour markets. *Journal of Ethnic and Migration Studies*, 30(2): 303–21.

Raghuram, P. (2016) Locating care ethics beyond the global north. *ACME: An International Journal for Critical Geographies*, 15(3): 511–33.

Raghuram, P. (2019) Race and feminist care ethics: intersectionality as method. *Gender, Place & Culture*, 26(5): 613–37.

Rai, S.M. (2019) Reimagining the state: Marxism, feminism, postcolonialism. In Cooper, D., Dhawan, N. and Newman, J. (eds) *Reimagining the state*. Oxford: Routledge: 37–56.

Raynor, R. (2017) Dramatising austerity: Holding a story together (and why it falls apart …). *Cultural Geographies*, 24(2): 193–212.

Raynor, R. (2021) Hopes multiplied amidst decline: Understanding gendered precarity in times of austerity. *Environment and Planning D: Society and Space*, 39(3): 553–70.

Reynolds, T., Erel, U. and Kaptani, E. (2018) Migrant mothers: Performing kin work and belonging across private and public boundaries. *Families, Relationships and Societies*, 7(3): 365–82.

Ribbens McCarthy, J. and Hooper, C.A. (eds) (2013) *Family troubles? Exploring changes and challenges in the family lives of children and young people*. Bristol: Policy Press.

Robinson, D. (2005) The search for community cohesion: Key themes and dominant concepts of the public policy agenda. *Urban Studies*, 42(8): 1411–27.

Robinson, F. (2020) Resisting hierarchies through relationality in the ethics of care. *International Journal of Care and Caring*, 4(1): 11–23.

Robinson, K. and Sheldon, R. (2019) Witnessing loss in the everyday: Community buildings in austerity Britain. *The Sociological Review*, 67(1): 111–25.

Robinson, S., Hall, E., Fisher, K.R., Graham, A., Johnson, K. and Neale, K. (2021) Using the 'in-between' to build quality in support relationships with people with cognitive disability: The significance of liminal spaces and time. *Social & Cultural Geography*: 1–20. https://doi.org/10.1080/14649365.2021.1950824

Rose, G. (1997) Situating knowledges: Positionality, reflexivities and other tactics. *Progress in Human Geography*, 21(3): 305–20.

Rose, N. (2000) Community, citizenship, and the third way. *American Behavioral Scientist*, 43(9): 1395–411.

Roseneil, S. (2013) Beyond citizenship? Feminism and the transformation of belonging. In Roseneil, S. (ed) *Beyond citizenship?* London: Palgrave Macmillan: 1–20.

Rose-Redwood, R., Kitchin, R., Apostolopoulou, E., Rickards, L., Blackman, T., Crampton, J., Rossi, U. and Buckley, M. (2020) Geographies of the COVID-19 pandemic. *Dialogues in Human Geography*, 10(2): 97–106.

Routledge, P. and Derickson, K.D. (2015) Situated solidarities and the practice of scholar-activism. *Environment and Planning D: Society and Space*, 33(3): 391–407.

Rowland, S. (2019) Understanding the deindustrial body: The legacies of occupational injuries and disease in the former Kent coalfield. Doctoral dissertation, University of Kent.

Russell, W. and Stenning, A. (2020) Beyond active travel: Children, play and community on streets during and after the coronavirus lockdown. *Cities & Health*: 1–4. doi: 10.1080/23748834.2020.1795386

Sabsay, L. (2016) Permeable bodies: Vulnerability, affective powers, hegemony. In Butler, J., Gambetti, Z. and Sabsay, L. (eds) *Vulnerability in resistance*. Durham, NC: Duke University Press: 278–302.

Sargsyan, N. (2019) Experience-sharing as feminist praxis: Imagining a future of collective care. *History and Anthropology*, 30(1): 67–90.

Secor, A. and Linz, J. (2017) Becoming minor. *Environment and Planning D: Society and Space*, 35(4): 568–73.

Shaheen, F (2020) Remaking the system. Fabian Society, 9 December, available at https://fabians.org.uk/remaking-the-system/

Sharp, J., Routledge, P., Philo, C. and Paddison, R. (2000) Entanglements of power. In Paddison, R., Philo, C., Routledge, P. and Sharp, J. (eds) *Entanglements of power: Geographies of domination/resistance*. Abingdon: Routledge: 1–42.

Shaw, I.G. (2019) Worlding austerity: The spatial violence of poverty. *Environment and Planning D: Society and Space*, 37(6): 971–89.

Smith, A. (2021) Sustaining municipal parks in an era of neoliberal austerity: The contested commercialisation of Gunnersbury Park. *Environment and Planning A: Economy and Space*, 53(4): 704–22.

Smith, G., Sylva, K., Smith, T., Sammons, P. and Omonigho, A. (2018) Stop start: Survival, decline or closure? Children's Centres in England, 2018. Sutton Trust, available at https://www.suttontrust.com/wp-content/uploads/2018/04/StopStart-FINAL.pdf

Solnit, R. (2020) The way we get through this is together. *Guardian*, 14 May, available at https://www.theguardian.com/world/2020/may/14/mutual-aid-coronavirus-pandemic-rebecca-solnit

Spade, D. (2020) *Mutual aid: Building solidarity during this crisis (and the next)*. London: Verso.

Springer, S. (2020) Caring geographies: The COVID-19 interregnum and a return to mutual aid. *Dialogues in Human Geography*, 10(2): 112–15.

Staeheli, L.A. (2008) Citizenship and the problem of community. *Political Geography*, 27(1): 5–21.

Staeheli, L.A. and Thompson, A. (1997) Citizenship, community, and struggles for public space. *The Professional Geographer*, 49(1): 28–38.

Stenning, A. (2020) Feeling the squeeze: Towards a psychosocial geography of austerity in low-to-middle income families. *Geoforum*, 110: 200–10.

Stenning, A. and Hall S.M. (2018) On the frontline: Loneliness and the politics of austerity. *Discover Society*, 6 November, available at https://discoversociety.org/2018/11/06/on-the-frontline-loneliness-and-the-politics-of-austerity/

Stephens, C. (2011) Narrative analysis in health psychology research: Personal, dialogical and social stories of health. *Health Psychology Review*, 5(1): 62–78.

Stewart, E. (2019) A sociology of public responses to hospital change and closure. *Sociology of Health & Illness*, 41(7): 1251–69.

Strong, S. (2019) The vital politics of foodbanking: Hunger, austerity, biopower. *Political Geography*, 75: 102053.

Strong, S. (2020) Towards a geographical account of shame: Foodbanks, austerity, and the spaces of austere affective governmentality. *Transactions of the Institute of British Geographers*, 46(1): 73–86.

Strong, S. (2021) Facing hunger, framing food banks, imaging austerity. *Social & Cultural Geography*: 1–18. https://doi.org/10.1080/14649365.2021.1921247

Sullivan, H. (2002) Modernization, neighbourhood management and social inclusion. *Public Management Review*, 4(4): 505–28.

Svenhuijsen, S. (1998) *Citizenship and the ethics of care*. London: Routledge.

Swyngedouw, E. (2007) The post-political city. *Urban Politics Now*: 58–76.

Tarrant, A. (2013) Grandfathering as spatio-temporal practice: Conceptualizing performances of ageing masculinities in contemporary familial carescapes. *Social & Cultural Geography*, 14(2): 192–210.

Tarrant, A. (2018) Care in an age of austerity: Men's care responsibilities in low-income families. *Ethics and Social Welfare*, 12(1): 34–48.

Taylor, F.M. (2020) Cumulative precarity: Millennial experience and multigenerational cohabitation in Hackney. *Antipode*, 53(2): 587–606.

Thane, P. (2016) *The foundations of the welfare state*. Oxford: Routledge.

Thomson, R. and Kehily, M.J. (2011) *Making modern mothers*. Bristol: Policy Press.

Tosh, J. (2013) Women and austerity: Beyond 'make do and mend'. *Psychology of Women Section Review*, 15(1): 46–52.

Tronto, J.C. (1993) *Moral boundaries: A political argument for an ethic of care*. Hove: Psychology Press.

Tronto, J.C. (2010) Creating caring institutions: Politics, plurality, and purpose. *Ethics and Social Welfare*, 4(2): 158–71.

Tronto, J.C. (2015) *Who cares? How to reshape a democratic politics*. Ithaca, NY: Cornell University Press.

Trussell Trust (2020) Latest stats, available at https://www.trusselltrust.org/news-and-blog/latest-stats/

Twigg, J. (1999) The spatial ordering of care: Public and private in bathing support at home. *Sociology of Health & Illness*, 21(4): 381–400.

Twigg, J. (2000) Carework as a form of bodywork. *Ageing & Society*, 20(4): 389–411.

Tyler, I. (2020). *Stigma: The machinery of inequality*. London: Bloomsbury.

Vacchelli, E., Kathrecha, P. and Gyte, N. (2015) Is it really just the cuts? Neo-liberal tales from the women's voluntary and community sector in London. *Feminist Review*, 109(1): 180–9.

Vaiou, D. and Kalandides, A. (2017) Practices of solidarity in Athens: Reconfigurations of public space and urban citizenship. *Citizenship Studies*, 21(4): 440–54.

Varley, A. (2013) Feminist perspectives on urban poverty: De-essentialising difference. In Peake, L. and Rieker, M. (eds) *Rethinking feminist interventions into the urban*. Oxford: Routledge: 125–41.

Wallace, A. (2010) New neighbourhoods, new citizens? Challenging 'community' as a framework for social and moral regeneration under New Labour in the UK. *International Journal of Urban and Regional Research*, 34(4): 805–19.

Warner, J. (2013) Social work, class politics and risk in the moral panic over Baby P. *Health, Risk & Society*, 15(3): 217–33.

Warren, J. and Garthwaite, K. (2014) Biographies of place: Challenging official spatial constructions of sickness and disability. In Soldatic, K., Morgan, H. and Roulstone, A. (eds) *Disability, spaces and places of policy exclusion*. Abingdon: Routledge: 129–43.

Watt, P. (2016) A nomadic war machine in the metropolis: En/countering London's 21st-century housing crisis with Focus E15. *City*, 20(2): 297–320.

Way, A.K., Kanak Zwier, R. and Tracy, S.J. (2015) Dialogic interviewing and flickers of transformation: An examination and delineation of interactional strategies that promote participant self-reflexivity. *Qualitative Inquiry*, 21(8): 720–31.

Webb, C.J. and Bywaters, P. (2018) Austerity, rationing and inequity: Trends in children's and young peoples' services expenditure in England between 2010 and 2015. *Local Government Studies*, 44(3): 391–415.

Wengraf, T. (2001) *Qualitative research interviewing: Biographic narrative and semi-structured methods*. London: Sage.

Wilkinson, E. and Ortega-Alcázar, I. (2019) The right to be weary? Endurance and exhaustion in austere times. *Transactions of the Institute of British Geographers*, 44(1): 155–67.

Williams, A., Goodwin, M. and Cloke, P. (2014) Neoliberalism, big society, and progressive localism. *Environment and Planning A*, 46(12): 2798–815.

Wills, J. (2016) *Locating localism: Statecraft, citizenship and democracy*. Bristol: Policy Press.

Wolch, J.R. (1989) The shadow state: Transformations in the voluntary sector. In Wolch, J. and Dear, M. (eds) *The power of geography: How territory shapes social life*. Abingdon: Routledge: 197–221.

Women's Budget Group (WBG) (2020a) Crises collide: Women and COVID-19. 9 April, available at https://wbg.org.uk/wp-content/uploads/2020/04/FINAL.pdf

Women's Budget Group (WBG) (2020b) Creating a caring economy: A call to action. 20 October, available at https://wbg.org.uk/analysis/creating-a-caring-economy-a-call-to-action-2/

Wood, H. and Skeggs, B. (2020) Clap for carers? From care gratitude to care justice. *European Journal of Cultural Studies*, 23(4): 641–7.

Wood, L., Swanson, K. and Colley III, D.E. (2020) Tenets for a radical care ethics in geography. *ACME: An International Journal for Critical Geographies*, 19(2): 424–47.

Woolvin, M. and Hardill, I. (2013) Localism, voluntarism and devolution: Experiences, opportunities and challenges in a changing policy context. *Local Economy*, 28(3): 275–90.

Worth, N. (2011) Evaluating life maps as a versatile method for lifecourse geographies. *Area*, 43(4): 405–12.

Wright, M.W. (2007) Urban geography plenary lecture: Femicide, mother-activism, and the geography of protest in northern Mexico. *Urban Geography*, 28(5): 401–25.

Wright, M.W. (2009) Gender and geography: Knowledge and activism across the intimately global. *Progress in Human Geography*, 33(3): 379–86.

Yuval-Davis, N., Wemyss, G. and Cassidy, K. (2018) Everyday bordering, belonging and the reorientation of British immigration legislation. *Sociology*, 52(2): 228–44.

Index

Page numbers in *italic* refer to figures.

A

Abraham, M. 30
activism 1–3, 23, 31–2
  see also anti-austerity activism; feminist activism; local action/activism; national level activism; political activism; scholar-activism
Adey, P. 71
affect 33, 34
affective activism 31, 46
affective atmospheres 128–30
affective labour 51
agency 27, 28, 43, 44, 48
  see also political agency
Ahmed, M.H. 20
Ahmed, S. 126
Alam, A. 21, 33, 61, 135
Anderson, B. 23, 65, 103, 128, 129
Andrews, G.J. 99
animations 91, *92*
anthropology 75
anti-austerity activism 28–9, 60, 61, 74
  Children's Centres 77–98, 125, 136
    background 77–9
    care within 79–80
    evaluating stories in court 92–7
    and national campaigns 131
    online spaces 88–9, 124
    political subjectivity 123
    storytelling at national level 87–92
    storytelling in council meetings 84–7
    storytelling during public protests *81*, 82–4
Arendt, H. 75
Askins, K. 31, 34, 121
austerity 5–6, 7, 59
  Children's Centres 62, 63, 65, 69, 73;
    see also Children's Centre activism
  food redistribution project 13
  impact on women 8, 19, 44
  and mental health 126
  and neighbourhood action 49–53
  and public services 60–1
  and the welfare state 17–20
  see also anti-austerity activism
austerity governance 26–9
austerity localism 77, 88, 95, 134

B

babies 79–80
Back, L. 121, 122
Bailey, S. 115
Bambra, C. 20
Baraitser, L. 80
Barford, A. 5, 17
Barnes, M. 21, 26
Bassel, L.
  Black and minority ethnic women 19, 28, 58, 124
  care 13, 44, 47, 63, 125
  failed care 18, 65, 69
  politics of listening 34
  women of colour 21
Bell, S.E. 47
Belsky, J. 63, 98
Benhabib, S. 75
Berlant, L. 34–5, 99
Bezanson, K. 14
Black and minority ethnic neighbourhoods 50
Black and minority ethnic women 19, 58, 124
  see also minority ethnic women's organisations; women of colour
Black organising 31
Blair, T. 24
Bock, J.J. 28
border work 15, 21, 25, 26, 38–9, 44, 49, 55
Bosco, F.J. 39
Bowlby, S. 12, 20, 21, 66, 99, 101, 130
Boyer, K. 19
Braun, Y.A. 47
Bregman, R. 132
Brenner, J. 14
Brexit referendum 35
Brickell, K. 20, 99, 101, 102
Briggs, A. 27
Brown, G. 101, 125
Brown, K. 65
Brown, W. 14, 49
Bunnell, T. 123
burnout 58, 114–15, 125–6
Burrell, K. 40, 41, 123
Butler, J. 32–3
Butler, P. 27
Bywaters, P. 18, 91, 96

C

Cameron, D. 26
Cameron, E. 33, 69, 75–6, 84, 87, 91, 124
Cammaerts, B. 29, 78, 80
capitalism 16, 17

Index

humanitarian 36
Cappellini, B. 19
care 2–3
　and austerity 60
　capacious approach to 58
　Children's Centre activism 79–80
　Children's Centres 62–3
　　shifting rationalities of 65–6
　ethics of 12, 13, 14, 18, 62, 94
　and inequalities 13–15
　infrastructures of 12, 21, 61, 135
　　and austerity 49, 73
　　and mental health 126
　　mutual aid networks 104–10, 112, 116
　　shadow care infrastructures 133
　　and vulnerability 32–3
　during lockdown 102, 104–10
　everyday practices and caring labour 111–15
　and motherhood 54
　new vision of 21
　politics of 11–13, 62–3, 65, 94, 122–7, 128, 132
　as resistance and political agency 21
　and the welfare state 15–17
　　austerity 17–20
　as work 116
Care Collective
　capacious approach to care 58, 123
　care as burden 125, 126, 127
　COVID-19 pandemic 20
　feminist analysis 12, 13
　mutual aid networks 114, 116
care-givers 13–14, 15, 16, 46, 126
caring institutions 21, 32, 135
caring masculinities 14, 47
'caring with' approach 12
caringscapes 12, 21, 66
Centre for Cities 17, 27
Chambers, D. 124
Chatzidakis, A. 102
childcare 46, 53, 62, 79–80, 88, 102, 114
Childcare Act 2006 94
Children's Centre activism 77–98, 125, 136
　background 77–9
　care within 79–80
　and national campaigns 131
　online spaces 88–9, 124
　political subjectivity 123
　storytelling
　　in council meetings 84–7
　　evaluating stories in court 92–7
　　at national level 87–92
　　during public protests 81, 82–4
Children's Centres 3, 5, 6, 8–9, 25, 61–73
　as places of friendship 66–9
　policy discourses 63
　politics of care 62–3, 65

politics of closures 64–5
reflections 121
shifting rationalities of care 65–6
as spaces of recognition and safety 69–72
Chung, C.K.L. 102
citizenship 23, 29–32, 39, 43, 44, 122–7, 134
citizenship acts 30, 36
Clarke, J. 5, 15, 17, 35, 135
Clayton, J. 18, 27, 134
Cloke, P. 3, 27, 28, 59, 133
Closs Stephens, A. 15, 65
Coastal Arts project 28, 40, 58, 137
　burnout 114–15, 125
　emotional governance 132
　emotions 35
　empathy and solidarity 53–7
　lockdown 105, 106–10
　period poverty project 8, 38, 55, *56*
Cohen, S. 28, 59, 134
collective emotional atmospheres 103–4
community 23–4, 127–33
　action *see* local action/activism
　cohesion 50
　development 24
　groups 7–8, 26, 27
　organisations 18, 25
　organising 124
　programmes 25
　projects 39–40, 136–7; *see also individual projects*
　and the third way 24–6
community workers 26, 49
Conradson, D. 66
Conservative governments 26
consultation 95–6, 97
'Contradictions of capital and care' (Fraser) 15–17
convergence spaces 64
Cooper, D. 21, 32, 110, 122, 135
cotton wool metaphor 3, 65, 72
council meetings 84–7
counter-public spheres 30, 33
court case 92–7
COVID-19 pandemic 6–7, 9, 19–20, 99–118
　affective atmospheres 128
　Coastal Arts project 56, 57, 105, 106–10, 114–15, 125
　home space 101–4
　local care 104–10
　　everyday practices 111–15
　mental health 126
　post-pandemic welfare 116–18
　reflections 121
　restricted mobility 130–1
　social media 33
Cox, R. 14

159

Craddock, E. 19, 31, 60
Creative Care packages 107
crises 72
Cushman, M. 27

D

Dasgupta, R. 102
Davidoff, L. 12, 29
Davidson, E. 60
Davies, G. 91
Davies, W. 34, 35, 76
Denning, S. 103, 128
Derickson, K.D. 7, 9, 64, 75, 101, 121
DeVerteuil, G. 2
digital spaces 33, 124, 130, 131
  see also Facebook; online spaces; social media
digital technology 102
Dobson, A.S. 130
Dobusch, L. 20, 102
domestic sphere see private sphere
domestic violence 42, 54, 70, 71, 80
Dorow, S. 131
Dwyer, C. 91

E

Early Help services 97
Early Help Strategy 96
economic value of care 14
economy 14
edgework see border work
effect 32
Eisenstadt, N. 62
Elliott, K. 14, 47
Emejulu, A.
  Black and minority ethnic women 19, 27–8, 58, 124
  care 13, 44, 47, 63, 125
  failed care 18, 65, 69
  women of colour 21
emotional governance 132
emotional labour 42
emotions 32, 33
  discourses of 108
  during lockdown 56–7, 103–4
  in the public sphere 34–6
  and situated solidarities 64
empathy 35, 40, 53–4, 132
empowerment 29–30, 43–4, 48, 58, 122–7, 135
Erel, U. 30, 41
ethics of care 12, 13, 14, 18, 62, 94
ethnicity 5, 13–14, 50
  see also Black and minority ethnic women; minority ethnic women's organisations; women of colour
Evans, M. 16
everyday care 19

everyday life 72
  politics of 4, 10, 14–15, 21, 23, 36–7, 119
  and citizenship 29–32
everyday practices, mutual aid 111–15
evictions 28–9
evidence-based practice 63

F

Facebook
  Children's Centre activism 79, 82, 83, 88–9
  migrant women 124
  mutual aid project 106, 107, 113, 117
failed care 18, 65, 69
families 70–1, 102–3
Family Centres 96
family hubs 77, 88
family identities 47
Farnsworth, K. 5, 17
Featherstone, D. 18
feminism 16, 17, 58
feminist activism 124
feminist analysis 11, 12, 13, 14, 15, 29–30, 30–1
Fenton-Glynn, C. 93
Fincher, R. 31, 131
Fink, J. 15, 16, 116, 134
Fisher, B. 11
flexible working 17
Focus E15 mums 28–9
food insecurity 2
food redistribution project 1, 12–13, 50–1
foodbanks 3, 27, 28, 109
foundational economy 14
Foundational Economy Collective 14
Fraser, N. 15–17, 20, 29–30, 116, 134
free school meals 117–18
friendship 66–9, 82, 123

G

Garthwaite, K. 3, 27, 45
gender 58
gender identities 14
  see also men; women
gender roles 41–2
geographies of care see landscapes of care
geography 75–6
Gerbaudo, P. 82, 124
Gibbs, J. 65
Gibson-Graham, J.K. 128
Giddens, A. 24
Gilchrist, A. 24, 49
Gill, R. 126
Gillies, V. 18, 96
good care 126
Gould, D.B. 34
Gray, M. 5, 17
Greco, M. 34

Greer Murphy, A. 19
Griggs, S. 25
Gunaratnam, Y. 16

H

Hall, E. 17, 66
Hall, S.M.
  care 60
  embodiment 120
  emotions 35
  friendship 123
  infrastructures of care 21
  research methods 6, 7
  social reproduction 14, 19
  storytelling 92
Hardwill, I. 31, 124
Hastings, A. 17, 18, 26, 27, 61
Held, V. 127
Helgeson, J. 124
Hitchen, E.
  anti-austerity activism 74
  austerity 6, 18, 28, 60
  austerity cuts 63, 73, 78
  council meetings 84
  service improvement 95
Holt, L. 80
home space 101–4
Homes, H. 19
homeschooling 100
Honig, B. 135
Hooper, C.A. 73, 91
horizontal activism 31
Horton, J. 6, 18, 28, 60, 63, 65
hostile environment 41, 123
housework 14
Houston, D. 21, 33, 61, 135
Howard, A. 31, 46
Hubbard, P. 77, 93
Hughes, S.M. 31, 39
Huish, J. 79
human geography 75–6
humanitarian capitalism 36

I

ill-health 45–6
Imrie, R. 2, 24, 48
Ince, A. 32, 35, 59, 110, 122
inequalities 126–7
  and care 13–15
infrastructural support 32–3
infrastructures of care 12, 21, 61, 135
  and austerity 49, 73
  and mental health 126
  mutual aid networks 104–10, 112, 116
  shadow care infrastructures 133
  and vulnerability 32–3
Insin, E. 30
interventions 18

invisible families 70–1
Irving, Z. 5, 17
Ishkanian, A. 80

J

Jensen, T. 55
Jordan, A. 14
Joseph, M. 23
judging subject 32, 35, 36
Jupp, E.
  austerity 20, 28, 60
  Children's Centres 62, 63, 65, 66, 71, 77, 82–97, 88, 94, 95
  citizenship 31
  community development workers 48, 49
  crises 119, 122
  emotions 35
  everyday life 72
  family identities 47
  home space 101
  ideologies of care 19
  infrastructures of care 135
  local action 132
  local activism 25
  mobility 130
  parenthood 123
  PhD thesis 120
  public/private divide 34, 38–9
  research methods 6, 7
  storytelling 69, 76
  trauma 41
  welfare services 18, 21

K

Kalandides, A. 7
Katz, C. 32, 123
Kay, J.B. 102, 103
Kehily, M.J. 72, 122
Kent 8
Kern, L. 74
Kiely, E. 60, 63, 95, 126
kindness 108, 132–3
Knight, D.M. 51
Koch, R. 36, 106, 117, 131
Kraftl, P. 63, 71
Kreissl, K. 20, 102

L

landscapes of care 12, 21
Laslett, B. 14
Latham, A. 60
Lawless, P. 25
Lawson, V. 21
Layton, J. 60
leaf-printing 100
Lees, L. 77, 93
legal challenges 92–7
Levitas, R. 24, 26, 127

Lewis, G. 16
Lewis, S. 102
library services 60–1, 95
lifecourse 8, 31, 53
Linz, J. 32
listening 34
Lister, R. 25, 29, 30, 62
Little, G. 79
Little, J. 71
local action/activism 23
  atmospheres and spaces of 127–33
  and austerity governance 26–9
  and citizenship 122–7
  and gender 38
  and the lifecourse 31
  during lockdown 104–10
    everyday practices and caring labour 111–15
  projects 39–40
  and the third way 24–6
  and the welfare state 133–5
  see also neighbourhood action; progressive localism
local authorities 27
local care 104–10
  everyday practices and caring labour 111–15
lockdown
  affective atmospheres 128
  home space 101–4
  local care 104–10
    everyday practices and caring labour 111–15
  politics of 117
  and post-pandemic welfare 117–18
London 8, 39
Lonergan, G. 13, 40, 44
Longhurst, R. 120
longitudinal research 6
long-term illness 45–6
Lopes, A.M. 21, 61
Lorde, A. 13, 126
Lowndes, V. 18, 26
Lupton, D. 72, 84, 126
Lupton, R. 25
Luxton, M. 14

M

MacLeavy, J. 6, 10, 14, 19, 30, 32, 36, 60, 116, 122
Manley, D. 6
marginalised groups 75, 91, 102, 127
marginalised voices 33
marginalised women 58
marginality 5, 12, 29, 40
Marshall, T.H. 30
Martin, D.G. 23, 31, 38, 60, 132
McCall, B. 75
McCaughie, K. 18
McDowell, L. 13, 54
McGrath, L. 65, 72, 84, 126
McKie, L. 12
McLean, J. 74
media genres 34–5
Mee, K.J. 12, 135
Meegan, R. 24
men 14, 46–7
mental health 48, 67, 68, 70, 84, 85–6, 125–6
mental health crisis 72
methodological background 4–7
methods 120–2
Middleton, J. 62, 80
migrant mothers 30, 40, 122–4, 136
migrant parents 8, 15
migrant women 5, 8, 13, 39, 41–4, 58
migration 31, 41
Milbourne, L. 27
Miles, S. 36, 106, 117, 131
Milligan, C. 66
minority ethnic women 19
  see also Black and minority ethnic women
minority ethnic women's organisations 27–8
Mitchell, A. 24
mobility 130–1
Morrow, O. 21
Morse, N. 18
Moss, P. 120
motherhood 41–2, 53, 54, 66–7, 72
  see also parenthood
mothering identities 46
mothers 30, 40, 79, 83–4, 122–3, 136
Mouffe, C. 76
Muehlenbach, A. 36, 51
Munro, E. 18
mutual aid networks 100–1, 105–10, 132, 137
  affective atmospheres 129–30
  emotional governance 132
  everyday practices and caring labour 111–15
  infrastructures of care 116, 133–4
  online spaces 124
  post-pandemic 117–18
  reflections 121

N

narration *see* storytelling
national level activism 87–92
Neal, S. 130
neighbourhood action 45–9
  under austerity 49–53
  see also mutual aid networks
neighbourhood governance 52
neighbourhood management 25
neighbourhood programmes 25, 48
neighbourhood renewal 2

neoliberalism 16, 17
New Labour government 52, 62
  the third way 24–6
Newman, J.
  austerity localism 77, 95
  border work 21, 38, 44, 55
  evidence-based practice 63
  feminism and neoliberalism 17
  local action 28
  New Labour government 25, 26
  populism 35
  welfare state 15, 17
Nielsen, G.M. 30
Nussbaum, M.C. 35

O

Okely, J. 122
Okolosie, L. 124
online media 57
online spaces 33, 44, 88–9, 124
  see also digital spaces; Facebook; social media
Orgad, S. 126
Ortega-Alcázar, E. 28

P

Pain, R. 48, 99
Panelli, R. 31, 131
parenthood 70, 122–3
  see also motherhood
Parker, B. 21
Parr, H. 126
Parry, K. 35, 131
Pateman, C. 12, 29
Paterson, M. 2
Pedersen, S. 72, 84, 126
Pedwell, C. 35, 54, 132
Peña Saavedra, A. 80
Penny, J. 27, 61, 63, 74, 77, 78, 88, 95, 134
period poverty project 8, 38, 55, 56
Petts, R.J. 20
Phipps, A. 124, 127, 134
Pickerill, J. 101, 125
political action 124, 127–8
political activism 35–6, 108–9, 110, 131–2
political agency 21, 29, 30, 36
  see also citizenship
political economy 14
political parties 124
politics 32
  and emotions 35
politics of care 11–13, 62–3, 65, 94, 122–7, 128, 132
politics of everyday life 4, 10, 14–15, 21, 23, 36–7, 119
  and citizenship 29–32
politics of kindness 132–3
politics of lockdown 117

populism 35
Pottinger, L. 31
poverty 8
  see also period poverty project
Power, A. 17, 66
Power, E.R. 2, 12, 133, 135
Pratchett, L. 26
Pratt, G. 14
prefigurative politics 32, 133–5
Prior, D. 21, 26
private sphere 11–12, 15, 19, 34, 71, 91, 102, 113
  see also public sphere; public/private divide
progressive liberalism 16
progressive localism 18
progressive universalism 62
Prügl, E. 14
psychology 75
public/private divide 102
  see also border work
public protests 81, 82–4
public services 60–1
public spending 25
public sphere 12, 33, 71
  emotions in 34–6
Puig de la Bellacasa, M.P. 2, 62, 65–6, 94, 99
Pykett, J. 35, 50

Q

quiet activism 31

R

race 13–14, 16
  see also ethnicity
Raco, M. 2, 24, 48
Raghuram, P. 13, 14, 40, 43, 126
Rai, S.M. 134
random acts of kindness 108, 132–3
Raynor, R. 5, 6, 45, 50
Reavey, P. 65, 84, 126
recognition 122, 126
reflections 120–2
relationships see friendship
re-privatisation of social reproduction 19
research methodology 4–7
  reflections 120–2
research projects 39–40, 136–7
  see also individual projects
researcher self 101
residents' groups 24, 25, 45–9, 136
  austerity 49–53
  local authority support 58
resistance 21, 28, 31, 32
Ribbens McCarthy, J. 73, 91
Roberts, M. 25
Robinson, F. 14, 50, 61
Robinson, K. 7
Rose, G. 120

Rose, N. 24
Roseneil, S. 29
Rose-Redwood, R. 99, 130
Routledge, P. 7, 9, 64, 101, 121
Rowland, S. 45
Russell, W. 105

S

Sabsay, L. 33–4, 35, 36, 76, 127
sacrifice zones 102
Samanani, F. 62, 80
sanitary products 8, 27, 55
  see also period poverty project
Sargsyan, N. 33
scholar-activism 7, 9, 121
Schweyher, M. 40, 41, 123
Secor, A. 32
self-care 43, 126
self-sufficiency 1, 2
shadow care infrastructures 133
Sharp, J. 4
Shaw, I. 73
Shaw, I.G. 60
Sheldon, R. 7, 61
Sisters Uncut 80
situated solidarities 64
Skeggs, B. 104
Smith, A. 60
Smith, G. 61, 62, 77, 88
social distancing 101, 105
social enterprises 8, 27, 28, 51, 52, 57
social investment model 25, 62
social media 128–9, 130, 131, 132
  Children's Centre activism 79, 82, 83, 88–9
  Coastal Arts project 55, 58
  COVID-19 pandemic 33, 105
  migrant women 124
  see also Facebook
social reproduction 14, 16, 20
  re-privatisation of 19
social welfare *see* welfare services
social work 18
Solnit, R. 105
Springer, S. 109, 117, 134
Staeheli, L.A. 23
Stenner, P. 34
Stenning, A. 19, 105
Stewart, C. 51
Stewart, E. 64
sticking plaster metaphor 1, 2–3, 51, 57
stigma 48
Stoke-on-Trent 1, 5, 6, 39
  community 128
  infrastructures 59
  PhD thesis 120–1
  residents' groups 7–8, 24, 45–9, 136
    austerity 49–53
    local authority support 58

  see also food redistribution project; residents' groups
storytelling 69, 74, 75–7, 124
  in council meetings 84–7
  evaluating stories in court 92–7
  at national level 87–92
  during public protests *81*, 82–4
  and vulnerability 33–4, 36
stranger intimacies 106, 117, 131
Strong, S. 27, 28, 114
Sullivan, H. 25
Sure Start Children's Centres *see* Children's Centres
Sutton Trust 77
Svenhuijsen S. 12
Swyngedouw, E. 93

T

targeted interventions 18
Tarrant, A. 14, 47
Taylor, F.M. 6, 92
teenagers 46
Thane, P. 15
third way 24–6, 48
Thompson, A. 23
Thomson, R. 72, 122
Tosh, J. 19
touch metaphors 99–100
town mutual aid project 106–10
  everyday practices and caring labour 111–15
trauma 41–2, 48, 55
Tronto, J.C.
  care 11, 12, 98
  caring institutions 21, 135
  caring practices 127
  infrastructures of care 134
Trump, D. 35
Trussell Trust 27
Twigg, J. 32
Tyler, I, 127

U

UK Uncut movement 80
unemployment 45

V

Vacchelli, E. 27
Vaiou, D. 10
Varley, A. 58
visibility/invisibility 12
vulnerability 32, 33–4, 36, 76, 80, 86–7

W

Wallace, A. 25
Warner, J. 18
Warren, J. 45
Watt, P. 19, 93
Way, A.K. 101

Webb, C.J. 96
welfare benefits 45
welfare services 60–1, 116–18
welfare state
  care in 15–17
  and austerity 17–20
  infrastructures of care 133–5
  new vision of 21
  the third way 24–6
Wiles, J. 66
Wilkinson, E. 28
Williams, A. 26
Wills, J. 26
Wolch, J.R. 2, 133
women
  and care 11, 20, 42, 127
  in the welfare state 15–17
  citizenship 29–30
  COVID-19 pandemic 114
  impact of austerity on 8, 19, 44
  impact of COVID-19 pandemic on 19–20
  local activism 38–9
    case studies 39–40; *see also individual case studies*
  media aimed at 34
women of colour 13–14, 20, 21
  see also Black and minority ethnic women
Women's Budget Group (WBG) 12, 19, 20, 114
Women's March, Washington 2017 31
women's organisations 27–8
Wood, H. 104, 127
Woolvin, M. 31, 124
Worth, N. 8
Wright, M.W. 46

Y

young carers 55
young mothers 28–9
young people 46, 47
youth club 1
youth work 51
Yuval-Davis, N. 41

www.ingramcontent.com/pod-product-compliance
Lightning Source LLC
Chambersburg PA
CBHW071205070526
44584CB00019B/2929